THE FORMATION OF MODERN
KURDISH SOCIETY IN IRAN

Kurdish Studies Series

Series Editors

Zeynep Kaya, Middle East Centre, London School of Economics and Political Science, UK & Department of Development Studies, School of Oriental and African Studies, UK
Robert Lowe, Middle East Centre, London School of Economics and Political Science, UK

Advisory Board

Sabri Ateş, Dedman College of Humanities & Sciences, USA
Mehmet Gurses, Florida Atlantic University, USA
Janet Klein, University of Akron, USA
David Romano, Missouri State University, USA
Clemence Scalbert-Yücel, University of Exeter, UK
Güneş Murat Tezcür, University of Central Florida, USA
Nicole Watts, San Francisco State University, USA

Titles

The Kurds in a Changing Middle East: History, Politics and Representation, edited by Faleh A. Jabar and Renad Mansour
Kurdish Nationalism on Stage: Performance, Politics and Resistance in Iraq, Mari R. Rostami
The Kurds of Northern Syria: Governance, Diversity and Conflicts, Harriet Allsopp and Wladimir van Wilgenburg
The Kurds and the Politics of Turkey: Agency, Territory and Religion, Deníz Çifçi
Kurds and Yezidis in the Middle East: Shifting Identities, Borders and the Experience of Minority Communities, edited by Güneş Murat Tezcür
The Formation of Modern Kurdish Society in Iran: Modernity, Modernization and Social Change (1920-1979), Marouf Cabi

THE FORMATION OF MODERN KURDISH SOCIETY IN IRAN

Modernity, Modernization and Social Change 1921–1979

Marouf Cabi

I.B. TAURIS
LONDON • NEW YORK • OXFORD • NEW DELHI • SYDNEY

I.B. TAURIS
Bloomsbury Publishing Plc
50 Bedford Square, London, WC1B 3DP, UK
1385 Broadway, New York, NY 10018, USA
29 Earlsfort Terrace, Dublin 2, Ireland

BLOOMSBURY, I.B. TAURIS and the I.B. Tauris logo are trademarks of
Bloomsbury Publishing Plc

First published in Great Britain 2022
Paperback edition published 2023

Copyright © Marouf Cabi, 2022

Marouf Cabi has asserted his right under the Copyright, Designs and Patents Act, 1988, to be identified as Author of this work.

For legal purposes the Acknowledgements on p. ix constitute an extension of this copyright page.

Series design by Adriana Brioso
Cover image: Nahid Primary School, Saqqez, 1973. Courtesy of Shahla Fotouhi

All rights reserved. No part of this publication may be reproduced or transmitted in any form or by any means, electronic or mechanical, including photocopying, recording, or any information storage or retrieval system, without prior permission in writing from the publishers.

Bloomsbury Publishing Plc does not have any control over, or responsibility for, any third-party websites referred to or in this book. All internet addresses given in this book were correct at the time of going to press. The author and publisher regret any inconvenience caused if addresses have changed or sites have ceased to exist, but can accept no responsibility for any such changes.

A catalogue record for this book is available from the British Library.

A catalog record for this book is available from the Library of Congress.

ISBN: HB: 978-0-7556-4224-3
PB: 978-0-7556-4228-1
ePDF: 978-0-7556-4225-0
eBook: 978-0-7556-4226-7

Typeset by Deanta Global Publishing Services, Chennai, India

Series: Kurdish Studies

To find out more about our authors and books visit www.bloomsbury.com and sign up for our newsletters.

For Hamed (1968–1985)

CONTENTS

List of illustration	vii
Preface	viii
Acknowledgements	ix
Maps	x
INTRODUCTION	1
Chapter 1	
THE INTEGRATION OF KURDISH SOCIETY INTO MODERN IRAN	13
Chapter 2	
THE WHITE REVOLUTION: ORIGINS, AIMS AND ECONOMIC PLANS	53
Chapter 3	
THE SOCIAL CONSEQUENCES OF MODERNIZATION	75
Chapter 4	
THE POLITICAL AND CULTURAL CONSEQUENCES OF MODERNIZATION	103
Chapter 5	
THE MODERNIZATION OF GENDER RELATIONS	145
CONCLUSION. KURDISH SOCIETY: PAST AND PRESENT	167
Notes	175
Bibliography	203
Index	215

ILLUSTRATION

Figures

1	Qaneʿ	40
2	Kurdistan Province in the educational map of Iran (naqsheye maʿaref-e Iran), 1304/1925	43
3	ʿAziz Muluk Maʿrefat (Moʿtamedi)	92
4	The Iranian army displays Sulaiman Muʿeini's body, 1968	111
5	Kurdish university students in the 1960s	112
6	ʿUbeidulla Ayyubiyan's Kurdish calendar	120
7	Theatre in Kurdistan	137
8	Women: Past and present	157

Maps

1	Iran and its administrative divisions, 1977	x
2	Tribes and tribal areas in the early twentieth century	xi
3	Language varieties of the Kurds	xii
4	Iran (1990)	xiii
5	The region populated by the Kurds in the west of Iran	xiv

Tables

1	Administrative Divisions of Iran 1908–79	29
2	A Single-Dimensional Approach to Social Change in Kurdistan	48
3	A Multidimensional Approach to Social Change in Kurdistan	50
4	The Third Economic Plan (1962–8)	61
5	Primary and Secondary Schools in Some Kurdish Cities (1955)	85
6	Education Centres and the Number of Female Teachers in the Kurdistan Province	86
7	Primary and Secondary Schools in Iran (1955)	87
8	Educational Institutions in the Kurdistan Province	92
9	Iran's Healthcare Indicators for 1923 and 1976	94
10	Healthcare Facilities in Iran (1978)	94
11	Cultural Encounters in Colonial and Nation-state Contexts: Similarities and Differences	124
12	Radio Broadcasting, Cinema, Theatre, Library, Newspapers and Magazines, 1972–3	134

PREFACE

Kurds and Kurdistan attract both scholarly and popular attention, increasing quest for knowledge on a people connected with those concepts and engaged in an unceasing struggle to promote their positions in history, politics and culture. For centuries, these concepts have been parts of the dynamic histories of a volatile region which eventually came to be known as the 'Middle East' in the twentieth century. Modernity placed the modern states encompassing Kurdish societies on a new path, leading to profound socio-economic, political, cultural and geographical transformations. It is not an easy task to deal with such a subject. However, this book presents a study of the emergence of Iran's modern Kurdish society since the formation of Iran's national state, with a special focus on the period following the Second World War until the outbreak of the 1979 Revolution.

The subject of the consequences of modernity and modernization for Kurdish-Iranian society has been part of my academic studies. However, this only followed a concurrent personal and intellectual journey which had started with the outbreak of the 1979 Iranian Revolution. The revolution and its political consequences in Iranian Kurdistan shaped me as a young Kurdish boy who, imbibing the ideas of his time in a specific environment, that is, a Kurdish-Iranian context, continued to search for answers to many questions for which the journey had actually begun in the first place, eventually shaping my interest in social and cultural history. My academic studies in the UK have truly been a thrilling experience, and I hope this book, which is an important outcome of my studies and research, contributes to our understanding of Iran's Kurdish society.

ACKNOWLEDGEMENTS

Many people have been directly or indirectly involved in developing the ideas discussed in this book. I am grateful to Ali M. Ansari and Saeed Talajooy for their constant support and comments on my works during the last several years when I was studying at the University of St Andrews, Scotland. I extend my thanks to a group of enthusiastic Iranian academics at the university's Department of Modern Languages, with whom I had regular meetings about culture, history and literature during the same period and became friends. I am particularly indebted to Saeed Talajooy for offering guidance in my research of the subjects of culture and literature and engaging with my arguments actively. My thanks are also due to Kaveh Qobadi, Ahmad Mohammadpur, Farangis Ghaderi and Gabriel Polley, whose comments in different ways helped me to present my ideas more clearly. I thank Pouya Taheri for helping with maps and figures. For this book, I have benefited from the works of many Kurdish academics living in Iran, too. I have acknowledged their endeavours and studies of social change in Iranian Kurdistan by citing their works when relevant. My research on social change in post–Second World War Iran includes many interviews that I conducted with many members of that generation. I thank all of them for their insight, enthusiasm and the great hospitality they showed me. I would like to express my gratitude to many friends and my children Arash and Hannah, for being unwavering sources of encouragement and support. I am especially grateful to Azad Azimi who supported me during difficult times. Finally, I thank all the staff at I.B. Tauris, especially Yasmin Garcha and Sophie Rudland, as well as the reviewers of the book, for their friendly and fantastic support.

All the quotes from the Kurdish and Persian sources are translated by the author unless otherwise stated. For the transliteration of Kurdish and Persian words, this book follows the Iranian Studies scheme. There are two exceptions. First, for surnames ending in *deh* in Persian, *da* is used when referring to a Kurdish figure, for example, Sharifzada instead of Sharifzadeh, to preserve the Kurdish pronunciation. The second exception is the names of non-English authors of sources published in English. The Persian attributive ezafeh (-e) and Kurdish attributive izafa (-i) are used in the text but not necessarily with a dash in the references. The text uses established anglicized forms such as Kurdistan and Majlis (instead of Kordestan and Majles).

Map 1 Iran and its administrative divisions, 1977. Adopted from J. Amuzegar, *Iran: An Economic Profile* (1977).

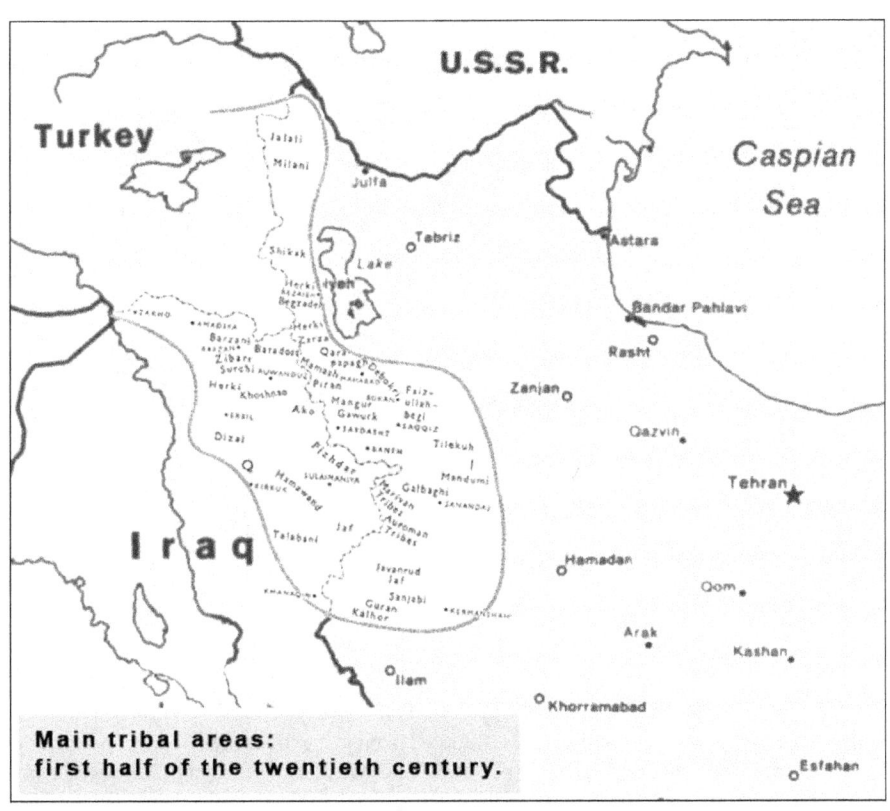

Map 2 Tribes and tribal areas in the early twentieth century. Adopted from W. Eagleton, *Kurdish Republic of 1946* (London: Oxford University Press, 1963), 19.

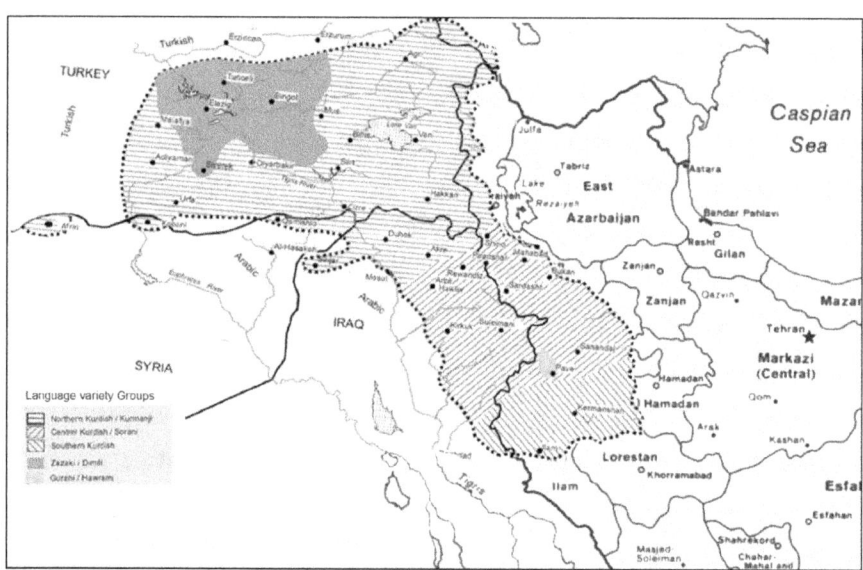

Map 3 Language varieties of the Kurds. Adopted from J. Sheyholislami, "Language Varieties of the Kurds," in Wolfgang Taucher et al. (ed.) *The Kurds: History-Religion-Language-Politics* (Austria: Austrian Federal Ministry of the Interior, 2015).

Map 4 Iran (1990).

Map 5 The region populated by the Kurds in the west of Iran. The inner borders indicate that the region is administered under different provincial centres (O). Cultural and linguistic borders become thicker as they meet the regions populated by Azari speaking communities in the north and northeast and by Persian-speaking communities in the south and southeast.

INTRODUCTION

This book examines the consequences of modernity and modernization for Kurdish-Iranian society in the twentieth century. It identifies a dual process of socio-economic transformation and homogenization of culture and identity, the dialectics of which (re)formed the economic, social, political and cultural structures of modern Kurdish society in Iran. As a result, socio-economically, Kurdish society became integrated into modern Iran, whereas it vigorously resisted homogenization of identity and culture; at the same time, it maintained porous cultural borders with other societies in Iran and continued to be shaped by mechanisms of modern cultural encounters. The socio-economic transformation of Iran strengthened and created new bonds between societies in Iran, while at the same time resistance and the struggle for political and cultural rights became permanent characteristics of Kurdish society. Modernization intensified in post–Second World War Iran, and the era of the 'White Revolution' of the 1960s and the 1970s is distinguished for the profound transformation of Iran it entailed. Therefore, an interpretation of the era constitutes the main concern of this book because, building on previous attempts to modernize Iran, the era was crucial in engendering profound changes in Kurdish society.

Modernity unleashed modernization and nation-building in Asian societies in an age when, as scholars have noted, Europe's cultural superiority had followed its military and technological supremacy over such societies since the beginning of the nineteenth century.[1] In twentieth-century multicultural Iran, where the Kurds had historically constituted a crucial component of the ethnic structure, this consisted of the above-mentioned process whose another consequence was modern *Kurdayeti* (Kurdishness), as both a national understanding of self and a movement for political and cultural rights, which took form, based of course (to borrow from Marx) on conditions inherited from the past. This dual process continued to be reconfigured according to the different historical and social contexts throughout the twentieth century.

There are several important historical conjunctures within the dual process. However, the intensification of modernization in the decades following the Second World War, including the era of the White Revolution, resulted in a profound transformation of Iranian societies' economic, social, political and cultural structures by the end of the 1970s. Although this era was the culmination of the preceding modernizing efforts, its impact on Kurdish society was revolutionary. From this perspective, this book follows its analysis of the consequences of modernity for Iran's Kurdish society in many chapters, which cover many significant aspects of modernization and homogenization.

Chapter 1 presents a background to the social and political integration of Kurdish society by drawing a link with pre-modern times. The transformation of power relations, modernization and centralization in the Ottoman and Qajar Empires, modernity, and, finally, the emergence of modern nation states, took place in a process that transformed the identity of the Kurds from a historical–cultural people, into an 'ethnic minority'. In Iran, this process was inextricably linked with the process of the formation of a national Iranian identity, a process in which the modern state, to borrow from a study on states' moral inclusion and exclusion, 'sought the monopoly over the right to define political identity' in addition to its other functions.[2] Finally, this chapter argues that the state-led modernization demonstrated a tendency to strengthen the social, economic and cultural bonds between various societies in Iran.

The next chapters follow the dual process and focus on the era of the White Revolution. *Chapter 2* presents a background to the ideas incorporated in the principles of the White Revolution, ideas that had been formed and pursued by various forces in Iran since the early decades of the twentieth century. It also presents a brief overview of development plans to explain that while they grew in sophistication and benefited from enormous financial resources, they became increasingly centralized and were devoid of economic plans for the provincial regions. *Chapter 3* discusses the social consequences of modernization in Kurdistan. Unplanned economic expansion and urbanization, and exodus to cities because of the White Revolution's land reform and economic transformation, had different consequences for different layers of society. Modernization raised standards of living for many, whereas new impoverished city neighbourhoods began to expand around Kurdish urban centres; it introduced and expanded education and healthcare provision, while in many ways it strengthened the disparity between urban and rural areas, city and village. Many became better off, enjoying increased income and forms of cultural capital. At the same time with no labour law in place, modernization created a modern Kurdish working class consisting of armies of urban unskilled labourers and seasonal workers; and forced poor rural families to migrate and work in terrible working conditions surrounded by unfamiliar circumstances, expanding child labour. Therefore, this chapter sheds light on a crucial dimension of Iran's rapid socio-economic change.

Chapter 4 analyses the political and cultural consequences of modernization by examining the way that the political and cultural structures of Kurdish society responded to homogenization. The political suppression of the Kurds and their resistance constituted two prominent characteristics of Kurdistan which continued during the decades linking the Second World War and Iran's 1979 Revolution. Modern education, urbanization and intellectual transformations were among factors that yielded networks of cultural and political activists and formed the nuclei of modern political parties. Interestingly, although the idea of armed struggle remained attractive because of its worldwide popularity at the time, and as a response to militarization and dictatorship, the political and cultural activism of the 1970s distinguished itself by distancing from theories of armed struggle, committing to theories of popular social revolution. Culturally, the argument of this chapter develops around two significant consequences of the modernization for Iran, being its cultural 'Westernisation' and, in Gramscian terms, the establishment of Persian cultural hegemony.[3] 'Westernisation' here refers to the state's imposition and inculcation of the preferred aspects of what was deemed as the 'Western' way of life because of its origin. In these circumstances, a democratic and progressive perception of modernity inspired a generation to engage actively in social change, adopt cultural innovations and enhance their societies' cultural achievements. Simultaneously, based on the notion of *Gharbzadegi* or 'Westoxication', nativism became a formidable force in Iranian politics. In Kurdistan, however, the new educated generation mainly inclined towards socialist critiques of modernization and distanced itself from calls to return to cultural purity, an idea increasingly cultivated by cultural critiques based on Islamic traditions and a Heideggerian critique of Western modernity.[4] Cultural, especially religious, distinctions functioned as effective barriers to imparting political Islam to Kurdistan, although evidence points to a nascent religious *Kurdayeti*, constituting the origins of Kurdish nativism. As regards Persian cultural hegemony, the era was marked by the establishment of the hegemony of the Persian language and culture in Iran. The emergence and proliferation of the new *visual* means of communication, for example, television and cinema, in addition to the existing audio means of communication, were crucial cultural developments for both the 'Westernization' of culture and the establishment of Persian cultural hegemony. Lastly, this chapter's arguments engage the scholarship for the first time on the theme of modernization's cultural consequences and, as crucially, also draw scholarly attention to the impact of the new means of communication in modern culture regarding, in this case, Iranian Kurdish society.

Finally, *Chapter 5* explores the modernization of gender relations in Kurdistan as another consequence of the modernization of Iran. Guided by gender theories and theories of change and transformation (see Theoretical and methodological considerations), this chapter adds yet another important dimension to studies of the formation of modern Kurdish society in Iran in the twentieth century.[5] It deliberately stresses the *modernization of gender order* against the notion of the *emancipation of women* to maintain a critical approach towards development theories that perceive women as a category for 'secularisation', regarded as a prerequisite to becoming 'modern'. Similarly, this chapter's examination of the transformation of the social status of women is a critical view of the Kurdish national narrative, which promotes the notion of women as a *national* asset, whose appearance and social place or action need to correspond to the need of the perceived nation. This chapter briefly highlights how the idea of a 'new woman' was part of modernity's ideological package, and therefore intimately accompanied the idea of the 'nation'. This is followed by identifying major factors, including women's agency, which affected the social status of women in Kurdish society. Furthermore, this chapter links social change in Kurdish society to social change across Iran, which partly forms a critical reading of, and a different approach to, national narratives which nationalize and categorize women as 'Kurdish' or 'Persian'. At the same time, this chapter transcends the limited boundaries of a popular Marxist approach which regards 'the woman question' as part of the class struggle and, therefore, secondary to the struggle of the working class. Lastly, it needs to be emphasized that, insofar as gender order is concerned, the era of the White Revolution is a crucial period for investment in modern education of women, the expansion of healthcare, and implementing legal reforms, for which the role of various women's movements was crucial.

Theoretical and methodological considerations

The literature on the Kurds contains many authoritative works.[6] Nevertheless, until very recently and with some exceptions, studies on the modernization of Iran had not been extended into analysing the social change in Kurdistan.[7] In the last two decades, however, a number of valuable studies on Iranian Kurdistan have appeared. These studies are attributed to a group of Iranian scholars in Iran, mainly but not exclusively Kurdish, who have begun to challenge the exclusive domination of political and elite Kurdish historiographies.[8] This book is another contribution to social change studies.

However, no studies of history, culture or social change can commence without determining their points of departure or presenting their theoretical foundations. To serve that purpose, the theoretical framework of this study consists of theories of change and transformation, which go against modernization theories, to serve a multidimensional approach to social change in Kurdish society; and of theories of nation and nationalism, to maintain a critical approach to Kurdish and Iranian national narratives. These are explained in the following sections. However, I need to point out that for writing the history of modern Kurdish society this book follows Illan Pappe's approach in studying the history of modern Palestine, itself owing much to studies on Asia and Africa in the 1960s and 1970s.[9] It does not intend to undermine, as Pappe rightly points out, the importance of factors such as industrialization, urbanization, hygienization, secularization, centralization and politicization of modern Middle Eastern societies.[10] However, it remains sceptical of such processes and challenges the connections between them constructed by modernization theories. On the other hand, the rejection of modernization theories extends to national narratives which, romanticizing the past, fail to understand the processes of change and transformation. Indeed, the critiques of modernization and nationalism go hand in hand. In contrast, this book depicts both an active Kurdish society and the past (as a resource to understand the present) as leading actors in the process of change. Additionally, Edward Said's critique of orientalism as a discourse, which in Foucauldian terms denotes notions and systematic statements to explain the world and is a manifestation of the link between knowledge and power, contributes to this study's historical perspective.[11] As regards the Kurds, orientalism as a discourse has, on the one hand, continued to reproduce a monolithic perception of the Kurds, for example, as tribal, rural and masculine with their own connotations which contrast with the idea of the 'modern'. On the other, highlighting elitist, national or political historiographies, orientalism has undermined the social histories of various Kurdish societies. Such misrepresentations of the Kurds have served discourses of power to undermine the political, cultural and religious rights of the Kurds in Iran and continue to shape ideological battlegrounds between opposing national narratives.

Furthermore, this framework is informed by several cultural critiques which enable us to understand both the cultural dimension of state formation and cultural consequences of modernization. Discussed mainly in Chapter 4, Antonio Gramsci's concept of hegemony is vital to understand the process of modern cultural encounters in multicultural Iran. Likewise, Raymond Williams's notion of 'residual' and 'emergent' cultures, a notion based on Gramsci, is employed to explain the ongoing tension between a hegemonic, powerful culture and marginalized cultures, and elucidate the process in which the hegemonic culture concedes ground to others or other cultures achieve better cultural positions. This is complemented by Pierre Bourdieu's definition of culture as a symbolic system and his concept of cultural capital. As a symbolic system, culture relies on social conditions and relations of power to produce and perpetuate meanings that safeguard the interests of the dominant social group or class. For socio-economic and political as well as cultural reasons, the era of the White Revolution profoundly affected social conditions and relations of power (see Chapter 4). The establishment of the hegemony of the Persian language and culture is one crucial consequence of the way such conditions changed. Insofar as the concept of cultural capital is concerned, it is one form of capital and refers to culture as economic practice.[12] Cultural capital includes products and practices which are not 'directly or immediately convertible into money' but accumulate in different forms in relation to the way society is formed;[13] therefore, restricting or expanding the access of different social groups to cultural capital becomes a means to achieve higher social positions. From this perspective, this study benefits from the concept of cultural capital for two reasons. First, it sheds light on regional and social disparities which either were not at least adequately addressed by economic plans in the 1960s and the 1970s or increased because of the plans' orientations. Second, its inclusion in this study aims to raise awareness of this concept in Kurdish social change studies. Finally, this study is indebted to John Thompson's analysis of the role of the new visual means of communication in modern society, because it makes possible an adequate interpretation of the way the cultural hegemony of Persian in multicultural Iran was established.

Modernity and modernization

Emerged as the outcomes of a series of international and political developments, modernization and development theories of post–Second World War played a crucial role in shaping the Iranian state's centralizing, urban-oriented economic plans.[14] At the same time, 'Modernization' and 'development' shaped a perception of change as a process of transition from a 'traditional' society to a 'modern' one.

Moreover, as Zachary Lockman argues (see Modernity and modernization), the duality of tradition and modernity was popularized by Max Weber sociology, from which (Kurdish) social change studies in Iran continue to suffer.[15]

This study challenges a transitional perception of change. 'Traditional' and 'modern' are not self-evident concepts, nor are they, as Reinhard Bendix explains, mutually exclusive. As John Stevenson argues in his study of social change in interwar Britain, 'all ages are ages of transition', and some of the most significant features of social change have their origins in the earlier period.[16] Therefore, Stevenson concludes, any understanding of an era involves recognizing that 'it was an end as much as a beginning, in which the concerns of the past have as important a part to play as those which foreshadow an emerging society'.[17]

In the eighteenth and nineteenth centuries, the term 'modernization' connoted social change. It consisted of 'the economic or political advance of some pioneering society and subsequent changes in follower societies'.[18] Social change resulted in modern sociology pioneered by Karl Marx, Emile Durkheim and Max Weber, which, as Bendix explains, 'developed almost wholly around the themes and antitheses cast up' by social change. However, an oversimplified view of tradition versus modernity developed too. This 'oversimplification resulted from ideological interpretation of the contrast between tradition and modernity, and from undue generalizations of the European experience'.[19] This generalization entailed a paradigmatic view of modernity as the new civilization of Europe and North America that has developed ever since. Modernity as a new civilization implies its uniqueness in human history and is based on a positive self-image that 'modern Western culture has most often given to itself'.[20] Modernity is generally perceived as 'a coherent system, a package deal, with a well-defined set of attributes'.[21] However, modernization in the post–Second World War era began increasingly to connote state-led programmes to modernize non-Western countries based on modernizing paradigms propagated by modernization theories. From this perspective, a profound socio-economic change that came to characterize Iran and its Kurdish society by 1979 cannot be merely explained in terms of such programmes, nor by some 'positive' and 'negative' ramifications.

Modernization theories promulgated 'a new and intellectually powerful way of thinking about social, political and cultural change', by which American social scientists tried to understand and predict social and political changes in the Middle East, as well as in Asia, Africa and Latin America.[22] This paradigm was 'rooted in a common set of assumptions about the character and trajectory of historical change'.[23] Intellectually, these theories were rooted in an intellectual tradition that imposed a sharp distinction between the West and the rest of the world. The older dichotomy between civilization and barbarism was replaced, in the works of Hamilton Gibbs and Bernard Lewis, by that between tradition and modernity, which stemmed from Max Weber's sociology.[24] According to Weber, the traditional societies of 'the East' must follow the linear path of civilization, which Western societies had successfully passed through, in order to be able to earn modern characteristics and end backwardness.[25]

Academically, modernization theories were a consequence of the political developments since the Second World War which were characterized by independence movements, the emergence of new, post-colonial countries, and crucially, the emergence of the United States as a new world power. Modernization became a fashionable term following the war when comparative social studies in the United States increased and produced a number of modernization theories.[26] These theories were founded on the theories of social evolutions, which, as Bendix explains, guided domestic studies in the United States, unlike in Europe where the theories of social evolution had been 'employed to interpret the encounter between the advanced industrial societies of the West and the peoples and cultures of colonial and dependent areas in Africa and the Orient'.[27] In the context of the Cold War, theories of political development were presented as an alternative to a dominant Marxism, which explained social and political predicaments by economic inequality, and advocated land reform, state-led economic development, etc., which were later picked up by pro-Western governments and implemented for political reasons.[28] Preparing a prescription for the modernization of traditional monarchies, Samuel Huntington has nonetheless rightly noted that while the aim of the modernizing monarchs of the nineteenth century was 'to thwart imperialism', the aim of those in the twentieth century was to 'thwart revolution'.[29] In the case of Iran, as scholars have noted, the White Revolution was initially a reaction to regional revolutions and coups, in order to preserve the Pahlavi regime and to prevent revolution from below.[30] This study derives from academic works, for example, on the ideological construction of the White Revolution and the interpretation of modernization that followed as uneven development.[31] However, this study contributes to this interpretation of the White Revolution as a revolution from above, by underlining the way the idea of a 'White Revolution' was exploited by the state, which adopted and then systematically implemented the existing reformist ideas in such regional and internal contexts, and analysing its consequences for Kurdish society in Iran.

With the intensification of state-led modernizations over the following decades in countries such as Iran, Turkey, Iraq and Egypt, as well as other Arab countries, modernization increasingly came to be perceived as a transition to a Euro-centric modernity, creating, as Bendix notes, certain prerequisites, since it was thought that 'regardless of time and place all countries must somehow create all the conditions characteristic of modernity before they can hope to be successful in their drive for modernization'.[32] However, Bendix maintains, to distinguish 'before and after' is 'an analytical tool, not a tool to predict "developing" countries'.[33] Concerning concepts of modernity, tradition and modernization, as far as modernization theories are concerned, Kurdish social change studies need to employ a critical view and distance from a transitional understanding of social change. This includes 'transitional modernisation' which, according to Daniel Lerner's *The Passing of Traditional Society* (1958), one of the most influential books in theories of modernization, is a 'passage' from an undesirable, backward situation to a more advanced, modern one. The passage is characterized by invidious dualities such as 'village *versus* town, land *versus* cash, illiteracy *versus* enlightenment, resignation *versus* ambition, [and] piety *versus* excitement'.[34] Transformation from one to the other, therefore, constitutes the passage from a traditional society.

Therefore, this book does not perceive 'modernization' as the transition to becoming 'modern'. Rapid social change has been popularly conceived as an inevitable result of a 'transitional phase'. Reflected in social change studies, this view is reinforced by ongoing intellectual debates which fortify a transitional perception of modernization, leading to an oversimplifying single-dimensional approach to social change. By contrast, this study argues for a multidimensional approach that invites us to adopt a critical reading of concepts and subjects involved. Lastly, this study's critique of the modernization of Iran does not intend to unduly demonize the state or the reigning Shah, nor intends to equal the state with the Shah. The state was crucial for the institutional transformation of Iran. However, the White Revolution's modernization was violently terminated because of the monarch's mismanagement of the process and dictatorship.

Nation, nationalism and Kurdishness

Theories of nation and nationalism can be subdivided into various subgroups which, from different perspectives, regard these concepts as both relatively modern and historically contingent phenomena.[35] As both ideology and movement, nationalism is founded on difference. Its historical consciousness rests on a national perception of history, throughout which the 'nation' maintains its cohesiveness despite historical changes and transformations;[36] historically, it obscures a good understanding of the past. In fact, nationalism usurps history in order to justify its distinctiveness from, and its cultural superiority over, others. One of the main reasons for the emergence of this modernist approach was the failure of theories of modernization.[37] On the other hand, perspectives on nation and nationalism continue to transform, while studies of the history of Iran from such perspectives have theoretically and considerably enriched our understanding of the histories and politics of modern Iran.[38] Regarding modernity, it is significant to note, as Andreas Wimmer rightly points out, that nationalism is not 'just a by-product of modern state formation [...]; rather, modernity *itself* rests on a basis of ethnic and nationalist principles'.[39]

However, unlike a vague and static 'Kurdish nationalism', this study employs the concept of *Kurdayeti*, defined as the struggle for Kurdish cultural and political rights, in order to simultaneously recognize such rights and be critical of the ideology of nationalism as such. Furthermore, the concept represents a dynamic process, serves a better understanding of Kurdish histories in Iran and reflects effective resistance against the homogenizing and oppressive policies of the modern Iranian state.[40] Like nationalism, *Kurdayeti* is also a world view based on a modern, national understanding of self and history. However, it is important to heed the cultural and historical affinities with the idea of Iran. Even when in an Iranian context a distinctive Kurdish nationalism emerged alongside Persian nationalism, it preserved aspects of *Iraniyant* (Iranianness) both to define itself and to construct an authentic past. For example, modern national Kurdish historiography has substantially relied on racial, 'scientific' and mythical, for example, Ferdowsi's *Shahnameh* and the Aryan myth, constructions of a national

Iranian past. It defines the Kurds, in Huzni's words, as 'an Iranian *qaum*', which prior to modernity's 'ethnic minority' only denoted kinship or a people who had distinct traits but (as a branch of a bigger family) also shared characteristics and origins with others.[41] On the other hand, for the Kurds, throughout the twentieth century, *Kurdayeti* developed as a popular and *legitimate* concept guiding various movements to achieve Kurdish ethnic rights within the framework of modern Iran, whereas nationalism, with the ascendancy of Marxism's class theories especially from the 1970s onward, came to be perceived merely as a source of belligerent stances aiming to divide human society based on 'nations'. It should be acknowledged that in many historical epochs Marxist or leftist Kurdish-Iranian organizations, fiercely opposing nationalism as such, have been the ardent advocates of the Kurd's political and cultural rights. Therefore, as it becomes more evident throughout this study, *Kurdayeti* is a more effective analytical tool for highlighting the dynamism of Kurdish history.

As regards modern nation-building and homogenization, in an Iranian context, homogenization refers to several strategies employed by the state-builders, including intellectuals who provided moral justification, to construct a unified Iranian political community based on the pillars of 'national unity' and 'territorial integrity'. As a violent process, homogenization has included the coercive practices of banning Kurdish, the forced settlement of tribes, and the overt suppression of revolts or any practices of self-rule, for example, the Kurdistan Republic of 1946 and the uprisings and political movements throughout the Pahlavi era. In short, homogenization has been tantamount to *stami milli* or national oppression, as popularly referred to by Iranian Kurds. However, as the modernization of Iran intensified during the post–Second World War era, the cultural hegemony of the perceived core-ethnocultural group, that is, the consensual acceptance of the cultural superiority of Persian culture and language, was established through the expansion of modern (Persian) education and, significantly, the mediatization of culture (see Chapter 4).

Based on studies of state formation and of the politicization of ethnicity, it can be asserted that the Kurds in Iran have faced different strategies of homogenization.[42] Generally speaking, the process of state formation in Iran is not merely characterized by systematic inclusion through, for instance, education or administrative divisions or forced inclusion, but also by attempts to create a normative state whose legitimacy is guaranteed by maintaining the cultural hegemony of Persian (see Chapter 4). Therefore, as Heather Rae rightly argues, 'state formation has a crucial cultural dimension' which needs to be analysed in studies of homogenization and modern nation-building too.[43]

Furthermore, 'Iranian Kurdistan' and 'Kurdistan' have political connotations. However, in this book, these concepts are used in a geographical sense to refer to the region occupied by the Kurds in the west of Iran. Moreover, referring to the province, 'Iranian Kurdistan' for the Iranian state has represented a discourse to sustain the relations of domination in favour of power. On the other hand, *Rozhhalat-i* Kurdistan, or Eastern Kurdistan, has become very popular among the Kurds as an alternative to the discourse of 'Iranian Kurdistan'. However, while it is a challenge to a dominant discourse that denies the cultural and political rights of the Kurds in Iran, 'Eastern Kurdistan' has the potential to become an act of spatialization, that is, the division of space, the flipside of periodization, which inevitably creates imagined lines between the Kurds and other Iranian societies, overlooking their shared historical, social and cultural bonds.[44] Therefore, this study adopts the concepts of Kurdish society (in Iran), which denotes an ethnic community residing in a specific geography, not in isolation but with intimate ties with other peoples or societies around them, and Iranian Kurdish society in order to acknowledge an independent existence of the Kurds in Iran on the one hand and emphasize the values shared by various peoples on the other.

Moreover, due to Iran's administrative divisions as a component of political modernization, many Kurdish cities are excluded from the Kurdistan Province. Kurdistan for the Kurds and most Iranians includes all Kurdish cities (in addition to many mixed Kurdish-Turkish, Kurdish-Lur and Kurdish-Persian cities), thus ignoring the administrative divisions. Furthermore, 'Kurdish society' in this book is employed without delineating ethnic and political boundaries or as a substitute for 'people'; it refers to an area where Kurds with a distinct language and culture have lived for centuries and their socio-economic, cultural and political ways of life have been shaped, especially in modern times, in connection with the other societies encompassing them.

Finally, there is a persistent tension in contemporary Iran over the concepts of *qaum* (an ethnic group) and *millat* (nation), which has become one of the primary battlegrounds in the clash of Iranian (Persian) and Kurdish national narratives. *Qaum* justifies the former's denial of the political and cultural rights of a community, which is, in turn, represented by the latter's definition of Kurds as *millat*, in need of recognition. On the one hand, the notions of national unity and territorial integrity, which constitute the pillars of Iranian national identity, continue to provide powerful grounds for the Iranian national narrative. On the other hand, the Kurdish national narrative continues to have historical and intellectual relevance in a situation in which the cultural and political rights of the Kurds in Iran are persistently and violently denied.

This confrontation over the concepts of *qaum* and *millat* in post-revolutionary Iran has emanated from the Islamic Republic's Constitution, which allows limited cultural rights for other ethnic communities (i.e. non-Persian speakers), defined as *aqvam* (sing. *qaum*) not as *millat*. The Constitution in this respect was based on a definition of the Kurdish community as an inextricable part of a unified Iranian nation. Nevertheless, it also reflected the pressure on behalf of various elements of the community to improve their cultural positions. Therefore, in the continuous clash of national narratives, *qaum* is redefined as an undeveloped nation, presumably not yet prepared to form an independent state. This is a meaning which has served power and continues to sustain the current relations of domination.[45] By contrast, the Kurdish national narrative endeavours to prove that the Kurds are a 'ripe' nation and justifies its claim to nationhood by referring to common descent, a specific land with a distinct history, language and popular culture. Any study of the Kurds in Iran, therefore, needs to treat such concepts not as self-evident but as power-serving ideas. In this regard, critical theories of nation and nationalism, which are followed by new perspectives on these concepts, provide firm foundations for an intellectual confrontation against national narratives, including their invented definitions and reconstructed histories, which are closely linked to both political power and political mobilization.

Source materials

A vast range of primary and secondary sources constitute this book's source materials. To sketch an image of Kurdish society in the early twentieth century, I have relied on travelogues, the memoirs of prominent literary figures and their literary works. I explored the valuable reference tools of the *Encyclopaedia Iranica* and the *Encyclopaedia of Islam*, both printed and the online second edition, and critically engaged with the interesting works of the earlier authors of studies on the Kurds. At the same time, I benefited from more recent statistical and informative works on the modernization of Iran. For primary sources on the era of the White Revolution, I have used official statistics, newspapers and scholarly journals of the time. These sources include books that contain statistics and information on, for example, development programmes and various state organizations. The National Archives (TNA) in London was particularly useful for its wide range of sources in the forms of correspondence and reports, which occupied me for weeks.[46] On the cultural and educational aspects of modernization, Iran's leading universities' academic journals and the Ministry of Education's educational reports and articles proved priceless, covering the entire Pahlavi era.

Furthermore, in addition to secondary literature, a critical reading of books published in the decades following the Second World War enabled me to gain a more comprehensive understanding of the era of the White Revolution. The literature in Iranian Studies concerned with the era provided me with valuable information and analyses of significant themes. In addition to historiographical works on the period, a case in point is Gholam Reza Afkhami's *The Life and the Times of the Shah*, which stands as a collective effort and contains valuable primary source information.

Finally, many interviews were conducted with members of the generation of the 1960s and 1970s who, in various capacities of teacher, judge, doctor and cultural or political activists, had witnessed the impact of the era of the White Revolution on Kurdish society. Memoirs form a significant part of Kurdish collective memory, while interviews help the researcher to understand the past. For this study, the published memoirs and interviews are, as Lynn Abrams argues, 'means of accessing not just information but also signification, interpretation and meaning'.[47] This study maintains this approach to oral history throughout the book.[48]

Chapter 1

THE INTEGRATION OF KURDISH SOCIETY INTO MODERN IRAN

Economy and society in early twentieth-century Kurdish society

Insufficient research and the lack of evidence hinder any attempt to depict social conditions prior to modern times, allowing generalization and speculation. Limited scope and slow pace of change until modern times did not connote the absence of change. Ever since the fifteenth century, the Kurdish region had been caught up in the rivalries between the formidable confederacies of Akquyunlu and Qaraquyunlu in the early modern times and then until the twentieth century between the Ottoman and Iranian (Safavid and Qajar) Empires, the policies of which shaped the Kurdish societies' social and political structures. Meanwhile, various Kurdish Emirates or principalities ruled over the Kurds, oversaw an economy exemplified by markets or handcraft industry and promoted cultural activities. Originated in philosophical, theological and literary movements of past centuries, religious education centres and literary innovations spread to more regions, embodied by an increasing number of literary figures.[1] Nevertheless, modernity distinguished itself by its unprecedented speed of social transformation.

In the nineteenth century, the region experienced major regional and imperial wars, which paved the way for the unprecedented political and economic presence of Britain and Russia in the Ottoman Empire and Qajar Iran. The Kurdish Emirates eventually faded away as the result of the empires' centralization policies which aimed to strengthen and modernize the state in the face of the military and political onslaught of European powers. The integration of the economies of the region into the world market by the end of the century resulted in an unequal trading balance with the effect that it made these economies exporters of raw materials and importers of manufactured goods.[2] Consequently, as Masoud Karshenas argues in the case of Iran, free trade led to the peripheralization of these economies in a world economy,[3] which by the end of the century, as Eric Hobsbawm explains, had been effectively and permanently divided into 'advanced' and 'underdeveloped' as the result of political and industrial revolutions.[4] Consequently, structural reforms in the regional states to modernize and strengthen the economy and society followed. As regards the Kurds, this subsequently transformed the pre-modern power relations based on Empire-Emirate with the effect that the rule of the 'autonomous' Emirates ended and the direct authority of the central state over the Kurdish regions through its representatives followed.

The integration of the Ottoman and Qajar Empires in the world market had undoubtedly engaged the Kurds in a wider regional trade. Mrs Bishop, a missionary, observed in her journey in Kurdistan around 1890:

> Long before reaching Sujbulak [modern Mahabad] there were indications of the vicinity of a place of some importance, caravans going both ways, asses loaded with perishable produce, horsemen and foot passengers, including many fine-looking Kurdish women unveiled, and walking with a firm masculine stride, even when carrying children on their backs.[5] Sujbulak, the capital of Northern Persian Kurdistan, and the residence of a governor, is quite an important *entrepôt* for furs, in which it carries on a large trade with Russia, and a French firm, it is said, buys up fur rugs to the value of several hundred thousand francs annually.[6]

In addition to the regional trade, the economy was characterized by an inter-trade system involving towns, tribal and village communities, which lived in conditions devoid of a sanitation system;[7] wheel-carts and quadrupeds were used as means of transportation. A nomadic and rural life had made people economically self-sufficient, while they continued to benefit from cross-border trades before its interruption by the modern state, which identified it as an act of 'smuggling' in order to make it illegal. Kurdish society was a feudal society under the yoke of *darabags* or *aghas* (landowners) who ruled over *ra'yats* (servants). The *agha* and the tribal chief owned both the land and the *jutiar* (Ku. peasant) class who cultivated the land. Although historically Kurdish societies (including urban, settled, nomadic and tribal) possessed distinct language and culture, socio-economically they were not radically different in comparison with other communities such as Baluchis, Lurs, Persians, Azeris and Turkomans who demographically contributed to the ethnic structure of Iran. According to *Sur Esrafil*, the bestselling periodical published in Iran between 1907 and 1908, a *ra'yat* in Iran had been condemned to the level of beasts of burden so that the landowner's acts of 'incarcerating, banishing, beating, and, sometimes, killing a *ra'yat* were seen as his natural and inalienable rights'.[8]

Based on nineteenth-century travelogues and anthropological accounts, it seems that until the expansion of trade in modern times, various nomadic, tribal and settled Kurdish social organizations were geographically scattered and socio-economically not compactly connected.[9] Nomads depended on cattle so were the tribes and settled communities whose economic resources also included cultivated lands, vineyards, orchards, fruit, wheat and barley. There were limited resources as regards cash crops and few markets. However, this began to change effectively with the expansion of trade, the emergence of a modern economy, urbanization and the availability of better roads with the effect that dairy products, meat and grain found new markets in growing urban centres. The expansion of trade and increasing movements of people upgraded economic trade, symbolized by inter-regional markets.[10] As regards the tribes, constant tribal conflicts originated in their desire to appropriate other tribes' territories, as well as their economic and military resources. Unsurprisingly, authoritarian centralizing modernization elicited strong opposition on behalf of powerful Kurdish tribes who had enjoyed a long-standing political authority legitimized in many cases by religion.[11] Moreover, wealth and military arsenals were in the possession of the *agha* or the *sheikh*, the chief religious authority. In contrast, the wider population suffered from harsh living conditions, economic exploitation of the ruling class and social injustice while notions of hygiene and healthcare were absent. James B. Fraser, who travelled to several regions in central and northwest Iran in the early 1820s, warns against exotic narratives wherein false impressions of that land 'are calculated to shut out all disagreeable impressions of poverty and misery, and to substitute for them those of population and riches'.[12] Applying to the whole land of Iran, Fraser's depiction of a situation, where 'the class of farmers and cultivators' lived 'continually under a system of extortion and injustice', illustrates distressing social conditions of the time.[13]

The structure of Kurdish society was characterized by powerful tribes, agricultural activity in the rural areas by non-tribal groups, small towns and a vast number of villages. The fact that Kurdistan up till the 1960s witnessed sluggish urbanization confirms this picture of early twentieth-century Kurdish society, although Reza Shah's forced settlement of the tribes and, in later decades, their more voluntary settlements benefited population growth in both village and city. Rural life was characterized by an unequal relationship between the landowner and the peasant who had to provide the former with various forms of rents in order to ensure survival, residency in the village and cultivate the land.

Kinship, clan and other ties characterized social bonds, while equally strong were also religious loyalties to genealogically authoritative *sheikhs* and spiritual adherence to various Sufi movements which originated religious orders and institutions such as *tariqa* and *khanaqa*, respectively.[14] *Shari'a* (Islamic law) and *'urf* (tradition) regulated the social and religious life, and, despite being mostly identified as the followers of the Shafi'i legal school in Sunni Islam, the Kurdish region religiously came to be known as very diverse, incorporating communities affiliated to other religions or schools of law. Although Kurdish culture was inseparable from religious values and institutions, *din* (religion) and *'ilm* (knowledge/science), as it was understood in pre-modern times, had historically coexisted and not opposed each other. Texts by Kurdish authors who were at the same time devoted religious individuals reflected this coexistence. In his history of Kurdistan (1597), Sharaf Khan defines history as *'ilm* which enhances 'wisdom to find truth' while, upon encounter with modernity, Haji Qadir Koyi's poetry at the end of the nineteenth century was distinguished by his appeal to science and reason in order to elevate the Kurds to the rank of a 'nation'.[15] Scientific subjects formed important parts of the curriculum in religious schools where, for example, astronomy and astrology, language and Aristotle's logic were taught.[16] However, this relatively harmonious coexistence was also partly because religion and the social position of its representative class had not yet faced the onslaught of modern natural sciences.

Furthermore, in a wider context, although illiteracy was widespread and education was 'in the hands of a few learned families',[17] there were many forms of learning literacy skills for different layers of society. For example, 'reading, writing, and the rudiments of arithmetic' were general among the merchant and bazaar class, while those who aspired to become Mirza or secretary also engaged with literature.[18] Education was primarily in the hands of the religious institutions, which also provided *madrassa* or college for those who pursued a profession in the priesthood, the law or medicine; many *hakims* or physicians obtained the profession by imitating their next of kin.[19] Especially since the middle of the nineteenth century, to the educational landscape were added new state colleges which, teaching 'the rudiments of a liberal education', prepared courtiers, diplomats, government employees and army officers for a new era.[20] On the other hand, as contemporaries observed, only 'the daughters of the rich and learned' had access to education, another factor which confirmed an uneven spread of educational opportunities among the population.[21]

As regards the Kurdish regions, attached to the mosque, *Hojra* and *khanaqa* (religious centres of education) trained *faqeh* (Ku. religious student) and *mala* (Ku. the teacher of *shari'a*) whom upon graduation led religious duties in villages.[22] They studied religious texts but also Kurdish, Persian and Arabic literature.[23] Both religious and literary figures built spiritual and intellectual bridges between regions until the emerging nation states effectively hindered the regional connection between peoples and created fixed, physical borders instead. Until the mid-twentieth century, the fabric of Kurdish literates was composed of mainly *hojra* -educated, who conveyed ideas and influenced thought. The modern states' modernizations had already begun to affect this composition by both introducing and popularizing a nationally inspired modern education, which gradually but effectively revolutionized the existing systems of learning.

The modern state also introduced notions of healthcare and hygienization. Orientalist accounts on the nineteenth and early twentieth centuries claim that the Kurds were almost unaware of healthcare and did not pay attention to hygiene while infectious diseases among them were widespread and the nomads suffered from rheumatism.[24] The foundations of public education and healthcare in Iranian Kurdistan – this applies to other peripheral regions as well – were laid down in the reign of Reza Shah (1925–41); however, these institutions spread in the second half of the twentieth century, specifically in the era of the White Revolution (1963–79).

A weak infrastructure in a mountainous land hindered communication and had a negative effect, as noted by Ervand Abrahamian, also on the expansion of trade.[25] These contributed to the isolation of villages which thus had to rely on a self-sufficient economy. In the course of the nineteenth century, the movement of multilingual Kurdish literates, poets and religious educated had compensated for the absence of the means of communication, and their literary endeavours intertwined with social and political developments in Kurdish societies under the Emirates.[26] Their journeys and the ideas they conveyed were significant for spreading knowledge and connecting various regions.[27] However, this does not conceal a closed structure of Kurdish societies which seemed to be uninformed about important political upheavals of the time. For example, Kurdish literature (represented mainly by poetry) did not reflect the impact of movements such as Sheikhism and Babism in the first half of the nineteenth century that preceded later movements of the century and ultimately that of the Constitutional Revolution of 1906. The lack of data can also be attributed to the ignorance of researchers who have been conventionally more interested in the origins and genealogies of peoples and ruling families. Nevertheless, an ineffective communications system, or complete lack of it, made these regions politically isolated.

Women were active participants in agriculture, animal husbandry, the village and nomadic life, and the upbringing of the children. While approaching a Kurdish town around 1890, Mrs Bishop observed 'Kurdish women unveiled, and walking with a firm masculine stride, even when carrying children on their backs'.[28] Orientalist accounts depict Kurdish women capable of 'hosting strangers in the absence of the men of the household', brave and active.[29] Carpet weaving based on women's labour satisfied the *agha* household's luxurious needs and the existing carpet trade as well. This craft continued to remain a permanent aspect of Kurdish rural life.[30] Women also rose to preeminent literary positions but only among the literate, the upper class and ruling elites of Kurdistan. Mastura Ardalan (1804–48), known as Mastura Kurdistani, in the ruling Ardalan family was a historian and poet. Other ruling families such as Soran and Jaf also yielded ruling women. In the course of the sixteenth century when the Ottoman governor imprisoned Suleiman *bag*, the *mir* (Ku. ruler) of the powerful Soran Emirate, Suleiman's sister, Khanzad, ruled the Emirate for a few years.[31] 'Adila Khanim, the governor of Halabja in the early twentieth century, came from the famous Jaf tribe. Both are remembered by posterity as just and capable rulers.

In many respects, for example, administration and demography, as Abrahamian has noted, 'the nineteenth century remains the dark age for Iranian statistics'.[32] This, as regards the Kurds, extends to 1956 when the government carried out the first official census. Moreover, porous geographical and cultural boundaries between various communities in that century render it difficult to collect data on a society that had not yet been defined as 'Iranian Kurdistan'. It is nonetheless estimated that of a population of nearly 7 million living in Qajar Iran in the 1850s, 800,000 were Kurds.[33] This high number also includes the population that resided in regions that later did not form parts of Iranian Kurdistan. According to *Vaqaye ' Negar-e Kordestani* (Kurdistan Gazette), the Kurdish region under the Qajar rule had a population of 600,000 in 1874. It was administratively divided into seventeen blocs, each comprised of a *qasaba* or small town administering several villages, and a city, that is, Sanandaj with a population of 24,744.[34] Bishop, who published her memoir in 1891 after travelling to Kurdistan, claims that Sauj Blagh (modern Mahabad), an economically important town in the northern part, had a population of 5,000.[35] Lastly, to these figures on the number of the Kurdish population we should add other Kurdish communities who lived in other parts of Iran, for example, in Khurasan in the northeast and Mazandaran in the north.

Therefore, such dominant socio-economic features, a landowner–peasant relation, geographical obstacles, weak infrastructure and ineffective means of communications, a self-sufficient, predominantly rural and illiterate society continued to characterize Iranian Kurdistan until the first half of the twentieth century.

Modernity

The Constitutional Revolutions of the early twentieth century in both Qajar Iran and the Ottoman Empire marked the effective encounter of the Kurds with *modernity*, a framework in which European ideas assumed cultural superiority. Modernity introduced the notions of law, progress, education and representation. It also inaugurated ideas of nation, nation state and fixed border, reflected in later political developments. Consequently, the political landscape of the Kurdish region was profoundly altered in the decades following the Constitutional Revolution. Documents pertaining to the constitutional years until the outbreak of the First World War demonstrate the impact of the revolution and its ideas throughout the Kurdish region. Correspondence exchanged between the *Majlis* and *anjoman-e Eyalati* or the provincial representative body of Kurdistan along with complaints made by guilds and prominent figures to the *Majlis* are framed around such concepts to justify their works, support their critiques and present their demands more effectively.[36]

In general, two aspects of Kurdish society, tribal and non-tribal, began to be reshaped in different ways. Historiography and anthropology have been lopsided on Kurdish tribal history. This is understandable because a large portion of the population lived under the rule of the tribes, which were known for their military prowess, economic resources, and territorial possessions (see Map 2). The political changes in Iran elicited resistance on behalf of the tribes such as the Kalhors and the Shikaks. The Kalhor tribes presumably preferred the status quo and in 1911 'supported the abortive military move of Salar ad Dola against the Constitutionalist government in Tehran'.[37] Located in the northwest of Iran and estimated to have numbered around 2,000 families in 1921, the Shikak confederacy under the leadership of the famous Simko continued to challenge the Iranian government's authority with demands to secure a 'Kurdish' rule.[38] Although the ideas of 'nation' and 'nation state' inspired the rebellion of Simko in Kurdistan, in retrospect it did not demonstrate political cohesiveness in that direction. The confederacy spread over a vast region between the Ottoman and Qajar Empires. It consisted of two main branches of 'Abduiy and Kardar, each of which was divided into eight and thirteen tribes, respectively. The Shikaks were nomads and were engaged in animal husbandry as their source of economic power. According to Sanar Mamedi, one of the later leaders of the powerful Mamedi tribe (in the Kardar branch), 'until 1941 the Shikaks disdained agriculture. They looked down at the Kirmanjs [settled, farming Kurds] and considered them as their own servants while coercing them into forced labour'.[39] The confederacy lost unity and its political power with the emergence of modern, centralized states. The quelling of the rebellion of Simko by the early 1930s was followed by forced, and later more voluntary, settlements of the Shikaks and their forced migration to other parts of Iran. Moreover, modern territorial borders resulted in the division of the confederacy and reorientation of its sub-tribes' loyalties to different states.

Moreover, based on contemporary appeals addressed to the *Majlis* for help, Kurdish tribes interrupted the processes of the formation of provincial administration and political participation of the population in the Kurdish region because these went against their political and economic powers.[40] However, decisively defeated by Reza Shah, Kurdish tribes in Iran re-emerged with his abdication following the outbreak of the Second World War. They played a crucial role in the formation of the Kurdistan Republic of 1946, which, ironically, both as an idea and a political platform *was not* the culmination of tribal politics. They formed the Republic's military backbone, and their chiefs were engaged in negotiations with the Soviet, the Azerbaijani and Iranian governments.[41] Tribal interests, however, prevented unity in action and even caused defection and further intertribal conflicts.[42] The end of the Republic in January 1947 and the intensification of the modernization of Iran effectively diminished their political power.[43]

Insofar as non-tribal Kurdistan was concerned, Iran's Constitutional Revolution inspired the formation of *anjoman*s or societies by Kurdish literates, for example, in major cities like Sanandaj, Kermanshah and Sauj Blagh, followed by the publication of irregular journals.[44] It engaged the Kurds with the ideas of law, *Majlis* and representation.[45] It inspired many to attempt to spread modern schools, a process which was interrupted not only because of political instability but also because of lack of support.[46]

Furthermore, nationalist movements and ideas began to spread manifest in various Kurdish political movements, which exerted regional impacts too. The modern Iranian nation state's educational, political and socio-economic requirements shaped a Kurdish urbanized (non-tribal) environment from which a new educated generation emerged. Organizational and ideological approaches attest to this fact and are symbolized by the first political organization, *Komala-i Zhiyanawai-i Kurd* (Ku. the Organization of Kurdish Revival, 1942–5) or *Zhe Kaf*. This nationalist, progressive organization was founded by a group of urbanized educated or, in Eagleton's words, 'middle class citizens' who also paved the way for the formation of the Kurdistan Republic of 1946.[47] Furthermore, the modern administrative structure of the Republic differentiated its functions in various ministries such as health, education, economics, labour, justice, road and agriculture. This simultaneously reflected preoccupation with reforms and economic plans, as well as with ideas which tribal politics could not have and did not intend to induce.[48] Furthermore, political demands increasingly began to reflect socio-economic and political transformations. For example, the ideas of self-determination and autonomy within the framework of Iran had gained grounds in political vocabularies by the early 1920s. As regards these ideas and resulting from prolonged political instability, a contributing factor was intensifying tension between a growing will for centralization of power and decentralization represented by provincial councils.[49] Simultaneously, although nationalism inspired separatist demands, these demands gradually lost touch with reality, that is, socio-economic and political situations. In contrast, *autonomy within the framework of Iran* increasingly reflected the dual process of modernization and homogenization of identity, which reproduced the tension between centralization and decentralization. This process paradoxically accelerated socio-economic integrations of ethnically distinctive societies in modern Iran, on the one hand, and created conditions for the survival of their ethnic identities through ethnic struggle, on the other.

Finally, new borders and their fixation shaped modern Kurdish societies territorially. Borders were redefined as the result of two processes: first, the idea of a powerful centralized state which, in turn, would end cross-border tribal conflicts; and second, attempts to serve socio-economic interests of Britain and Russia and secure the production of oil – this was done with absolute neglect of the tribal populations' socio-economic interests.[50] Indeed, the famous Sykes-Picot Agreement had been preceded by a common commission, authorized by Russia and England and led by Vladimir Minorsky and Sir Arnold Wilson, between December 1913 and October 1914.[51] Oil had become a primary factor, and 'it mattered less where the line should lie that it should be laid down definitely somewhere, for, until that had been done no development [in oil wells] was possible'.[52] In this respect, 'a strong central government' was advocated to put an end to 'inter-tribal feuds and raids' that had desolated the land and ruined villages.[53] Territorially, therefore, fixed geographical and cultural borders replaced hitherto permeable ones, effectively separating Iranian Kurdistan from other Kurdish societies, which were each ultimately redefined as a nation state's Kurdistan – modern Turkey and Syria did not recognize Kurdistan, whereas Iran's and Iraq's administrative divisions, albeit for different reasons (see the following paragraphs), included a Kurdistan Province.

The impact of the Great War

Meanwhile, the Great War effectively interrupted the constitutionalist movement in Iran and paralysed attempts to implement modernizing reforms. The legacy of the war proved to be enduring. Regions occupied by the Kurds suffered immensely and the presence of Russia, Britain and the Ottoman Empire in Iran, and their rivalry in the north and northwest, where the Kurds lived, made this region one of the battlefields of the Great War. *Kaveh*, a contemporary journal published by a number of Iranian intellectuals in Berlin, included regular war reports and maps, which illustrated the Kurdish region in the heart of the belligerent sides' rivalries.[54] In the aftermath of the war, journals in the mid-1920s still reported 'widespread poverty and unemployment', urging the government to establish factories and pay more heed to agriculture.[55] During the war, the Kurds suffered hunger and death on a great scale while mass migration in search of food took place several times: 'waves after waves of [Kurdish-speaking] people from Iran arrived in Sulaimaniya [in Ottoman Kurdistan] where the death toll had already reached ten per day. They begged and, in some cases, women sold their bodies in order to survive.'⁵⁶ By the end of the war, Sulaimaniya 'had dropped from it[s] prewar population of 20,000 to 2.500'.⁵⁷ According to Muhammad Zaki Beg, the renowned Kurdish statesman and historian, probably over half a million Kurdish civilians perished during the war.⁵⁸ Nevertheless, in many respects, the war had only exacerbated political and economic situations. Contemporary correspondence of the pre-war years from Kurdistan province complained about a sense of being abandoned 'in the hands of *estebdad* [despotism] of the local rulers' and, in the face of the devastating impact of the presence of the Ottoman forces since the mid-1900s in some areas, frequent pillages and insecurity. Moreover, they uncover many cases of corruption and refer to the interruption of the expansion of *mo 'aref* or (modern) education by closing down schools in many areas.⁵⁹

Famine and hunger, cold winters and bad harvests in the 1920s and 1930s soon were to be followed by the outbreak of the Second World War, the drastic consequences of which exacerbated living conditions. The government introduced a system of rationing of staple food such as sugar, tea, bread and cotton in Tehran in 1941, and later Ministry of Food is claimed to have issued ration cards to the senior officials in the provinces.⁶⁰ However, the absence of census data and widespread bribery and fraud rendered the system and also the distribution of food and ration cards insufficient and ineffective.⁶¹ Geographical barriers and war presumably created additional hindrance for such efforts. Moreover, bread riots and political instability destroyed the system in many towns.⁶² The exception was the Kurdish region administered by the Kurdish Republic in 1946, where the shortages of staple food were to some extent overcome due to the good harvest of 1944, the sale of the entire Kurdish tobacco supply to Russia and the collection of taxes.⁶³

However, lingering inflation and shortages of food, exacerbated by weak infrastructure and a fragile economy, continued into the Second World War and outlasted the reign of Reza Shah. For example, a widespread famine in Kurdistan which had followed the cold winter of 1947 brought about inhumane economic practices. As soon as the news reached Hemin, who became a renowned Kurdish poet, that a young girl was being bartered for a sack of flour, he recalled in his famous *Tark u Run* (Dark and light), he embarked to investigate and began to ask 'a group of village women what was happening [. . .] they started to spit in the other man's face who had intended to buy the girl, and [then] run to bring as much flour as they could find [to prevent the trade]'.⁶⁴ Referring to all humanity and highlighting the consequences of the war in his region, Hemin Mukriyani (Muhammad Amin Sheikhuleslami, 1921–86) maintained metaphorically that 'while mankind in the twentieth century had created and used atom, radars, and even invaded the moon, I witnessed how human beings grazed in the grazing fields'.⁶⁵

In brief, a Kurdish man and woman in the nineteenth and early twentieth centuries was under the yoke of *agha* or tribal chiefs, and the literature mainly represented their class and ruling families. A self-sufficient economy and a weak infrastructure characterized the Kurdish region which was mainly rural with a number of small towns. Facilities to ameliorate social conditions were absent, so was the state itself except for its military ventures. The political developments since the early twentieth century originated political processes which, influenced by the dissemination of new ideas, war and political instability, began to reshape Kurdish tribal and non-tribal societies in Iran. Moreover, modern state and border effectively separated the Kurds in Iran from other Kurdish communities in adjacent regions while modernity in the shape of modern institutional, social and political ideas yielded an urbanized, educated generation who added a new aspect to Iran's Kurdish society hitherto dominated by tribes and the *agha* class. By the mid-twentieth century, the tribes' military and political power declined as the result of a centralizing and modernizing state's oppressive policies, as well as socio-economic transformation. However, their ownership of the village and the peasant in an oppressive economic structure, ensured by their monopoly of the legitimate use of violence against the poor, survived. In general, redefined as an 'ethnic minority', socio-economic and political transformations facilitated the Kurds' socio-economic transformation into modern Iran. The next section deals with this unequal integration.

The integrating modernization and social change

The state-led modernization and socio-economic change since the 1920s maintained their tendency to strengthen social, economic and cultural bonds between various societies in Iran. The prevalent modernizing discourse of the time, reflected in contemporary journals such as *Ayandeh*, advocated the integration of Iranian Kurds by expanding socio-economic developments. Two other manifestations of this tendency included the Kurds' political and cultural demands, which began to revolve around autonomy *within the framework of Iran* and not *independence* in different historical conjuncture, and the intensified social change during the era of the White Revolution, which profoundly changed Iran in the same direction. In fact, this tendency determined the course of both state-led modernization and transformation in Iran throughout the twentieth century with the effect that by the time of the 1979 Revolution Kurdish-Iranian society had become both socio-economically and culturally inseparable from modern Iran. However, the growth of such inseparable qualities never negated cultural or political demands embodied in *Kurdayeti*. This probably refers to a paradox rather than a contradiction and to the way the relationship between modernization and identity was determined by both these integrating tendencies and the resistance of *Kurdayeti*.

As the outcome of the relationship between modernization and Kurdish identity, the modernization of Iran did not render *Kurdayeti* (Kurdishness) irrelevant but reshaped and reinvigorated it along modern national lines. Modernization ensured *Kurdayeti*'s continuous presence in the political field of modern Iran rather than inducing the assimilation of the Kurds and the disappearance of Kurdish identity.[66] Put simply while modernization succeeded in creating a shared, strong socio-economic and political field, attempts to create a homogenous entity failed in eradicating *Kurdayeti* in both perception and practice. In an expanding, shared socio-economic base the Kurds in Iran began, and continued, to define themselves as Iranians. Nevertheless, the suppression of Kurdish identity and its resistance to a hegemonic Persian culture continued to generate a prolonged tension between a homogenizing state and the Kurds in Iran. This paradox of socially integrating but ethnically resisting has formed a Kurdish identity that socio-economically and culturally maintains a sense of belonging to Iran, on the one hand, and to *Kurdayeti*, on the other.

Kurdayeti should not be perceived as a fixed term but rather as both a politico-cultural stance and a practice.[67] In both theory and practice, it continued to enjoy a formidable base for its existence and also for the formation and transformation of the values to which the Kurds adhered. Modern *Kurdayeti* is a national perception of self formed as the result of nineteenth-century literary transformation in the wake of the cultural superiority of Europe. However, practically, it has been shaped and reshaped in reaction to the advance of other nationalisms and the formation of modern states, crucially in the context of decades of socio-economic and political developments in such states. Distinctive ethnic and cultural characteristics necessitated this transformation, while subjugated political status and the impoverished social conditions of Kurdish societies, expressed explicitly by poets such as Koyi at the end of the nineteenth century, made progressive, educational and evolutionary ideas the necessary concomitant of a national conception of self and history. Moreover, the demise of the Kurdish Emirates as a result of modernizing centralizations contributed to a process in which the Kurds were conceptually redefined as 'ethnic minority' in the nation state. In fact, both the processes of the transformation of the Kurds into an 'ethnic minority' in a modern nation state and refashioning self took place simultaneously.

Culturally, *Kurdayeti* owes its existence to many formidable elements, above all perhaps religion, as both a way of life and a mechanism of ethnic persistence and language. The Sunni religion of the Kurds is a way of life different from that of the state-sponsored Shi'a religion in Iran and has been one of the most salient components of Kurdish identity. It has also provided resistance against homogenization.[68] In this sense, religion has had at least two major effects. First, historically it continues to serve a Kurdish ethnic identity distinctive of an Iranian one which favours Shi'a Islam. Here religion, rather indirectly, creates a bulwark for Kurdish ethnic identity. Quite interestingly, religion has followed and confirmed Kurdish identity because it provides a distinguishable Kurdish way of life. In addition to this, in the modern history of the Kurds in Iran political and literary lives of the prominent politico-religious figures, as well as the *hojra*-educated activist-intellectual, for example, poets, historians and journalists, attest to the fact that Kurdish ethnic identity is prioritized over the religious identity.[69] For example, membership in Zhe Kaf was free for the adherents of different faiths, but it was conditioned on swearing allegiance to Qur'an for Muslims or 'to anything sacred' if members were believers of other faiths such as Yazidis.[70] In this case, religion as a means to ensure the faithfulness of the members served to legitimize Kurdayeti. Indeed, the prioritization of the ethnic sentiments continued throughout the process of modernization in later decades with the effect that with increasing secularization of thought and also the growing influence of Thirdworldist ideologies on Kurdish political groups in the 1960s and 1970s, religion lost such a contributory role. However, a nascent religious Kurdayeti or nativism towards the end of the 1970s in Iran could be detected (see Chapter 4).

Second, distinctive religious beliefs left the Kurds generally unaffected by theological transformations in the Shi'a thought at least since the eighteenth century, which provided formidable ideological foundations for later Iranian nativist ideologues who equated modernization with Westernization.[71] Predominantly as Sunni Muslims, the Kurds have followed a different religious hierarchy than that of the Shi'a Muslims, and this includes immunity against concepts such as *ijtihad* (interpretation) practised by a *mujtahed* (interpreter of the Shari'a) and, most importantly, *marja'e taqlid* (source of emulation). The latter has the potential to become *Imam* who is infallible in his leading of the *umma*. This is not to suggest that Shi'a identity has historically overshadowed an Iranian national identity. Quite the contrary, pre-Islamic mythology plays a fundamental role in shaping a modern Iranian identity with the effect that in historical conjunctions its mythical figures and stories are Islamicized; here it is the religion that needs legitimacy.[72] Comparatively, while Kurdish mythology has heavily borrowed from Iranian mythology and its pre-Islamic legends, it has largely served an ethnic, and not religious, Kurdish identity.

Therefore, not being influenced by either theological transformations or existing religious rituals in Shi'a tradition, Kurds as a religious minority under a religiously biased state in Iran have inclined towards 'secularism' and non-religious political movements. Therefore, insofar as religion is concerned, any analysis of the nationalization and modernization of Iran ought to consider those two aspects that pertain to the relationship between ethnic and religious identities. In what ways this relationship is maintained or transformed when both the state-led modernization and social change intensify is a question for later chapters. For the moment, it can be asserted that the indirect impact of a distinctive religious tradition, religious prejudices and direct impact of secular movements shaped and reinforced a rather secular *Kurdayeti* in its struggle for ethnic rights. However, with the intensification of modernization in the second half of the twentieth century, it seems that a religious *Kurdayeti* gradually becomes another distinctive contributor to the struggle for those rights.

The Kurdish language is another salient feature of Kurdish identity. The literature is pioneered by Hassanpour's *Language and Nationalism in Kurdistan*, in which the author presents a history of linguistic oppression by modern nation states including that of Iran. A distinct Kurdish language and endeavours to preserve it were factors that ensured the persistence of the Kurdish language in the face of the Persianization of language and culture in Iran. However, many factors distinguished the state's linguistic policies, for example, from Turkey where outright linguistic purification and annihilation occurred.[73] These include historical and cultural bonds, as well as the simplification movements which affected linguistic policies and preceded modern linguistic oppression, respectively. Indeed, the exigencies of a modern state in Iran to create military and, later, medical and educational vocabularies also guided linguistic policies. Including these factors allows us to broaden our understanding of the processes of both linguistic simplification and purification in Iran and gauge the radicalism of linguistic policies in the time of Reza Shah compared to a much more radicalized one under his son, Muhammad Reza Shah (1941-79).

Therefore, while the Kurdish language in modern Iran began to suffer in the sphere of literature, education and administration, such factors reduced barriers for those who enhanced *Kurdayeti*'s linguistic capacities. Thus, benefiting from history and individual endeavours, the Kurdish language in Iran continued to function as a distinctive feature of Kurdish identity and served *Kurdayeti* in its struggle for ethnic or national rights.

Kurdistan and the politics of modernization, 1920-60

The reign of Reza Shah (1925-41) followed the constitutional era as another significant period in Iran's modern history for its politics of modernization, laying the foundations of modern institutions, despite the sluggish socio-economic change, and modernizing the political structure of Kurdish society along national lines. Politically, as the reign of Reza Shah regressed from parliamentary rule and liberalism to an authoritarian and nationalist monarchy, it marked the end of the ideals of the Constitutional Revolution and the formation of a centralized state[74] – a state which came to be firmly based on the pillars of modern Iranian identity, namely national unity (one nation one language) and territorial integrity.

The modern social and political structures of Kurdish society were shaped by the process of the formation of a centralizing and rationalizing nation state in Iran, the requirements of which determined its policies in Kurdistan. The early decades of the modern Iranian state were significant for an effective start towards the social integration of all linguistically and culturally distinctive societies in modern Iran. Politically integrating elements comprised both rationalizing and coercive institutions, namely an efficient bureaucracy and a national army, while socially integrating elements included, but were not restricted to, educational, socio-economic and judicial reforms. Such reforms originated in the ideas and reforming efforts at least since the Constitutional Revolution. Indeed, reform was the main theme of all the periodicals of the time.[75] *Sur Esrafil* reminded its readers that 'Everybody demands education and wants a regular army. All try to find a way to expand the industry, improve transportation, and increase factories. All agree on the benefits of agriculture. And finally, all the focus of [the people of] this land is on this same word of reform, endeavouring to fulfil this sublime motivation.'[76] Efforts to reform continued following the second constitutional *Majlis* in 1909 after Muhammad 'Ali Shah's anti-constitutional coup failed, and he was subsequently abdicated.[77] In addition to war, as many intellectuals argue, the absence of 'national unity' and, crucially, the absence of 'public education' and resistance to European culture and ideas were explained as obstacles to reform and progress.[78] Nevertheless, while in the spiritual sphere religious and secular thought yielded varied opinions on the roots of the 'backwardness' of Iran – in the material sphere there was a consensus to employ European advanced technology – a personified, central power never featured in such arguments.[79] An influential journal such as *Kaveh* (1916–22) continuously emphasized Iranian national unity, Europeanization of culture, public education and Persian language.[80] Noted by historians of Iran, in the intellectual sphere the argument was usually for a central authority, and this was also voiced by Kurdish intellectuals such as Muhammad Mardukh, who, celebrating Nowruz in 1919, wondered 'why has not this strong and erudite [Iranian] state been able to end the chaos [in Kurdistan] in recent [post-constitutional] years?'[81]

However, the emergence of Reza Khan (later Reza Shah) induced inclinations towards a powerful centralized state in order to end political instability, implement reforms and ensure national unity and territorial integrity of Iran. Along with the intellectual persistence of likes of Mahmud Afshar, able statesmen such as Abdolhossein Taimurtash, Ali Akbar Davar and Muhammad Foroughi regarded Reza Shah as vital for the creation of the modern, Iranian nation state, and although constitutionalists, including Hassan Taqizadeh, a veteran of the Constitutional Revolution, opposed the change of the dynasty for constitutional reasons, they regarded Reza Khan in the same way.[82] As an illustration of this popular attitude towards Reza Khan, in the struggle to establish a modern judicial system to introduce and enforce new laws, many prominent figures had strived against cultural and religious obstacles until, as Foroughi recalls, 'there was a total change of fortune [in their favour] with the rise of Reza Shah Pahlavi'.[83] Support for the establishment of the dynasty also came from other layers of society. As Homa Katouzian concludes, in 1926 the emerging Pahlavi state claimed 'a broad support among the country's various influential elites' such as landlords, provincial magnates and leading merchants.[84]

The state in much of the first Pahlavi era endeavoured to fulfil the requisites for a modern, centralized nation state as the institutional condition for the realization of the long-standing will to reform, constantly interrupted by the presence and rivalry of the great powers in Iran and political instability.[85] Indeed, its efforts, however oppressive, were also dictated by historical facts – a prolonged instability and indirect colonialism – as well as by the need for a modern state to function effectively. Ultimately, however, both Pahlavi eras witnessed the concentration of political authority in the monarch, whereas many Iranian intellectuals had stipulated a progressive (*erteqayi*), constitutional system to tackle 'the unsteadiness of the central government, the chaos of the central administration, political instability and insecurity' against a 'regressive' (*qahqaraiy*) administration under previous Qajar kings.[86] Instead, except for the period between the outbreak of the Second World War, which entailed severe financial and political crisis with paralysing effects, and the coup of 1953 against Muhammad Musaddeq, the state turned into a powerful, centralized authority surrounded by a cult of personality.[87] Therefore, Reza Shah purged those who had been pivotal for the formation of the Iranian nation state, and Muhammad Reza Shah (1941–79) sidelined planners, appropriated their ideas and found around himself uncritical statesmen, legitimizing his political involvement on the grounds of 'the deficiency in the political system'.[88] Ultimately, both the Shahs overlooked collective efforts in favour of the glory of a nationalist dynasty. Although between 1941 and 1953 the *Majlis* and the press managed to manoeuvre more freely, the state remained politically oppressive in Kurdistan. For example, the cultural and political revival of the early 1940s ended when the army finally suppressed the experience of Mahabad in 1946, subsequently forcing a considerable number of political and cultural activists into prolonged exile, while, with the help of the landowners, the state brutally quelled the peasant uprising in the region around Bukan (1952–3).[89] In fact, the poet Hazhar's ('Abdulrahman Sharafkandi, 1921–91) memoirs entitled *Cheshti Mijawir* is an account of him and many others, who spent three decades in exile following the end of the Kurdish Republic of 1946.

Against this background, policies and reforms in the process of the formation of the Iranian nation state under the Pahlavis began to alter the social and political structures of Kurdish-Iranian society. To avoid simplifying the politics of modernization into mere adversarial attitudes towards the Kurds, one can identify at least two issues surrounding the state's linguistic policies to demonstrate how the linguistic policies of the state derived from its linguistic requirements: first, the continuation of the drive for linguistic simplification since the early nineteenth century and the lack of a *radical* purification of Persian until well into the second Pahlavi era;[90] and second, the need of a modern state for new legal, economic, scientific and educational vocabularies. For example, the 1935 Constitution of the First Academy (1935–41) calls for replacing unsuitable foreign words with equivalents used among 'the artisans [. . .] in poetry or local songs'.[91] Moreover, suggested vocabularies for various professions, specifically the army but also for the sciences corresponded to institutional reforms. However, one familiar with such vocabularies will notice that a considerable number of the suggested words were never popularized nor did they ever replace the old one.[92] Undoubtedly, anti-Arabic and Turkish sentiments, as well as a pride in Persian, inspired such efforts, though they divided opinions too.[93] The state banned using Kurdish as the language of education and administration but instruction and communication in Kurdish between teachers and students and also in government offices continued despite early encouragements to speak only Persian. However, a persistent *Kurdayeti* and, despite intermittent coercive measures, the absence of both *radical* linguistic oppression and total ethnic denial in Iran, as it was the case, for example, in contemporary Turkey, helped Kurdish to flourish, embodied in continuous literary activities. A more in-depth reading of the role of language in the formation of the Iranian national identity since the end of the nineteenth century highlights a dual process of linguistic simplification and a modest, rather than a *radical*, linguistic purification until the 1970s.

In addition to oppressive linguistic policies, the politics of modernization comprised other significant measures such as administrative division and the constant presence of the gendarmerie to ensure the consolidation of the central authority and the political integration of the Kurds into modern Iran – by now gendarmerie had been deprived of its constitutional functions and radically reshaped in the wake of Khyabani's and Lahuti's rebellions.[94] With no regard to ethnic rights and guided by political considerations, the constant practice of administrative division of Iran established a precedent for arbitrarily (re)division of the Kurdish region in Iran among the neighbouring provinces. Prior to the modern border, the contours of the existing and old ruling Kurdish Emirates or principalities delineated a map of Kurdistan divided among its ruling Emirates. The Kurdish region, which later became 'Iranian Kurdistan', comprised the regions under tribal confederacies such as the Shikak and the ruling Emirates of Mukrian, Ardalan and Baban. As additional centres of power, there were other ruling families in and around Kermanshah. This division of power naturally left a legacy for later administrative and electoral laws of succeeding Iranian governments since the Constitutional Revolution until Reza Khan's coup of 1921. In addition to this, geographical proximity (in the absence of effective means of communication and a weak infrastructure) and existing economic relationships, rather than the idea of modern border and identity, were behind such decisions and laws.

Administrative policies under various ruling dynasties since the early modern period had attempted to pacify the local powers and ensure the effective collection of revenue (e.g. custom and land tax) needed to maintain the court, bureaucracy and the army.[95] However, as an important break with the way administration was organized in the past, the impact of Europe on nineteenth-century Iran resulted in the expansion of bureaucracy under the Qajars and later the introduction of new electoral laws after the Constitutional Revolution.[96] The first law concerning administrative division was passed in this period and divided Iran into several self-governed *ayalat*s which included *velayat*s (sub-*ayalat* regions with an important city). Factors of *modern* border and *national* identity did not shape provincial policies, although, presumably, the Ottoman Empire and the ruling Iranian dynasties had constantly perceived Kurdish *ethnic* identity as a threat to their central authorities because of the role Kurdish ruling families could have played in imperial rivalries. Indeed, such modern factors gained ascendancy when, in the process of forming the *Iranian* nation state in the 1920s and 1930s, Kurdish ethnic identity became inimical to the 'national unity' of Iran. For example, it seems that the electoral law of 1909 allocated Sauj Blagh (modern Mahabad) as a constituency in the Azerbaijan province mainly because of history, electoral convenience and geographical proximity rather than political motivation.[97] Sauj Belagh and the surrounding region had been historically in close connection with the Turkish-speaking region in its northwest stretched to Tabriz, itself an important economic, cultural and, in modern times since the early nineteenth century, also an ideological hub.

The ascendancy of political considerations that served an Iranian national unity began effectively with the rationalization of administrative division in the process of the formation of the Iranian nation state. Moreover, the expansion of modern bureaucracy and population increase resulted in the country being re-divided into new provinces based on a new system of nomenclature more compatible with modern times. Iran's National Council divided Iran into four *ayalat*s (provinces) and twelve *velayat*s (sub-provinces). The new law of December 1937 replaced the *ayalat*s with ten *ostan*s. This was followed by gradual changes in which Iran was finally divided into fourteen provinces in 1339 (1960–1), which were recognized by names instead of numbers as was the case under the law of 1937. Meanwhile, Kurdistan Province was created in 1336 (1957–8). Prior to this, Kurdistan, that is Sanandaj and a few other cities, and Mahabad were major cities that were allocated to the Fifth and Fourth Provinces, respectively; other minor Kurdish cities were administrated by these cities as *bakhsh* (sub-city). However, Mahabad is allocated to western Azerbaijan to this day, and Kurdistan Province does not represent the region dominantly populated by the Kurds in the west of Iran either. Modern administrative divisions defied notions of Kurdish ethnic and geographical unity and served 'national unity' of Iran. The rationalization of Iran's administrative divisions began no later than the Radical Party's manifesto of 1923 under Ali Akbar Davar.[98] This was the first step to reform the administration according to the exigencies of a modern state. However, although there are only little studies on this subject, they show that administrative divisions throughout the twentieth century have been mainly arbitrary, economically and politically unproductive, and failed to serve decentralization, while ignoring, for example, the connection between local identity and geography (see Table 1).[99] In later decades, and with the emergence of a more organized *Kurdayeti*, administrative divisions explicitly became a political act to safeguard the central authority against potential Kurdish political movements. Moreover, from the outset, some intellectuals believed that administrative division should serve the same purpose as uniformity in 'language, moral, [and] dress' did to achieve 'national unity', and asked to avoid the existing ethnic names of the provinces too (see The political structure of Kurdistan).[100]

Consequently, the 'Kurdistan Province' began to comprise a smaller number of Kurdish cities and population under successive governments (see Map 5). Guided 'mainly by security considerations', the modern state aimed to interrupt linguistic

Table 1 Administrative Divisions of Iran 1908–79

Year	Number of provinces (ostans)	Titles and the provinces which included Kurdish cities
1908	4	Azerbaijan, Fars, Khorasan, Kerman
31 December 1937	10	The 4th Ostan: Khuiy, Rezayie, Mahabad, Maragheh, Bijar.
		The 5th Ostan: Ilam, Shahabad, Kermanshah, Sanandaj, Melayer, Hamadan.
1957–8 (1336)		The Kurdistan Province is created by excluding many Kurdish cities.
1960–1 (1339)	14	Numbers are replaced by names.
1979	24	The Kurdish region in the west of Iran continues to be divided between different provinces, including the Kurdistan Province.

() = Iranian calendar

and ethnic commonalities between the Kurds inside Iran and the Kurdish residents of adjacent countries, and in this way diminish the impact of 'external' political movements.[101] Although this politically motivated policy never resulted in ethnic assimilation of annexed cities and regions into other provinces nor was it successful in diminishing Kurdish identity, it created a condition to deny individuals the right to prosper because of their ethnicity and ingrained prejudices. As crucially, it continued to conceal the sufferings of social and religious groups, such as the Faili Kurds, who geographically found themselves in the margins of Kurdistan.[102] Therefore, the history of the administrative division of Iran is also a history of denying millions of Kurds opportunities to prosper socially and economically. As significant, it also created conditions prone to ethnic animosity in the time of political crisis among, for example, the historically mixed communities of the Kurds and Azaris in the north and Faili Kurds and others in Ilam in the south. The administrative division of Iran corresponded to a centralized modern state, and the White Revolution was the heir to such policies and their outcomes.

Finally, the reign of Reza Shah marked the emergence of Kurdish political societies in the Kurdish region in Iran. This was exemplified by the Organization of the Kurdish Revival and its active political and intellectual engagements in the early 1940s. The Kurdish Revival effectively paved the way for the formation of the Kurdistan Republic of 1946, which marked a significant turning point in modern Kurdish history. The Republic was a result of a period of foreign occupation of Iran (1941–6) in which Kurdistan had been experiencing political freedom as well as cultural revivals since the outbreak of the Second World War in 1939. These political developments were originated in at least three decades of major social and political developments since the Constitutional Revolution. The authoritative histories of Iran have contributed to a chronology in which the Republic is treated too briefly as a 'secessionist' attempt, thus avoiding other important factors along with favourable circumstances, caused by the presence of the Soviet Union in Iran, in its formation. The Republic was the outcome of several decades of political developments and socio-economic, cultural and intellectual transformations since the Constitutional Revolution, in general, and the outbreak of the Second World War, which weakened the central state, in particular. It was a democratic experience that grew to reflect the dual process of modernization and homogenization, undertaken by a modern state which, enjoying the monopoly over the right to define identity, explained the Kurds as an inextricable part of modern Iran in order to guarantee territorial and moral boundaries of Iranian political community. The presence of a friendly Russian army, in the same way as a debilitating central government, undeniably favoured the formation of the Republic and led to close relations that involved taking advice and conducting trade. Furthermore, the Kurdish Revival's *Nishtiman* and *Kurdistan*, published in the early 1940s and since the formation of the Republic respectively, reflected not only intellectual transformations or the advance of Kurdish national desires, but they mirrored a dynamic and transforming society that was embracing modern progressive ideas. That said, this book places the Republic in the dual process and explains its formation, programme and legacy in light of broader socio-economic, political and intellectual transformations which manifest the formation of Iran's modern Kurdish society. From the proclamation of the Republic onwards the Kurdish movement is unmistakably Iranian as it defines itself within the framework of Iran. The Republic was announced a few months after the foundation of the Democratic Party of Iranian Kurdistan in September 1945, the manifesto of which included 'an autonomous Kurdistan within the frontiers of the Persian Iranian State'.[103]

Reforms and economic developments

The modern Iranian government undertook unprecedented social, institutional and economic reforms between 1925 and 1941. This marked the start of deliberate, centrally directed development in Iran. As Jahangir Amuzegar has noted, these reforms were 'the outcome of a philosophy and a policy, rather than of a concrete program or strategy'.[104] Although these reforms did not entail profound alteration of the social structure of Kurdish society, they were significant because they (1) laid the foundation of new institutions into that society, reshaping its social and political structure and (2) maintained the tendency to socio-economic integration. The pace and scope of many aspects of such reforms as, for example, the spread of modern schools, healthcare, infrastructural development and the provision of modern facilities to ameliorate living conditions remained limited. Moreover, the chasm between village and city persisted as the latter began to benefit from reforms and feel the impact of social and technological transformation too; the prevalent *agha-jutiar* (landowner–peasant) relationship survived and continued to characterize an agricultural, rural Kurdish society. Moreover, the Second World War and the political developments that followed Reza Shah's rule at best interrupted both a sluggish state-led modernization and the amelioration of living conditions in Kurdistan. In fact, economic conditions in Kurdistan under Reza Shah deteriorated, and his rule did not entail any profound alteration in the social order of society concerning social stratification, gender relations, living conditions, healthcare, communications and transportation.[105]

Insofar as the state was concerned, two main factors were responsible for these unimpressive results. First, the state was present as a political and coercive power rather than a socially modernizing and inclusive authority. Second, as scholars have noted, the economic objectives of Reza Shah comprised rapid industrialization and infrastructural development, which mostly benefited the centre, tended to fulfil the state's military requirements and served to produce a modern, progressive and independent image of Iran.[106] For example, economic development plans ignored agriculture and contained an ambitious, extravagant but uneconomical railway system from the Persian Gulf in the South to the Caspian Sea in the North. The cost fell on people while oil reserves could have been used to provide foreign loans.[107] Moreover, the economic plans did not effectively deal with geographical hurdles (vast arable lands, lack of rivers and roads), though one can infer that such a hostile environment in addition to Iran's fragile infrastructure were serious hurdles to overcome by any government in favour of agriculture. Therefore, the orientation of the economic plans and the neglect of agriculture disadvantaged a periphery region like Kurdistan, which relied on agriculture and had a fragile infrastructure. Moreover, Kurdistan continued to suffer under the centralizing tendency of the modernization whose second development plan (1956–62) effectively marked the triumph of centralization in its tension with decentralization or more province-oriented plans.

Reports and books on the general socio-economic condition across Iran make amends for the lack of statistics on Kurdistan under Reza Shah. Although this period witnessed an increase in the state's influence and size in the economy, comprehensive economic plans were only introduced after the Second World War. Indeed, the role of the state in the economy before 1921 was confined to granting concessions to foreigners in order to stimulate the use of natural resources. Nevertheless, based on unequal terms, these agreements to a great extend formed the basin for later economic development and finance, for example, in the oil industry, telegraph, bank and railways.[108] Until the end of the 1960s, the lack of revenue was one of the main reasons which continued to paralyse economic plans and delay their effective executions. As a positive aspect, however, this period witnessed the coming of age of a generation of Iranian political leaders and activists who initiated important principles of later reforms including the White Revolution. Furthermore, in addition to the existing literates, an emerging urbanized educated generation in Kurdish society compensated for the deficiencies of the state in many significant ways by actively engaging in social and political activities, which included the spread of literacy and the promulgation of social, political, gender and ethnic awareness. This was especially the case between 1939 and 1946 (see Social change, 1920–60). Meanwhile, socio-economic plans began to assume two common characteristics: they were confined to the centre and ignorant of agriculture, which in the 1930s employed up to 85 per cent of the labour force. Moreover, despite the expansion in transport and communication, contemporary observers' accounts confirm the ineffective role of the state in rural areas and provinces.[109]

Therefore, as a mainly rural and agricultural society, the Kurdish region suffered from the orientation and deficiencies of economic policies in this period. General observations of the Iranian economy in this period, as well as the writings of contemporary Kurdish literary figures, attest to the fact that by neglecting agriculture and prioritizing political objectives, socio-economic conditions in Kurdistan did not improve; for most people, it even deteriorated:

> In the time of Reza Shah, the economy was in a very bad state. In addition to the oppression of the gendarmerie, unemployment and poverty in villages increased economic burden. Peasants used oxen to plough the land. The most profitable crop was tobacco. A family of eight had to work long hours. However, in the end, either the crop was damaged by humidity or swallowed by the Tobacco Collection Centre. The remaining was at the mercy of the landowner.[110]

The above-mentioned political and geographical restrictions and the impact of the Great War generated little hope for immediate economic prosperity. Moreover, Kurdish society carried the scares of the war for many years, paralysed further by famine, cold and hunger, and the quest of powerful tribes such as the Shikak for political power over other tribes also increased the casualties of wars and conflicts. At the same time, Kurdistan's economic structure and its class relations perpetuated economic hardship and social miseries for many. The society was mainly characterized by an unequal and oppressive regime of the Kurdish *agha* (landowner class), which ensured the *agha*'s ownership of the land and the exploitation of the peasant. When the ownership of a village was transferred from one landowner to another, it included peasants' families as well. This social relationship differed from a slave-based economy in that the peasant shared a small portion of the harvest. *Agha* could expel a peasant not only from his village but also from the region under his jurisdiction. In addition to poverty, this forced many peasants and their families to be constantly on the move.[111] On the other hand, agriculture and agricultural techniques in this period in Kurdistan did not improve, while the production of grain across Iran decreased towards the end of Reza Shah's reign in 1941 with the effect that the government was forced to import wheat.[112] The situation was exacerbated by the increase in the population of Iran from ten million in 1925 to almost fifteen million in 1941. The 1934 budget allocated 42.2 per cent to war while the share of agriculture and public health was 0.4 per cent and 2.3 per cent respectively.[113]

Furthermore, observers in the 1940s reported:

> Agricultural labour force and their living conditions were very poor and for the most part illiterate. Public-health services were almost completely lacking, and clothing and fuel were scanty and hard to come by. The peasants were often in ill health, suffering from malnutrition, malaria, dysentery, typhoid, typhus and cholera.[114]

G. Black also observed in 1948 that 'the ground [was] ploughed by oxen dragging a crooked stick, [. . .] The grain [was] cut with stickle and threshed upon clay threshing floors by beaters pulled in a circle by oxen. The grain is separated by winnowing.'[115] Confirmed by many contemporaries such as Hemin and Hussami, such living conditions and agricultural techniques aptly applied to Kurdish rural and village communities. Therefore, as the result of neglecting agriculture and prioritizing political objectives, Kurdistan did not considerably benefit from economic policies under Reza Shah while political oppression and the constant presence of gendarmerie remained striking aspects of his rule. However, this period is distinguished for its significant contribution to social change through the foundation of modern institutions such as schools and healthcare, the introduction of new means of transportation and the rationalization of administration. Such institutional and technological changes provided the base for a more profound transformation of the society during the era of the White Revolution.

Social change, 1920–60

Until the 1960s, the socio-economic change in Kurdistan was a sluggish and prolonged one. However, the emergence of a number of modern institutions and trends marked the beginning of a new era. The state, whose policies corresponded to the need of a modern state, was the main contributor in this process except where non-state agents of change were crucial, for example, for simultaneously spreading literacy and promulgating social awareness. These revealed the interaction of various factors in reshaping society.

In addition to the gradual spread of modern education and healthcare, the new era was going to be characterized by the emergence of wage labour, including seasonal workers, and the formation of an urbanized middle class which accompanied urbanization with its impact on Kurdish urban centres, the transformation of cultural values and norms, and technological changes. As regards social stratification, an urbanized middle class emerged in the 1950s and 1960s. In rural areas, an abject lack of a health system and public education continued to characterize life in both rural and urban centres. In the 1930s and 1940s, modern education had not become widespread and a weak infrastructure prevented it from reaching rural areas. However, adding the itinerant literates to this category, this period marked the emergence of an educated, urbanized generation who reflected modernization and modern education. Their impact alongside the *hojra* educated on political developments, for example, by founding societies and publishing journals.

Modern urbanization did not radically begin in Kurdish cities until after land reform in the 1960s, which entailed an exodus to cities. A Kurdish city was mainly characterized by a military base, a bazaar (market) in a mercantile economy based on agriculture, and *mahallas* (neighbourhoods) which evolved around the main congregational mosque and the bazaar, the main components of an unindustrialized self-sufficient economy.[116] Towns had two important components: *caravansaries* that constituted the focal point of overland trade and commerce; and *mahalla*, the physical borders and gates of which, despite the psychological bonds of its residents, were eroding. However, a Kurdish city or town was not merely typified by a 'traditional', implying an immobile, way of life. Before the vast migration of the 1960s and 1970s, people moved between villages or resided in cities as the result of many push factors such as the oppression of *agha*s and poverty, as well as pull factors, including the existence of free, that is, not owned by *agha*s, and culturally attractive cities. The industry was mainly limited to craftsmen but also craftswomen. Women worked in agriculture, animal husbandry and carpet weaving, in addition to demanding household tasks. Although the conspicuous absence of adequate research related to gender studies characterizes Kurdish studies, circumstantial evidence and public knowledge refer to a history of the hardship women endured as unrecognized labourers in carpet weaving, agriculture and the production of dairy for cities.

Finally, whereas one of the main characteristics of the Kurdish region was the village-city discrepancy, it was shockingly maintained, including in the era of the White Revolution, despite institutional, economic and infrastructural changes. As noted earlier, a profound change of this aspect of life or more precisely a radical alteration of social life in the rural area depended upon the main contributor's, that is, the state's, socio-economic, cultural and political policies. It did not imply that life in cities was more prosperous but that villages could not benefit from reforms also due to an inadequate transportation and communications system. The Pahlavi modernization maintained the tendency to ignore rural areas, whereas in this period the majority of the Kurdish population lived in the countryside without sufficient access to modern facilities, such as education, health and communications. On the other hand, each Kurdish town was surrounded by a great number of villages in which *agha* ruled, and the state was effectively absent for the provision of economic, social and educational needs. Instead, it insured its physical presence through growing gendarmerie bases.

Healthcare

As Byron Good argues, studies on the history of healthcare in Iran tend to link the transformation of healthcare to economic, political and social transformations rather than the diffusion of Western medical knowledge.[117] The centralization of power under Reza Shah marked both the beginning of the centralization of the healthcare system, including the institutionalization of the imperialist legacy of quarantine services and the control of hospitals. This included the transformation of the Constitutional Sanitary Council into a Department of Public Health and the introduction of new services such as vaccination, provincial medical offices and licensing regulations.[118] The impact of this on the Kurdish society of the time is reflected in including a Ministry of Health in the ministries of the autonomous Kurdistan Republic, attesting to the growing awareness of the population to public health.[119] This awareness, however, did not necessarily confirm the existence of any effective health system. For example, in 1925 the Iranian government's director of public health, Dr Amir Alam, stated:

> For the last two years the general sanitary situation of the country has left much to be desired. Provincial Medical Officers of Health, having failed to receive for several months their salaries, have for the most part abandoned their posts. An indifference, a *laissez aller*, truly regrettable reigns with regard to all questions of public health. Our plans, our schemes, our cries, have had no chance of finding an echo in governmental or parliamentary circles.[120]

The modes of practice included *hakims* (an unqualified 'doctor', apothecary), bazaar shops, which provided herbal medicine, curator prayers, pray writers, fracture healers and visiting sacred shrines. Also crucial were holy places and celebrated *sheikh*s whose religious prestige and genealogy provided unmatched authority. Historical medical knowledge and books guided practitioners while religious beliefs allowed many such forms to continue to exist. It seems that the role of missionary doctors was restricted by the influence of religion with which *hakims* or healers were closely connected.[121] The connection of religious figures and medicine (advanced chemical or herbal), to benefit from Gramsci's insight on the role of the intellectuals in society, reveals how *sheikhs* were seen as healers and *hakims* as possessing divine power.[122] As noted in studies on the history of healthcare in Iran, the structure of healthcare can be characterized as decentralized, relatively self-sustaining and autonomous from central powers.[123] This structure corresponded to the political and economic structure of a society that was politically ruled by powerful tribal chiefs and economically was characterized as dominantly self-sufficient and geographically restricted. The absence of both transportation networks and an effective communications system isolated village and town communities from not only each other but also major urban centres. Modernization and socio-economic transformation were going to cause structural change in this respect, too, with the effect that modern medical institutions gradually replaced known modes of medical practices.

However, the introduction of modern healthcare in Kurdistan was slow and ineffective, while illiteracy, the lack of facilities and cadres hindered its expansion. Although the 1930s witnessed licensing regulations, the requirement of diploma for physicians, the establishment of a Ministry of Health with provincial offices, there is no indication of any health programme in Kurdistan in this period. Moreover, as noted in the study of other regions, the provision of healthcare prioritized the requirements of the military and 'reflected the basic interests of Reza Shah and the elite'.[124] Sir Harry Sinderson confirmed in 1935 that 'in this [medical programme] the civil population was regarded as secondary in importance to the army'.[125] The first hospital in the provincial city of Sanandaj was 'a military hospital, the construction of which between 1927 and 1931 was concurrent with the establishment of a *padegan* (army base)'.[126] Events surrounding the establishment of this hospital demonstrated the slow progress of healthcare. After its destruction as the result of a fire in 1321 (1942–3), it was only reopened in 1340 (1961).[127] *Rega*, published by the remnants of the fallen Republic in exile, provided further evidence of the prioritization of the military and the unavailability of modern healthcare for the population. In its first and the only issue published in autumn 1949, *Rega* reported:

> Red Lion and Sun Society has been taken over by the *Tip* (army brigade) in Mahabad and it accepts only people close to itself. [The Society] has opened a branch for the population merely to pretend that it serves people. Across Kurdistan, in Bukan, Saqqez, Baneh, Sardasht and Naghadeh, as well as in villages, there are no doctors nor are there any medicine available.[128]

Instead of more adequate institutions of healthcare, Kurdish cities in the 1950s and 1960s embraced *Tazriqat va Panseman* (Injection and Bandage) which were set up by, for example, previous army medics with preliminary medical knowledge; pharmacies run by graduated doctors are phenomena of the 1970s. (According to official statistics for 1352 (1973) by administrative divisions, there were twenty-six dependant and independent pharmacies in Kurdistan Province.)[129] Therefore, Kurdistan in this period continued to be characterized by the absence of an effective health system and its requirements, including trained personnel. Geography, however, was not the only hurdle to the expansion of modern healthcare. The tendency of the state-led modernization to rapid urbanization and industrialization left out vast disconnected rural areas and further delayed the promotion of social consciousness and the provision of healthcare and sanitation.

Crucially, a significant aspect of social change was efforts to raise awareness on such issues, which were carried out by non-state agents of change who were influenced by humanitarian and social ideas of the time. Receptivity to progressive ideas of the time influenced social activists across Iran. For example, in the early years of the Iranian nation state *Alam-e Naswan* (The world of women), one of the earliest periodicals published by and for women, 'concentrated on such matters as health and hygiene, care of children, domestic science, cookery, dress, and fashion'.[130] This paper, which 'was enthusiastic and hopeful about reforms for women carried out by the state', faced the fate of many other journals and was ironically shut down by Reza Shah in 1934 as he 'consolidated more power and authority'.[131]

In Kurdistan too, war and political upheavals quickly caused a profound change in attitudes and actions. They inspired cultural revivals in the forms of literary activities and publications, which drew attention to social conditions too. *Nishtiman* and *Kurdistan* promoted awareness of social issues in the early 1940s. However, the forceful end of the political experiences which allowed their publications interrupted activities that aimed to ameliorate living conditions. Finally, complementary to these efforts was the state's contribution to the promulgation of social awareness of health issues since the 1920s by introducing plans to form provincial medical centres and ministries. These efforts remained limited in scope and did not entail profound change. However, the ideas remained and laid the foundation for later attempts to establish a more effective health system. Consequently, Kurdish society gradually began to receive new ideas and practices in healthcare.

Literacy and modern education in Kurdistan

In the second decade of the twentieth century, the famous journal *Kaveh* regarded illiteracy in Iran as *om ol-ma'ayeb* or the mother of all faults.[132] Literacy was restricted to main urban centres; historically, it was a luxury of wealthy families, a prerogative accorded to people, including a percentage of women with a wealthy background, in the upper echelons of society. Before the advent of state schools, mosques and other worshipping places were centres of learning. Religious establishment under the Safavids and Qajars maintained the role of providing literacy and religious education until modern *madrasas* in Iran overtook traditional educational centres, which saw their demise as a consequence of the socio-economic transformation of Iran at the end of the 1960s and 1970s.

In Kurdistan *maktab* and *hojra* were attached to the mosque, and *khanaqa* was a centre for the upkeep of *tariqa* (a non-orthodox religious sect) and a place where

Tasawuuf or Sufism was studied. *Khanaqa* belonged to a sheikh who taught his followers by employing *Mullahs* in the *khanaqa's hojra*. The *sheikhs* of Borhan and Zanbil in the vicinity of Bukan ran *khanaqas*, where many notable families sent their sons for religious education. *Faqeh* was a religious student who learnt under a *Mullah* in the mosque's or *khanaqa's hojra*. According to Hemin, who spent four years in a *khanaqa*, the diversity was remarkable:

> In those years khanaqa was densely populated. People could freely visit khanaqa. The disparity between its inhabitants was negligible [. . .] it was like Noah's Ark. There were people from different ethnicities. Wanderers, socially isolated, worshippers, Muslim, Mullah, Sayyed, learned, educated, robber, thief, illiterate, crazy, idle, disabled, blind, limping and even atheist all lived together under the same roof. Afghanis, Persians, Turks, Azeris and even Indians could be seen there. [There were] Kurds with their dialects from different parts of Kurdistan. Men who later became well-known such as Fauzi, Saifi Qazi, Peshawa Qazi Muhammad [the head of the Kurdistan Republic of 1946], haji Mullah Muhammad Sharafkandi, 'Ali khan Amiri, and especially the literate aghas of Faizulabegi visited khanaqa and stayed for several months.[133]

However, the mosque's *hojra* embraced more men from the lower strata of society with the effect that those from poor families constituted the majority of *faqehs*. According to Hazhar,

> The majority of *faqehs* are [either] the sons of widows [or] poor peasants. Once in *hojra*, they have to beg for bread and provide clothing from *ratura* [bursary]. In springs and autumns, they have to travel to villages to beg for cooking oil, cheese, tobacco, tea and sugar. People paid *faqehs zakat* [alms] by setting aside proportions from the harvest.[134]

Away from home, they used the mosques' resources for the duration of their religious learning; and the landowners' financial support was crucial for the maintenance of *hojras*. Free meal and accommodation were provided albeit at the expense of village inhabitants. An attendant of *hojra* around Bukan in the second Pahlavi era downgrades the role of *khanaqas*, which was mainly 'a place for rich and notables', in spreading literacy and science and in improving living conditions as long as a wider population is concerned. However, despite economic hardships endured by *faqehs* and the existing curriculum, religious schools were crucial for literacy as available centres of education. As regards both subjects and teaching methods, their deficiencies were illuminated by the spread of modern education. Hazhar complains,

> How is their [*faqehs'*] education? [It consists of] several age-old books which have changed a little. I mean the curriculum has not changed for centuries. Teaching is only the responsibility of those who have learnt from such books. [. . .] The educational discipline and quarterly or annual exams are unheard of.[135]

As a starting point for acquiring literacy and also a variety of scientific and religious knowledge, a mosque's *hojra* played a similar role in other regions of Kurdistan such as Mariwan where it was supported by landowners and *vaqfs* (religious endowment). Therefore, benefiting from the residency of a landowner family, many villages came to possess *hojra* as a centre of literacy. In many villages, the mosque provided both religious and some form of scientific education for around twenty students in the first decades of the twentieth century. After a few years, these students were qualified as *mala* and received a certificate to be able to carry out religious duties in a village. At the same time, the literates became bound to a system of patronage while in a village a landowner's resources were crucial for providing funds and shelter for recruited *Mullah*s. The *agha* class sought to continue its legitimacy in the eyes of the population by maintaining its link to religion.

The Qajar Empire (1798–1925) is recognized as an era when mosques and subsequently *khanaqa*s spread across Kurdistan with the effect that it increased interest in literacy. In this respect, we should recognize the importance of religious centres of education and also the accidental nature of acquiring literacy by individuals. Religious education centres produced literate individuals who later, in various capacities, spread literacy across the region. As stated earlier, the lives of many such literate individuals and poets illustrate how the interest in acquiring literacy and knowledge was promoted especially where the state was effectively absent. Qane' (Muhammad Kabuli, 1898–1965) is probably the quintessential example by illustrating how the life and activity of a literate person can simultaneously popularize the importance of education and promulgate social and political awareness. Despite economic hardship, he became an active person whose travel and literary activities made literacy a popular goal among the lower strata of society.[136] Crucially, the Great War and the October Revolution of 1917 were the cataclysms that caused reorientation in social outlooks. With later political upheavals, such events ended the isolation of Kurdish society and opened it to change and new ideas. In one of his poems, Qane' warns the landowner class:

> *Listen! Socialism has become widespread*
> *Is ever closer, your end.*
> *Your servants have realised*
> *you are their enemies*
> *Your fort is not formidable or unconquerable*
> *Because its walls are made of colonialism.*

And in another message to the masses, he demands:

> *Arm yourself with guns, shuffles and pens*
> *You, from the enlightened to shepherds.*
> *Let's demolish this rotten order*
> *Let's build the equality palace.*
> *Then the son of the Kurdish proletariat*
> *Will lead their homeland, Kurdistan.* [137]

As regards the accidental nature of becoming literate, several factors, such as family ties, location and a relative's attitude to life, were decisive in putting one on the path of acquiring literacy and obtaining available religious and scientific education. This applies to Qaneʻ, Hemin, Hazhar and many others who testify to this fact in their memoirs.[138] As another example, Karim Hussami (1926–2001), writer and political activist, became literate because of his father and another *Mirza* who were both in the service of the *agah*s of Qizilja in the Mahabad region[139] (Figure 1).

As a result of acquiring education through religious schools and by accident, literacy spread in circumstances influenced little by the state. Such a generation, exemplified by the likes of the above-mentioned poets, established themselves as the enlightened of twentieth-century modernizing Iranian Kurdistan. In addition to nationalist ideas, they carried a mixture of socialist ideas (except in the case of Hazhar) with the effect that when the illiterate masses learnt their poems, it simultaneously increased the will for the acquisition of knowledge. Poetry was probably the most attractive literary form for many reasons. Widespread illiteracy was not a barrier for its learning but was more accessible because listening to or encouraging short poems was easier than reading books. Furthermore, poetry was creative and most importantly a reliable source in which 'truth' could be cited. Such factors around poetry probably explained why the majority of the learned men in

Figure 1 Qaneʻ. 'The Pedagogy of the Oppressed': Qaneʻ at his best, ca. 1950. Author's collection.

this time became poets or acquired poetic skills, imitated their predecessors and conveyed the ideas of the time. Modern education could not conceal the history of literacy which provided conditions and agency for new education.

Modern education in Iran formally began with the establishment of primary and then secondary schools in towns as the result of pre- and post-constitutional reforms, which had been inspired by the idea of modern education. Upon contact with modernity, a progressive and scientific perception of education began to guide contemporary intellectuals.[140] This view originated in the Enlightenment and also, as scholars have noted, in the Whig perception of history as progress, influential in Victorian Britain.[141] Kurdish intellectuals perceived illiteracy as a social ill and regarded modern education as a means to elevate Kurds to the level of a (progressive) nation. The transformation of Kurdish poetry into a social discourse at the end of the nineteenth century was intellectually guided by modern concepts of nation and education, while modern Kurdish journalism and historiography vividly began to reflect the progressive conception of modern education.[142]

There were attempts at establishing modern schools in Kurdish urban centres at the end of the constitutional era; and like religious education, state education mostly benefited the male population. Educational efforts incited the reaction of some religious schools and figures when towns and cities such as Mahabad, Sanandaj and Saqqez began to acquire public primary schools in the 1920s.[143] Memoirs and biographies indicate the emergence of secondary schools much later. For example, in 1938 a male student from Mahabad, where an education department seems to have existed in these years, had to go to Urumia to finish his secondary education.[144]

The intrusion of modern ideas into the existing culture elicited the resistance of the religious institution, and the prevalent anti-modern education attitudes hindered the spread of modern schools. Moreover, despite the existence of *'motajadded'* (Pe. modernist) religious persons, the pressure of religious beliefs was constant. The era of the coexistence of religion and science in the education system of *hojra* had gone. Modern natural sciences and modern schools began to threaten the position of the clergy and also the validity of the religious texts.

> In 1927, I finished primary school in Mahabad. The situation was strange then. Non-religious education [was regarded] as wrong and a person who tried to enrol in a secondary school was seen as an infidel. If a person believed in spherical earth or said that it is the earth that goes around the sun, that person was considered as someone who was regressing towards the worship of fire.[145]

Opposed by *Maktab-e Quran* (Pe. A Quranic school), the first modern school in Saqqez was established around 1918 with the support of Sadr-ulama Mufti, the representative of Saqqez for the Majlis in three periods from the ascension of Ahmad Shah (1909) to the end of Reza Shah's rule (1941).[146] He was 'the founder of Ahmadia national four-class in 1921 [. . .] which eventually became a six-class school called Shahpour in 1925', followed by the foundation of a secondary school for girls in 1935.[147] The inception of modern education was, thus, marked by the efforts of individuals who carried with them the educational ideas of the Constitutional Revolution. In addition to the linguistic needs and educational policies of the modern Iranian state, its authority, despite a negligible budget, led to an increase in the number of elementary and secondary schools. Although the introduction of modern education was a significant development, primary sources indicate a slow process for the period between 1920 and 1940,[148] which was interrupted by the outbreak of the Second World War followed by the political crisis that Iran experienced until the coup of 1953. Nevertheless, in a society affected by abrupt regional and international upheavals since the Constitutional Revolution, the cultural revivals in Kurdistan between 1939 and 1945, symbolized by *Zhe Kaf* and its organ *Nishtiman* and then the short-lived Kurdish Republic, multiplied the impact of educational efforts. These inspired the population to participate in politics and engage more actively in educational, social and literary activities. Indeed, such upheavals proved to be crucial factors for creating widespread enthusiasm for social change in Kurdistan primarily because they created momentum for the popularization of modern ideas. At the same time, this period marked the emergence, or proliferation, of modern Kurdish intellectuals too who gradually parted with religious education. Therefore, as the result of ongoing social and political transformations, and modern education, these intellectuals were composed of either non-*hojra* educated or those who had been transformed into modern intellectuals possessing a strong social consciousness.[149] Influenced by modern progressive ideas and revolutions, the poetry of Qane' was transformed from love poetry into a socially and ethnically critical one, while, evident in their books, both Hemin's and Hazhar's poetic careers were propelled by the experience of the Kurdistan Republic, which signified profound intellectual transformations in a worldwide context.

The Constitution of 1907 'provided for public education [. . .] through the Ministry of Education'.[150] In the 1920s and 1930s, new educational laws were ratified and culminated in the establishment of Tehran University in 1935. 'Nevertheless, the modern education system [under Reza Shah] remained small, urban, formalistic, and elitist; it was barely able to meet the qualitative and quantitative needs of a modernizing economy.'[151] The education system in this period became centralized and continued to expand in the decades after the Second World War. By 1978 there were nineteen universities in Iran.[152]

In Kurdistan, the introduction of modern education by establishing public primary schools in the time of Reza Shah remained limited to towns and cities. *Ta'lim wa Tarbyiat*, published by the Ministry of Education since 1925, reported in its educational map for 1925 the existence of only one such school in Sanandaj, Sauj Blagh, Kermanshah and Urumia; there is no indication of any intermediary schools (Figure 2. However, memoirs refer to the existence of a primary school in other cities such as Saqqez in the 1920s. The first public school in Sardasht, another Kurdish city, was established in 1310 (1931/2) with twenty-five to thirty students.[153] Statistics of later periods also indicate, for example, a low level of primary and secondary enrolments until the 1960s.[154] Moreover, during the reign of Reza Shah, political considerations overshadowed educational and social concerns

1. The Integration of Kurdish Society into Modern Iran

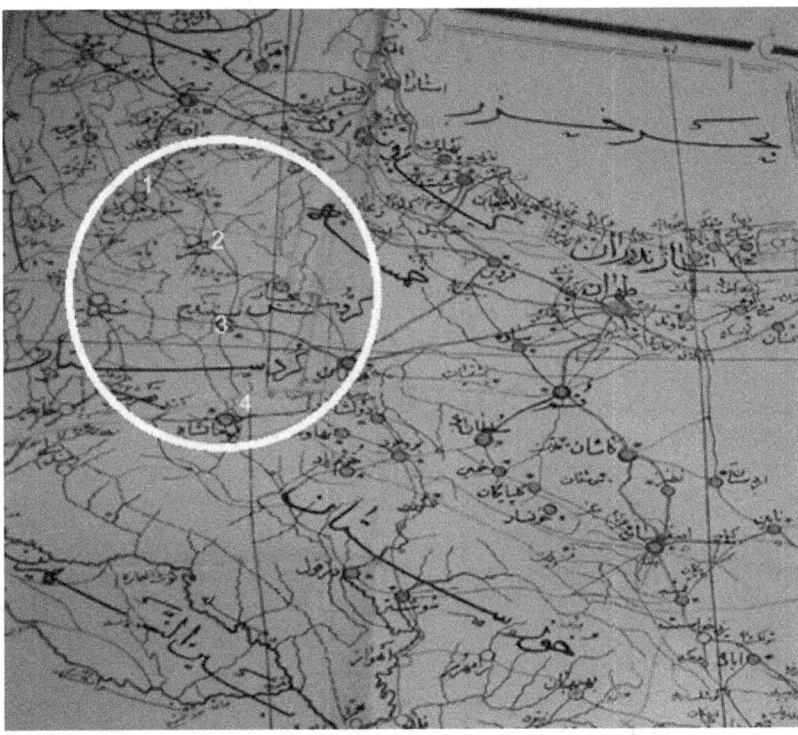

Figure 2 Kurdistan Province in the educational map of Iran (naqsheye ma'aref-e Iran), 1304/1925. *Source*: *Ta'lim wa Tarbiyat*. This educational map is modified by adding a white circle around an area including some more urbanized cities in the Kurdish region of Iran. Numbers 1–4 represent the cities of Mahabad, Saqqez, Sanandaj and Kermanshah respectively. * Public primary schools ∆ Three-year elementary schools ☒ Six-year elementary schools ∗ Iranian schools abroad

to a great extent. Persian became compulsory and therefore incited resentment towards the government and increased interest in Kurdish which was helped by the fact that it was not forbidden at schools in Iraq Kurdistan.[155] In the time of Reza Shah, except in a few villages for their military and strategic positions, rural areas were entirely deprived of modern educational centres. Instead, the presence of gendarmerie characterized this era. In the Hawraman region in south-western Kurdistan with a legacy of Zoroastrian culture, literacy was seen as a social duty also for women who to some extent managed to gain literacy through religious centres. Furthermore, the authority of the landowners was gradually used for the opening of modern schools since the 1960s. Their wealth had provided funds for *hojra*, and this time their permission was a prerequisite for the establishment of a school. This is another factor that explains the existence of, or the lack of, both religious and modern schools in rural areas. With the demise of the landowner's influence and wealth following the socio-economic developments in the late 1960s and 1970s, *hojra* lost its patronage and subsequently faded away. However, as discussed in the next chapter, they were not immediately replaced by schools in rural areas, and the absence of modern schools continued to characterize rural life in those decades. In addition to this, modern primary and secondary schools in cities reduced enthusiasm for traditional education; they became increasingly attractive by providing new means and paths to employment in the public sector.

To sum up, although the state's authority was crucial for educational changes, it was not a sole actor but, on some occasions such as the cultural revival of the early 1940s, also a barrier. In addition to (limited) modern education, agency was crucial for producing an urbanized new educated generation, who promoted social and political awareness in Kurdistan and became another social force alongside notables and tribal chiefs. Social change and transformation had assigned a historical role to the non-state agents of change to stamp their mark on social change. On the other hand, one can argue that the dialectics of religious and modern education in Kurdistan advanced and gradually popularized literacy which was not limited to the privileged anymore. *Hojra* remains crucial in the history of education. It produced Kurdish literary figures who, since the end of the nineteenth century, became the advocates of the popularization of modern education. Insofar as the state is concerned, the continuation of the constitutional educational reforms in the first half of the twentieth century, in the shape of modern primary and secondary schools, however limited, changed the educational landscape of Kurdish society. A complementary factor, which seems to be in many respects more responsible for the spread of literacy than the state itself, was undoubtedly the literate, the non-state agents of change.

The political structure of Kurdistan

The process of the consolidation of the central state through the militarization of public spaces by a new, conscripted army and the expansion of bureaucracy in the forms of various institutions shaped the political structure of Kurdistan. The modern political structure of Kurdistan began to be influenced by military considerations because of the region's potential to be dominated by political developments in other coterminous and ethnically similar societies, as Afshar warned.[156] On the rumours of 'the independence of the Ottoman Kurdistan', Afshar wrote in 1925:

> Our domestic policy should be so that the Iranian Kurds, who are from the Iranian race and their language is one of the Iranian languages, gradually but quickly integrate with [*amikhte*] other Iranians in order to eradicate any differences. Solutions include the establishment of [modern] schools in that region, the propagation of Persian, the teaching of the history of Iran, promoting a feeling of *Iraniyat* among the population and, finally, extending the railways from the central parts of the country to that region in order to create further social and economic relationships between the Kurdish and Persians speaking [peoples]. Whenever this task, i.e. 'the Persianisation of the Kurds' was carried

out, then the independence of the Ottoman Kurdistan and the existence of a racially Kurdish government [in that country] [located] between a Turkish state and us will not harm us.[157]

Moreover, the Reza Shah's rule became increasingly oppressive, and the suppression of the elements of Kurdish identity, which were perceived as inimical to a unified Iranian identity, was carried out by the gendarmerie in both urban and rural areas. 'In the time of Reza Khan Pahlavi', Hazhar recalls, 'no one could even think about writing in Kurdish' and people buried Kurdish books such as the *divan*s (anthologies) of prominent Kurdish poets in order to protect them.[158] It had become routine for the gendarmes to interrupt life in rural areas:

> When [I was living] in Taragha [in the vicinity of Bukan], the gendarmes visited that village on a daily basis. They regarded [wearing] Kurdish dress, [using] tobacco and [cigarette] paper, and any seemingly unfriendly gesture of people towards [both] themselves and their horses as a big sin.[159]

The consolidation of the state crucially included eradicating or debilitating local powers. At least the urban population welcomed the weakening of the powerful tribes' grips on their lives. The historian, Ayatullah Muhammad Mardukh, praised the 'end of chaos' in Kurdistan 'by this strong and erudite state' in his Nowruz celebration speech.[160] Hazhar also retells, ironically, the story of the Shikaks' pillage of Sauj Belagh in autumn 1921:

> The army of 'Smail agha Simko' raided Sauj Belagh to fight the *'ajams* [the Turks]. [It is claimed] that they went house to house and looted the Kurds. It seemed that in the same way that Smail agha had wanted to liberate us from the *'ajams*, he also wanted to liberate us from that we had [achieved] thanks to the *'ajams*. They pillaged everything [. . .] they even robbed the babies [. . .] they robbed women of their pyjamas and then, apologising, turned their faces away [in order not to see their naked bodies]. The Shikaks robbed the Kurds but did not kill them; they [however] killed any Turkish-speaking person [they came across].[161]

Nevertheless, both the disarmament and displacement of tribes, which were followed by building *padegan*s or military bases in growing towns and strategic villages, constituted various elements of a militaristic policy. A dozen of tribes with tens of *taifa*s or sub-tribes were forced to settle, while many others were robbed of their properties and sent to exile.[162] Facing violence and poverty, hundreds of families from the Galbakhi tribe in the southern part of Iranian Kurdistan, for instance, were sent to other parts of Iran as far as Kerman in the southeast of Iran.[163] The policy of compulsory settlement, called *takht-e qapu* (wooden door) instead of the 'black tent', forced many other tribes such as the Peshdaris to cross the border and reside in what is now Iraqi Kurdistan. This policy, which included the incarceration of tribal leaders even after being disarmed, was to some degree reversed in the early 1930s because of its negative economic impact, for example, on meat production.[164]

The social and economic plans in the time of Reza Shah were usually preceded by military expansions and considerations. This continued to restrict the capacity of the state to implement effective social programmes in order to improve social conditions in Kurdistan. The degree of the militarization of the public space fluctuated according to the existence or the absence of political crises in Kurdistan. However, the military gaze of the state became constant; and this is the precedent set by military policies and means in the reign of Reza Shah.

Furthermore, political participation through the election of *Majlis* deputies since the Constitutional Revolution was restricted or did not develop further, with the effect that the election of representatives eventually became a symbolic act by the 1970s. Moreover, the ascendancy of Persian as the official language of both education and administration created formidable obstacles for the Kurdish language to thrive in cultural and literary spheres. The number of journals or newspapers remained near zero until the 1979 Revolution. All these elements affected political participation negatively. However, in addition to the free space, which the Kurdistan Republic and the Musaddeq era created, the resolution of political and social activists to promote political and social awareness by publishing and distributing 'illegal' journals, books and pamphlets, which addressed issues concerned with politics, culture and literature, counterpoised dictatorship and the authoritarian modernization.

Therefore, a modernizing Kurdistan began to assume a political structure shaped by military considerations, reflecting the tension between *Kurdayeti* and the process of creating a homogenous nation state. Indeed, by claiming to protect borders, the state has ever since attempted to legitimize military considerations and policies. Although the administrative division of provinces revealed military and political motivations behind such policies, the emergence of discourses of power in the formation of the modern political structure of Kurdish-Iranian society merits a brief review.

Politically, the state's cultural and linguistic efforts to ensure a unified Iranian identity led to a period of political suppression, which included banning Kurdish in schools, introducing a dress code and persecuting literary activists.[165] The idea of *vahdat-e melli-e Iran* (Pe. the national unity of Iran) provided intellectual legitimacy for the state's linguistic policies. Affected by the political instability and wars, the Persian journals in the 1920s reflected a political culture in which a strong state and 'national unity' were advocated as core principles creating a politically stable and socio-economically advancing Iran. For example, Afshar defined national unity as 'the political, moral, and social unity of people living within the territory of Iran' in order to 'preserve the political independence of Iran and its territorial integrity'.[166] The national unity stipulated uniformity in custom and the eradication of diversity in dress, language and names.

> We believe that until national unity in language, morals, dress, etc., has been achieved, imminent danger to our political independence and territorial integrity

will always exist. [. . .] Some Persian-speaking *ilats* [tribes] can be transported to reside in foreign-speaking [i.e. non-Persian-speaking] regions [*navahi-e bigane zaban*], while foreign-speaking tribes can be moved to Persian-speaking regions. Foreign geographical names [. . .] must be replaced with Persian names. The country must assume new suitable [administrative] divisions and avoid using the [current] names of Khurasan, Baluchistan, Fars, Azerbaijan, and Kurdistan [for its provinces].[167]

Afshar, however, did not want to sound 'Chauvinistic' or 'imperialistic'. Indeed, such ideas emanated from an existing feeling of threat from outside of Iran, and also from a common wish of intellectuals and statesmen such as Muhammad Foroughi and 'Ali Akbar Davar to build an effective modern state. Afshar also defended 'deconcentration' as against both 'centralisation' and 'decentralization' and did not necessarily agree with any administrative divisions.[168] Nevertheless, he remained adamant about the unity and conformity of diverse Iranian communities under the banner of Iranian national unity in every sphere of life.[169]

The implementation of such ideas on behalf of an authoritarian state inevitably presupposed coercive means as it was going to face resistance against ethnic unity and conformity. As regards the Kurds, the tension between these hegemonic and resisting identities incited violence also on behalf of the Kurds and became the origin of modern armed struggle perceived as a legitimate form of resistance against ethnic oppression. Abbas Vali rightly observes that the suppression of Kurdish identity became the root of a continuing conflict with the central government and the violence in Iranian Kurdistan.[170] However, the modern Kurdish armed struggle in correlation with militarization is still largely understudied.

A powerful Iranian national narrative, which conceptually marginalizes the Kurds and their history, assumed an oppressive attitude towards cultural and political rights regarded inimical to a centralized, territorially defined modern Iran. Indeed, Kurdish identity became the victim of two historical factors. First, a painful memory of Iran's territorial loss in the hands of the great powers which inflicted severe damage to its territorial integrity and independence; the treaties of Golestan (1813) and Turkmanchay (1828) provide historical facts in this regard. Logically, therefore, the modern Iranian identity was based on the pillars of national unity and territorial integrity with the effects that the Kurds began to be judged by the above-mentioned principles, leading to ingrained prejudices against them. Second, this unified Iranian identity established the Persian community as the core-ethnocultural nation, and this resulted in the marginalization of other ethnic communities, including Kurdish.[171] Although in this unification 'differences' were not codified, for example, by issuing different *Shenasnameh* or ID based on ethnicity, as Brubaker has shown was the case in the *multinational* Soviet Union, it institutionalized difference.[172] All residents of Iran were defined as Iranian, but ethnic groups such as the Kurds became a modern *qaum* (ethnic community) as a constituent of the modern nation of Iran connoting an 'undeveloped nation' at the same time, as opposed to *mellat* (Pe. nation); and their cultural and political rights were defined in connection with 'Iran' as a unified nation. Moreover, the

Table 2 A Single-Dimensional Approach to Social Change in Kurdistan

Mechanisms of modernization according to modernization theories	Some major obstacles to development

• State as the sole actor
• Modernizing institutions
• Implementation of the elements of modernization
• A Western pattern of development
	• The absence of
	  ○ Big capital
	  ○ Technology
	  ○ Modern institutions
	  ○ Modern values
	• Cultural resistance
	• Existing religious and ethical values are not favourable to individuals aiming at material progress.

Traditional society • Static • Undeveloped • Rural; a passive peasantry • Simple division of labour based on 'mechanical solidarity' • Superstitious • Patriarchal • Backward-looking	**Traditional man** • Irrational • Exposed to traditional institutions and way of life • Undisciplined • Averse to new experience, perception and value • Engaged in an unspecialized simple division of labour

The elements of modernization (patterns of development are largely those of the United States and Western Europe)

	Institutional approach		*Sociopsychological approach*
Socio-economic elements • Industrialization • Demographic growth • Application of scientific technology • High specialization of labour • Urbanization • Modern education • Secularization • Hygienization • Developed media • Stratifications • Effective differentiation	**Political elements** • Rationalization of authority: ○ The replacement of traditional, religious, familial, secular, national political authorities • Centralization of power • The differentiation of new political functions (legal, military, administrative, scientific) and the development of specialized structures to perform these functions • Political participation via new institutions (e.g. political parties and interest groups)		Cultural and ideational elements (individual modernization) • 'Modern' is a syndrome of certain qualities • Modernization of ways of thinking and feeling • Change in behaviour, values and perceptions • The modern is a (Weberian) ethos • Modern is a spiritual phenomenon, a mentality

Becoming modern

Modern society	**Modern man**	*Required personal qualities*
• Centralized authority • Loyalty to the state • Urbanized • Industrialized (e.g. factory workers) • Disciplinary • Rational and scientific • Complex divisions of labour based on merit • Secular • *Strong* modernizing institutions (factory) with universal effect • Technologically developed • A developed media system • Democratized and globalized	• Industrial • Disciplined • Experiencing modern life • Employed in complex, rationalized, technocratic and bureaucratic organizations • E.g. factor worker, active worker • Possesses rewarding roles • Possesses exposure to modernizing elements • Shaped by industrial milieu (factory)	• Openness to new experience, ideas, feeling and acting • Readiness for social change • Intellectually able • Able to plan ahead • Rely on institutions • Valuing technical skills • Educated, aspired, appreciate science • Engaged in a complex division of labour

Table 2 (Continued)

Modernization will result in:
- The political authority of the state
- The universal response to institutional and individual modernization
- Making mostly irrelevant the uniqueness of culture and society
- Secularization: societies become more secular as they become more modernized
- 'Transcultural similarities in psychic properties of individuals create a basis for a common response to common stimuli'
- Independent nuclear family
- Women's rights
- Religious beliefs not being able to stand urbanization and industrialization

---

institutionalization of difference in favour of the Persian community is exemplified by the clash of definitions between the Iranian and Kurdish national narratives over the concepts of *qaum* and *mellat* which is originated in the processes of the formation of modern Iranian and Kurdish identities. *Qaum* justifies the Iranian national narrative's denial of the political and cultural rights of a community, which is, in turn, represented by the Kurdish national narrative's definition of itself as *mellat*, in need of recognition.

Therefore, the politics of modernization entailed an enduring clash between Iranian and Kurdish identities and their legitimizing national narratives. Except occasionally in the time of political crises, wars and revolutions, a powerful and stable central government has continued the oppression of Kurdish identity and guaranteed the ascendancy of the discourse of a unified Iran – a discourse which is in fact very divisive. Such claims and policies began to interrupt modus vivendi and encourage violent modes of resistance. Indeed, the political structure of Kurdistan began to be shaped by political and militarily motivated policies, on the one hand, and the resistance of *Kurdayeti*, on the other. The continuous resistance to power and its discourses as regards the Kurds thus originated in the process of the nationalization of Iranian identity. However, discussed in the next chapter, Kurdish society proved to be more receptive to socio-economic change with the effect that *Kurdayeti* found itself in a paradox of ethnically resisting but socially adaptive.

Conclusion

Against a historical background, this chapter aims to illustrate the integrating tendency of modernization and social change in Kurdish society since the early twentieth century. The crucial elements in this process are identified as attempts at socio-economic reforms, institutional changes and the state's politics of modernization. Although Kurdistan experienced a sluggish socio-economic change until 1960 and its social order did not radically alter, it witnessed the emergence of new socio-economic trends, affecting its social structure. The

Table 3 A Multidimensional Approach to Social Change in Kurdistan

Main mechanisms and socio-political dynamism of social change and transformation:
- State
- Economic plans
- Modernising institutions
- Non-state agents of change
- Historical conjuncture

factors of social and political integrations — *Factors resisting authoritarian modernisation and homogenisation*

State-led Modernisation (centralised, authoritarian)	Historical conjuncture	Non-state Agents of Change	Kurdish Culture and Identity
The early 20th-century Kurdish society	The impact of:	1. An educated generation generated by:	Modernisation included:
o social stratification based on the master-servant relationship	o Domestic, regional and international events, wars and crisis	o pre-modern education	o nationalisation of identity, based on a unified Iranian identity
o predominantly rural	o Mass communication (Radio, TV, publications)	o modern Education	o persianisation of culture and language
o widespread illiteracy	o Population movement	o modern ideas of education and progress	o politics of modernisation which included the militarisation of public space and modern administrative divisions
o the lack of a health system	o Culture in modern society	o state-led economic and political modernisation	
o economically self-sufficient	o Interaction between social forces	2. Social, cultural, and political activists whose worldviews were shaped and re-shaped by further worldwide and regional ideological transformations.	Nationalisation resulted in the
o patriarchal, exploitative gender relation	o Unequal opportunities	3. Intellectuals and their productions	o suppression and marginalisation of Kurdish identity
	o More globalised		o the banning of Kurdish as the language of administration and education
Modern nation-state preceding by:	o Dissemination of symbolic means of communication	Such factors have been crucial for:	o Persianisation of culture and language.
o Revolution, war, coup	o Perception, value, and behaviour are shaped by a wide range of factors and not by one single institution (e.g. 'factory'):	o the spread of literacy	
o Modern national and progressive ideas	o History, myths, tradition, religion, social change, politics of modernisation, political organisations, agents of change (state and non-state), intellectual transformation	o the promotion of social, political and gender awareness	*Kurdayeti* (Kurdishness) maintained its distinctive ethnic characteristics by formidable cultural and religious factors.
o A new political culture		o cultural production	
o New intellectuals	o Gender awareness, social and political awareness	o creating cultural exposure to change	
o State, the main actor of change			
o Economic plans			
o Modern education and health system			

In a multi-dimensional approach:

1. The outcomes of the interactions of the above factors are not generally predictable nor can be logically expected using development theories.
2. Positive and negative ramifications of the state-led reforms shape the social and political structures of society.
3. The crucial role of the non-state agents of change in social change is identified.
4. The inclusion and a critical analysis of other concepts and themes such as the following are required:

    o Traditional vs. modern
    o Modern education
    o The modernising and integrating institutions
    o Secularisation
    o Backlash to secularisation
    o Politics of modernisation
    o The gender order
    o Land reform
    o Industrialisation
    o Infrastructural development
    o Social displacement
    o Urbanisation and the modern city
    o Media
    o Political participation
    o Political, cultural, and armed resistance

state was the main authority in this process, and its policies were shaped by various historical and ideological factors as well as political exigencies. This socio-economic process laid the foundation of modernizing institutions such as education and healthcare. They did not become widespread under Reza Shah. Nevertheless, they were significant as foundations for reforms in later decades. Undeniably, based on a literary background, modern education yielded a new educated, urban generation which became a social and political force in political upheavals alongside tribal chiefs of tribal communities. Furthermore, the efforts of members of such a generation to simultaneously spread literacy and promote social, ethnic and political awareness of people highlight the crucial role of non-state agents of change. This becomes more evident in the way the political structure of Kurdish society continued to change according to the modern nation state's nationalistic and militaristic attitudes, on the one hand, and the resistance of *Kurdayeti*, now intellectually transformed by the second half of the century, to the state's 'national unity', on the other.

In this way, therefore, political and economic modernization seemed to succeed in determining the integrating tendency of Kurdish society, whereas the nationalization of Iranian identity not only failed to erase Kurdish identity, but it unwittingly motivated its perseverance. In this regard, many important elements of Kurdish ethnic identity such as religion and language continued to function in favour of *Kurdayeti* by reinforcing distinct ethnic characteristics. The nationalization of Iranian identity continued to provide legitimacy for *Kurdayeti* as a sense of both belonging to and struggle for the Kurds and Kurdistan – a sense which continued to be reinforced theoretically and practically by intellectual endeavours and political movements. Modernization, on the other hand, sustained its tendency to integrate Iranian societies into a distinct, Iranian socio-economic and political field which formed the source of defining self within the framework of Iran since the Second World War. That said, *Kurdayeti* did not remain as a rigid phenomenon but continued to reshape according to historical conjunctures and intellectual transformations in the second half of the century. However, it became more embedded within the framework of Iran as Kurdish society became socio-economically more integrated into that country because of the intensification of modernization and social change, especially in the era of the White Revolution.

Chapter 2

THE WHITE REVOLUTION

ORIGINS, AIMS AND ECONOMIC PLANS

The White Revolution is a social transformation unprecedented in Iran's three-thousand-year history.

Muhammad Reza Shah Pahlavi, 1962[1]

While the Westerner has become disillusioned and the Western culture is declining, we are marching behind the West [. . .] and keep boasting about the advances of the West and claiming that we will soon be one of the greatest advanced countries of the world.

Reza Barahani, 1969[2]

Introduction

This and the following chapters present an assessment of many significant aspects of Kurdish society's social transformation in the two decades following the inception of the reforms in the early 1960s. The Shah's Revolution, based on the existing ideas in Iran to reform the Iranian state and society, developed into a dream of making Iran a Great Civilization, while the spiralling oil revenues effectively contributed to the intensification of the state-led modernization. Political consequences notwithstanding, reforms profoundly changed Kurdish-Iranian society too. Therefore, it is the task of the following chapters to interpret and analyse the way this took place.

By the time the 1979 *popular* revolution began, the White Revolution had profoundly transformed Iran. The scale of this transformation extended to Kurdish society too, and therefore, an analysis of social change in Kurdistan in the two decades of the 1960s and 1970s is inevitably linked to change across Iran. The popular revolution did terminate the *Pahlavi's* modernization. However, the state and the society that emerged bore indelible marks of this earlier period because it had laid strong foundations for the continuation of future state-led modernization, regardless of the nature of the succeeding state. This chapter briefly contextualizes the White Revolution and identifies the origins of the ideas that led to its inception. This is necessary for three reasons. First, the historical context and reformist ideas, which were already in circulation, invite a critical reading of the White Revolution for us to identify its negative and positive ramifications as the result of a mixture of factors peculiar to contemporary Iran. Second, as regards Kurdish society, this critical reading assists us to place this period in the dual process we have been following, and not regard it as an inevitable transitory point in the age of modernity, let alone an unprecedented event in 'Iran's three-thousand-year history', ahistorical and inflated claim by the reigning monarch. Finally, this approach enables us to identify other contributing factors alongside the state in the process of change and transformation and engage in a critical assessment of the consequences of reforms too. In addition to an overview of the reaction to the White Revolution in Kurdistan, the conceptualization of the White Revolution is followed by presenting a general discussion of some other significant topics in the process of the socio-economic transformation of the Kurdish region: the Kurdish region in economic planning; land reform and its general consequences for the rural-class structure; and infrastructure.

An idea exploited

As an idea, the 'White Revolution' had been cultivated by Iranian intellectuals at least since the early 1940s.[3] It represented a non-violent transformation of Iran under a 'leader' who would also pacify the presumed perils of different hues of red, yellow and green (later black) menace, that is, communism, the far east and Islam, respectively. The initial meaning of the term served a 'parliamentarian regime' and aimed to create a 'balance between the executive and legislative powers'.[4] In contrast, the Shah's White Revolution primarily aimed to pacify the multifaceted threat to the monarchy in order to preserve and strengthen its foundations. Simultaneously, the ideas of land reform, the centrepiece of the Shah's White Revolution, had been advocated since the early 1940s, for example, by left-wing groups to curb the power of the landowner class and transform agriculture. The division of land in Iran had been previously attempted, for instance, under the autonomous government of Azerbaijan in the early 1940s;[5] and since it was a long-standing demand of the left, the monarch's Revolution hoped to neutralize 'the threat of communism' by accomplishing social reforms in general and the land reform, in particular. The White Revolution not only reflected a history of genuine desires of Iranians for reform pursued since the Constitutional Revolution (1906–11), but it also aimed to prevent social revolution from below. The fear of revolution from below originated in the crisis around the nationalization of the oil industry as early as 1949. As Roger Louis reveals, for the British officials such as Michael Wright, assistant under-secretary supervising Middle Eastern affairs, 'for a long time it had been clear that the situation of "political stagnation" in Iran could not continue indefinitely. Either the Iranian government would have to come to grips with far-reaching economic and social reform or there would be a Communist revolution.'[6] The White Revolution was a revolution from above.

The Shah's White Revolution denotes a set of principles in the process of the modernization of Iran. These principles were originally comprised of six points:

land reform, nationalization of forests, sale of state-owned enterprises to the public, workers' profit-sharing in 20 per cent of net corporate earnings, voting and political rights for women and formation of the Literacy Corps. These were extended to 19 points by 1977. These principles, which were formally presented by the Shah, first to the cabinet and then to the Congress of the Farmers of Iran in January 1963, included reforms that had already been introduced by successive Iranian governments, mostly during the previous cabinet under Ali Amini in the absence of the Majlis, recasting much of the ingredients of the Third Economic Plan (1962).[7] Land reform was a long-standing preoccupation of Iranian statesmen too, and the incorporation of a Literacy Corps in the principles for mandatory universal education had become law in October 1962.[8] The government had already started land reform in northwest Iran in March 1962.[9] This was also the case with the principle of voting and political rights for women. As an increasingly considerable social force in modernizing Iran, women activists had continued to pursue such rights since the 1920s and pressure the state and statesmen to conceive more rights, including the right to vote.[10] The Shah remained conservative especially when he faced a major challenge from the clergy.[11] Therefore, it was mainly the women activists who eventually forced informal participation of women in the election of 1962, without their votes being counted, which two days later made the Shah promise 'the right of women to vote in the future'.[12] Ali Amini, the incumbent prime minister, who had advocated land reform since the mid-1940s, had used the title 'White Revolution' when the land reform was passed, and for whom this reform, along with women's rights, constituted the pillars of that revolution.[13] The Shah added new ideas such as profit-sharing schemes for industrial workers, an idea he had conceived while observing life in the United States. As noted earlier, as an alternative to social theories of the left and as a modernizing programme to prevent social revolution, the White Revolution was quickly renamed 'The Revolution of the Shah and the People'; more points were added to the principles of the White Revolution in the following years.

That said, the novelty of the Shah's White Revolution was in its political dimensions, though it inaugurated a profound socio-economic transformation of Iran. While it was affected by the previous attempts at reform and the preceding economic plans, the political situation in Iran granted urgency to such reforms. Domestically the dynasty had been facing a protracted political crisis since the Second World War, embodied in short tenures of successive cabinets and ultimately the oil crisis which was culminated in the coup of 1953.[14] In the early 1960s and before the declaration of the principles of the White Revolution, a new wave of social unrest threatened the monarchy when religious and secular oppositions alike resurfaced. In effect, the Shah's Revolution attempted to thwart both the 'black and red menace'. Furthermore, economically, the Third Economic Plan seemed to have forged a rival power centre consisting of the so-called Harvard economic advisers, Amini and the Plan Organization under Gholamhosain Ebtehaj, whose performances were judged under the shadow of the Kennedy administration. This 'raised political concern for the Shah who wanted a strong army'.[15] Regionally, the toppling of the monarchy in Iraq (1958) and the military coup in Turkey (1960) further increased political pressure to intensify economic development for which the oil revenue and a strong military constituted its pillars. The White Revolution, therefore, aimed at preserving the establishment by providing alternatives to other social and political forces represented by an increasingly politicized religious opposition and various reformist movements, the existence or reconfiguration of which was due to the social transformation of Iran in general and the state-led modernizations in particular. Therefore, the White Revolution amounted to political dictatorship. This was anticipated by the National Front of the liberals, a significant oppositional force in the time, which, in reaction to the referendum for the White Revolution and under the slogan 'yes to reform, no to dictatorship', denounced it as illegal.[16] In *Mission for My Country*, the Shah stipulated 'positive nationalism' and 'political democracy' for economic development to simultaneously make the opposition irrelevant and promote Iran to an unprecedented status among the world's powerful nations.[17] As it turned out to be the case, he had to cross the path towards that imaginary status alone with dire political consequences for Iran.

Reaction to the White Revolution

There seems to have been two kinds of reaction to the announcement of the principles of the White Revolution and the referendum in Kurdistan: an initial general reaction and a more specific one put forward by organized Kurdish activists. The White Revolution created an unprecedented opportunity to effectively challenge the Kurdish *aghas*' authority over society and benefit from a more favourable context to affect poor socio-economic conditions. An initial positive reaction to the land reform explained the need to weaken the social and political power of the landowner class. However, the continuation of more organized opposition to the Pahlavi state and a *Kurdayeti*, intellectually more connected to the outside world, created mixed feelings towards the reforms.

The reaction of Kurdish political activists to the Shah's announcement of the White Revolution illuminated the political dimensions of the reforms in question. The increase in the number of Kurdish university students in Tehran had led to the formation of *Yakiyati Khwendkaran-i Kurd* (Ku. The Union of Kurdish Students), which was concerned with domestic and international political developments and began to expand in 1961–2.[18] An influential event of the time was the expansion of the Kurdish movement in Iraq which also attracted the support of the opportunistic Iranian government, which perceived Arab nationalism as a threat to its regional position. The state exploited this situation by organizing new but controlled Kurdish publications and radio programmes. However, the state unintentionally created opportunities for Kurdish activists and literary figures to practice the Kurdish language and literature. *Yakiati* 'identified itself with the Kurdish movement in Iraq with the effect that the movement's rise [in the early 1960s] and fall [in 1975] determined its fate too'.[19] Moreover, the National Front and Dariush Foruhar's Iran Party turned to the

Union to benefit from their active engagement in political and cultural activities and tried to absorb it.[20]

In these circumstances, Kurdish educated-activists treated the White Revolution as a political project and 'did not pay heed to its social promises'.[21] One activist, who founded a small bookshop called *Danesh* (Knowledge) in 1966, explains the opposition to the Shah's White Revolution in the international, regional, and domestic contexts of the time. For example, the rise of the United States as a world power, the collapse of the monarchy in Iraq and the advance of the Kurdish movement in Iraq 'shaped their initial opposition to the reforms without having a deep understanding of its contents'.[22] However, attitudes to social issues addressed in the principles of the White Revolution changed in the 1970s, when the opposition to the Pahlavi regime increased.[23] Moreover, while many members of *Yakiyati* voted to participate in the referendum, some others, among them engineers, voted against it mainly because of '*Kurdayeti* and the social status of some members' who came from wealthy landowning families.[24] Nevertheless, while political dispositions were shaped according to the ideas and context of the time, 'the oppressive and inhumane socio-economic regime of the Kurdish *agha* was another factor to welcome the land reform'.[25] Moreover, participating in the referendum for the White Revolution was considered a shrewd move 'to cover political activities and safeguard the organisation against SAVAK'. That said, the common characteristic of these mixed attitudes can be identified as a superficial understanding of the events which were taking place. For example, according to an activist, using *dehqan* (peasant) instead of newly adopted *keshavarz* (Pe. farmer) only amounted to an oppositional gesture to the Shah and thus demonstrated 'a lack of deep knowledge of the principles concerned with social issues'.[26]

In contrast, the popular reaction to the White Revolution was more enthusiastic.

> It had a good impact on the population living in villages under the yoke of the *agha*. It upset the landowners. The idea of land reform and attempts to divide the land were not new and dated back to the time of Musaddeq [prime minister 1951–3], who also demanded the landowners to move to cities. During his tenure, many villages in the Gawirk region founded *Shura* [Ku. Council] to run the village. Ultimately, *Shuras* were brutally suppressed as another outcome of the 1953 coup.[27]

The popular enthusiasm was understandable. Villagers lived under the brutal regime of the *aghas* devoid of any basic rights. The *rashaiy*, the Kurdish serf and *jutbanda* (Ku. sharecropper), who formed the lowest layers of the village social structure, 'lived like slaves'.[28] Therefore, people, including students, teachers and staff in public offices, participated in the demonstration organized to support the referendum. Even the clergy, 'unlike their Shi'a counterparts, did not oppose the White Revolution at least publicly'.[29] However, as time proceeded, the negative and positive ramifications of the reforms became more evident. The division of land proved to be unequal because the landowners were able to keep good quality lands while the *rashaiy* remained landless and was forced to migrate to cities. As a result, popular discontent increased, reflecting Kurdish activists' growing political and social awareness, too.[30] However, this is undeniable that the White Revolution triggered unprecedented interaction and movements of people and connected the confined village life to the outside world, modern education, healthcare and new ways of life.[31] In attracting further rural and urban public support, the expanding, extremely attractive 'radio played a crucial role by promoting awareness on social issues such as healthcare, in various local dialects'.[32] Both the big and small landowners remained suspicious of the White Revolution, while the state continued to remind them of the peaceful nature of the Shah's Revolution, ensuring compensation for the lost lands. According to oral history, *Khorde-malik* (the small landowner) lost more in possession and status than the big landowners.[33] However, the latter's social and political power had been dealt a severe blow, too.

Therefore, the reaction to the inception of the White Revolution can be assessed as follows. Political activists opposed or supported the reforms for different *political* reasons which, as we discussed earlier, also explained the White Revolution's raison d'etre. At the same time, the initial enthusiastic reaction of the wider population, including the educated and activists, however sceptical, originated from the oppressive regime of the Kurdish *agha*s which the land reform had now begun to imperil. The state's authority was crucial to implement the long-craved reforms, which began to materialize through more sophisticated economic plans. However, while the plans' directions and contents made sense in a political context, perspectives on how to transform Iranian societies had a long pedigree.

The potential and directions of economic plans

The era of the White Revolution is distinguished by two completed Third (1962–8) and Fourth (1968–73) Development Plans, followed by an aborted Fifth Development plan (1973–). As scholars have noted, the previous modernizing attempts of the interwar years were 'outcomes of philosophy and policy, rather than of a concrete program or strategy'.[34] The First (1949–55) and Second (1955–62) economic plans were at best paralysed by political instability and the shortage of revenue, whereas the spiralling oil revenue since the 1960s, and especially in the early 1970s, made possible the execution of more ambitious and sophisticated economic plans. The Second Plan spent, out of a budget of 82.3 billion Rials, 75.2 million mostly on transportation and communications.[35] Owing to increasing oil revenue, which reached $958 million in the mid-1960s and rose to a staggering $20 billion by 1973,[36] these plans coincided with the most significant socio-economic developments that Iran had ever witnessed. Although they continued previous infrastructural and agricultural works, improved transportation and built dams for electrical output, they concentrated on industry, mining and human resources.[37] Consequently, Iran began to experience unprecedented economic growth. As another illustration of this, $6.9 billion was spent during the Third and

Fourth plans and GDP grew from at an annual rate of 8 per cent in 1962–70 to 14 per cent in 1972–3 and then to 30 per cent in 1973–4.[38]

Furthermore, this period is distinguished for embracing more effective organizations and centres to spur economic development and conduct research.[39] This was, as Afkhami has noted, embodied in 'the development tripod' of the Ministry of Economic Affairs and Finance, the Plan Organization and the Central Bank which 'became a synergic force for development' and their chiefs enjoyed a good degree of harmony.[40] In addition to this, economists along with reports by Plan Organization and the Central Bank point to an increase in national income during the Second Plan despite political instabilities in the early 1960s. During this period a combination of foreign public and private loans, as well as grants and credits, with a significant contribution of the oil industry helped a capital formation of about $3,500 million.[41] Moreover, the government's oil revenue increased, of which $810 million helped finance the Second Plan.[42] In effect, both the First and Second Plans 'were essentially financial allocations set aside for public sector projects'.[43]

During the Second Plan, the Plan Organization became a more established entity in economic development in Iran. Claimed as an incorruptible individual who eventually resigned as the head of the Plan Organization in 1958, Abolhasan Ebtehaj contributed immensely to the reorganization and transformation of the Plan Organization. As a prelude to economic actions, he generated what was sometimes regarded as controversial or prolonged studies on economic needs of Iran and its various regions; in addition to 'qualified' Western-educated Iranian economists, he employed Western economists through the World Bank, for which institutions such as Harvard topped its list.[44] The significance of the Second Plan, according to Ebtehaj, was the foundational and organizational basis that it laid for later expansive economic plans. Nevertheless, during the plan asphalted and railroads were also expanded across Iran while new factories and dams went under construction.

As regards provincial development, according to Javad Mansur, the Public Relation Officer of the Plan Organization, 'the [Second] Plan had more than enough projects [. . .] [but] no further funds to devote to provincial surveys of the EBASCO [Electric Bond and Share Company which provided engineering and construction services] type, as these crucially involved heavy additional financial commitment'.[45] As a result, this forced 'Ebtehaj to go slow on further provincial progress for the time being'[46] and subsequently assign the development of provinces to various foreign firms. Though unsuccessful, this included dividing Iran into five regions allocated to four foreign companies to assess their economic and infrastructural needs and engage in their developments.[47] This project enticed a *scramble* for Iranian provinces by American, French, Japanese, Italian and British firms which looked for 'the most suitable areas'.[48] In addition to increasing political pressures on Ebtehaj, the project failed because foreign companies sought propitious areas whereas the undesirability of a region such as Khurasan in the east of the country deterred, for example, British and German companies, which had not been initially included, to commit themselves and invest in that region. Instead, they pressed for a share in other regions with the French or other projects in more central regions such as Fars and Isfahan.[49] Even in this case, UK companies were not 'required to invest in the social development of the area, e.g. [building] schools [and] hospitals'.[50] This meant investment in certain and not properly *planned* social projects. Moreover, political considerations and economic interests on both sides shaped their approaches to provincial projects. For instance, while the Shah and Ebtehaj insisted that the interested British firms should invest in the neglected region of Khurasan because of its rich potential,[51] the British considered their economic interests, regional and international political positions to avoid lagging behind others.

The end of Ebtehaj's reign, which followed a government proposal to bring the Plan Organization under the control of the prime minister, revealed to some extent the prevalent contemporary trends in the economic development of Iran, on the one hand, and the start of more centralized planning which was going to coincide with the centralization of political power in one individual, on the other. The origin of centralizing development planning went back to the Second Plan and the dispute between the incumbent prime minister, Razmara and Ebtehaj. The former was in favour of an economic plan which provided the provinces with financial help in order to enable them to undertake their development projects, whereas the latter's stringent attitudes restrained such decentralizing attempts and mainly intended to attract foreign capital through his ideas for provincial development.[52] Ebtehaj's rejection of both the plan and demand of the representatives of Khuzistan, dominantly an Arabic-speaking region in the south, for a share in the oil revenue exemplified his centralizing approach, favoured by the Shah.[53] Instead of adopting a welcoming attitude, Ebtehaj rebuked them for not speaking (i.e. presenting their case in) Persian.[54]

However, as it can be inferred from a foreign office document, the fate of Ebtehaj was sealed when disagreements between various functions of the government, for example, the cabinet, the ministries and the Plan Organization, revealed impatience with his meticulous methods and disregard for military expenditure.[55] In any case, Ebtehaj embodied the government's will for centralization of economic development, and it can be surmised that he set a precedent in this regard too.[56] Although economic development in Iran before Ebtehaj had been inclined towards centralization, he effectively blocked initiatives from the provinces. Moreover, his plan for *omran-e shahri* (Pe. city development) stipulated provinces to provide 50 per cent of the budget, whereas the other half he projected to come from oil revenues.[57] However, Ebtehaj became increasingly unpopular with politicians for other reasons, which included his long-term planning, being both 'indifferent' to the present distress of the population and, according to some views, extravagant, so that he came to be known as someone who preferred foreign experts and loans, and an 'uncooperative, obstinate and arrogant' person, who spent four years surveying and planning.[58] That is why the incumbent prime minister claimed in the early months of 1959 that 'Iran had the Plan Organisation as well as a Ministry of Road, but still no road'.[59] By April, 'the various schemes for regional development initiated by the Plan Organisation [were] in suspense [. . .] EBASCO was told to go home'.[60]

Development plans after Ebtehaj

Enabled by spiralling oil revenues, post-Ebtehaj more comprehensive and cogent economic plans continued economic growth and ushered in the profound socio-economic transformation of Iran. Moreover, encouraged by income and growth, economic planning resulted in formulating another long-term plan of Twenty-Year Perspective based on a Plan Strategy whose ideas had French origins. The plans also signalled the fear of the depletion of oil as the blood of Iran's economy. The axis was the Plan Organization under Khodadad Farmanfarmaian (the end of 1960s–1972) and Abdolmajid Majidi (1972–7). An overview of the next economic plans demonstrates both the growing economic capacity of the state and how the plans maintained a centralizing approach devoid of specific provincial plans.

In the view of some economists, the Third Economic Plan (1962–8), whose framework was formulated by the new Economic Bureau, outclassed the previous ones by being 'truly the first comprehensive attempt at scientific planning in Iran'.[61] Its objectives included an average annual increase in the gross national product of 6 per cent; maximum employment based on the annual population growth rate of 2.5 per cent; improvement in national income distribution through socio-economic reform; and maintenance of reasonable price stability.[62] In contrast to the previous plan, which was 'simply a list of investment programs and projects' and faced 'the lack of both statistical data and familiarity with methodological planning and techniques', the next development plans were going to be prepared in more favourable economic circumstances.[63] Politically, although Iran was going to experience a period of stability, modernization also intensified the opposition of an increasingly politicized religious force that had turned against the monarchy and was eventually attracted to the ideas of *vilayet-e faqih* (Guardianship of the Islamic jurists) and Islamic government[64] (Table 4).

The Fourth and Fifth Development Plans distinguished themselves for being even more comprehensive in both quantitative and qualitative terms and containing clearly defined objectives. They accelerated the pace of industrialization and privatization by huge investments.[65] As scholars have noted, any economic ambivalence on behalf of the Shah was finally resolved when Iran's annual income from oil reached from $200 million in 1957 to $20 billion by 1973.[66] Up to $10

Table 4 The Third Economic Plan (1962–8)

	The Third Economic Plan's budgetary allocations	%
The Third Plan envisages a development scheme to the tune of $3,066 million for the public sector, to be matched with $2,000 million of the private investment. It was financed mainly by oil revenue (55% in 1962 and 80% in 1968).	Communication	25
	Agriculture and irrigation	21.5
	Electric power and fuel	15.8
	Industry and mining	12.3
	Education	7.9
	Health	6
Source: Amuzegar, 'Capital Formation,' 70–1.	Others	11.5

billion, which was channelled into the plans, aimed to accelerate the pace of modernization in all sectors 'but particularly through heavy industrialization'.[67] Other qualitative aims included 'a more equitable distribution of income through the extension of welfare services, particularly education, health, rural rehabilitation and urban development'; 'export diversification in order to reduce heavy dependence on oil income' and the modernization of techniques and administrative reforms.[68]

Moreover, the continuing increase of the shares of the oil sector and industry in GNP had made possible the inexorable pace of modernization, albeit at the expense of agriculture and export diversification. The Fifth Plan superseded the previous one in being 'the most comprehensive' with more emphases on industrialization and privatization, regarded as positive economic developments in Iran because, for example, privatization had become an accepted concept well ahead of other countries such as Egypt, India and Indonesia.[69] In contrast to the early 1960s, the development plans of the first half of the 1970s coincided with a period of political and economic stability, which made possible a more effective execution of their programmes. In this context, as becomes more evident in the following chapters, what it assumes to be a *culture of change* across Iran surfaced, reflecting both a popular and an intellectual enthusiasm for socio-economic change.

That said, development plans continued to retain their concentration on the expansion of modernization from the centre and lack any specific provincial development planning. The plans' emphases on industrialization or privatization left out regions that lacked resources or ignored their potential while the dramatic growth of GNP between 1963 and 1977 benefited 'the central regions, particularly Tehran, more than the outer provinces'.[70] In the peripheral Kurdish region, therefore, the state's modernization was tangible through the expansion of welfare services by government ministries and these ministries' provincial offices such as *Rah* (Road) and *'Omran* (Development). With the same token, the impressive growths of GNP and per capita income were palpable as employment in the public sector increased alongside the population's spending power. In addition to the bazaar as an integral constituent of the economy, the capital and workforce in this region became heavily concentrated in the construction industry. Indeed, in the absence of 'industrialization', the predominant mode of production continued to evolve around conventional artisanship and handicraft, and this pushed the workforce towards the construction industry, which owed its expansion to a relentless pace of urbanization. Moreover, demographic change and population movement had made the economy more dynamic with the effect that bazaar or the existing mode of production expanded. Iran's economic growth was indeed very impressive. However, in the absence of provincial planning, modernization was felt through its reverberations that originated in the capital. Instead, overshadowing economic and political contradictions, ambitious plans such as the Twenty-Year Perspective (1972–92) marked the determination of the Shah to take Iran towards a 'Great Civilization', a dream based on oil reserves. Ironically, as scholars have noted, the perspective was designed based on a pessimistic view of the world and urged the Iranians to act fast and take the opportunity to develop before Iran's 'oil was depleted'.[71] According to Manucher Farmanfarmaian, 'oil *was* Iran's economy' and defined its future because 'oil was not just a commodity for Iran; it was the blood of its earth and means to catapult its people into the twentieth century' and after.[72] Perspective was based on an ambitious Spatial Strategy Plan, an idea of French origin, to deploy the population in relation to natural resources and deal with every region. 'Rapid growth', the plans shrewdly acknowledged, 'leads to imbalance between groups, regions, and economic sectors'.[73] The economic crisis of 1977 forced the Shah to embrace such a strategy knowing that it would not restrain his power; perspective and strategy also inspired the Six Economic Plan, which was terminated with the outbreak of the popular revolution of 1978–9.[74]

Kurdistan in development plans

The general improvement of socio-economic conditions in Kurdistan depended on the effectiveness of development plans to address infrastructure, transportations, communications, healthcare and education across Iran. In this respect, the development plans of the 1960s and 1970s were more effective than their predecessors. However, these plans were centralizing, exclusive and lacked province-specific planning. While economic planning changed the face of Iran in general, their aims and directions did not directly benefit a peripheral region like Kurdistan for three main reasons. First, development plans and projects had been initially paralysed by the shortage of revenue and, when oil revenue meteorically increased in the early 1970s, its increase emboldened the grandeur desires of the Shah. As a result, the plans became increasingly dependent on how the Shah decided to spend oil revenues. Second, as we noted earlier, economic planning in Iran historically developed amid political instability; they were politically motivated. Finally, insofar as peripheral regions were concerned, these plans served centralized planning to the detriment of provincial planning. These three aspects affected the nature and the outcome of economic planning in both the centre and peripheries. Therefore, Kurdistan as a periphery benefited from the state-led modernization as much as the state's infrastructural and industrial efforts expanded from the centre towards its peripheries. Dependency on oil is discussed in other parts of this study to some extent; the following is an elaboration of the last two aspects.

Political instability not only exerted a negative impact on economic planning but also inspired politically motivated reforms. The White Revolution, as we discussed earlier, was itself the outcome of the fear of ominous perils of internal forces and thus intended to preserve the monarchy. Although the ideas which embellished its principles were already in circulation, so was widespread the will to change Iran through an overarching reform process, both the state and the Shah provided platforms for the implementation of reforms. Moreover, domestic and international political developments in the 1970s, just like the pressure from the Kennedy administration did, continued to shape the plans and affect their outcomes. In effect, the uncertainty over Iran's oil reserves and the Shah's hubris further made reforms in the service of politics. As studies have noted, all projects became 'means to an end, the fulfilment of the Shah's dream of the Great Civilisation'.⁷⁵ Moreover, as the White Revolution advanced, the Shah sidelined those with a more critical mind. All these functioned against plans or projects based on studies or the needs of the population of Iran, the peripheral regions and subsequently these regions' rural areas which were certainly the most deprived. Probably no other topic can better highlight planning deficiencies and deprivation than the sustained city–village disparity in the peripheral regions. Insofar as the Kurdish region is concerned, the disparity between urban and rural areas was sustained throughout the era of the White Revolution and no economic plan, which aimed at urbanization, industrialization, modern healthcare and education, addressed that issue effectively. As discussed in the following chapters, this aspect of life kept out most of the Kurdish population from the benefits of modernization. This is confirmed by Afkhami's collective study – and in this respect, it distinguishes itself from many other studies on this period – that rapid industrial growth increased 'already widening urban-rural disparities'.⁷⁶ However, no industrialization was pursued in Kurdish urban areas and consequently a bazaar-artisan economy continued to characterize the region's economic life. Moreover, an industrially feeble Kurdish city relied on trade with a village, lucky for its proximity to urban centres, to survive, without promoting the rural economy. Crucially, amid increasing urbanization, the lack of rural and urban development plans in the aftermath of land reform made expanding Kurdish cities encircled by deprived *mahallas* or neighbourhoods. Interestingly, as regards these districts, the nomenclature resembled a division of labour: *Hammal Awa* (Porters Quarter), *jutiaran* (Peasants), *Sangborran* (Stonecutters), *Qarachi Awa* (Gypsies Quarter), *Spour Awa* (Sweepers Quarter). To this, one can add many more such as *Kiwer Awa* (Blinds Quarter) and *Diz Awa* (Thieves Quarter). Modernization continued to maintain the chasm between city and village, depriving the latter of the benefits of social change and economic programmes effectively. In contrast, as regards the process of planning, in retrospect it seems that Ebtehaj's Plan and Budget Organization, a pre-White Revolution reforming body, pursued reforms that served the social and economic needs of Iranian societies. Simultaneously, it could take credit for being the continuation of the previous attempts by Iranian statesmen and intellectuals at economic planning since the Second World War. Additionally, it was not inspired, at least entirely, by later political concerns or grandeur ideas, which were more obsessed with producing a progressive image of Iran through superficial and showy achievements than with socio-economic problems of the whole country. As the threat of both internal and external political upheavals loomed large by the end of the 1950s, Ebtehaj's meticulous methods and prolonged studies proved to be too much for the fragile nervous system of the Iranian politicians to take. However, as regards the Kurdish region, Ebtehaj's centralizing tendency and his demand that the provinces should contribute immensely to the budget did not go in favour of such a region that had a weak infrastructure and lacked financial resources. Finally, political considerations overlooked many other crucial aspects such as Kurdish culture and identity with the effect that they remained areas prone to tensions and conflicts (see Chapter 4).

Finally, the tendency to centralization outlasted Ebtehaj's era with the effect that economic plans, perspectives and strategies that followed, served a centralizing state and an absolute monarch. Consequently, economic planning and social reforms in the peripheries reflected the overall trend across Iran and made these regions the terminus of economic expansion from more central regions. It is beyond the scope of this study to present a comparative study. However, the formation of Iran's modern Kurdish society was not an exceptional process, radically different from the processes which reshaped other Iranian societies. Nevertheless, in many respects, each region reacted to change differently based on its history, culture and socio-economic structures. Moreover, the idea of 'provincial development', however inadequate, did not survive into the White Revolution, whose increasing principles did not simply bother to address different regions in different ways. Therefore, politically concerned development plans, the misuse of revenue and the preoccupation with centralization hindered socio-economic change in peripheral regions such as Kurdistan and Khuzistan and determined the scope and pace of change – as discussed earlier, Ebtehaj's Plan Organization rejected a plan by the latter's representatives. This was also the case, as we will see, with the expansion of modern institutions such as healthcare and education. On the other hand, the state became even more political in those regions where distinct culture and identity continued to create reasons for concern. Consequently, whereas the Persianization of culture and language through modern education, and, by the 1970s, audio and visual means of communication ensured the suppression of distinct identity, it was no coincidence that the White Revolution enhanced the role of SAVAK, the secret intelligent service (established in 1957), as a brutal force to quell political and cultural activism.

Effective mechanisms of modernization

Land reform, infrastructural developments and modernizing institutions such as modern education and healthcare were effective mechanisms of modernization, which entailed a profound socio-economic change in Kurdistan by the end of the 1970s. Modern education and healthcare are discussed in Chapter 3. The following section presents an overview of the other two processes.

Land reform

The literature on land reform in Iran is relatively vast, and they provide a general understanding of its historical background, implementation and consequences; the literature is also supported by some extensive studies on land and landowning in Iran.[77] Published in 1979, Baqer Momeni's *Land Question and Class Struggle in Iran* in Persian presents a detailed account of the historical backgrounds to land reform, including previous attempts by different social and political forces which pursued their economic or political interests since the Constitutional Revolution; it demonstrates how land and landowning becomes a crucial subject in the context of rapid socio-economic and political changes throughout the first half of the twentieth century.[78] Despite differences in approach, it seems that there is a consensus on both the purpose and the consequences of the reform during the era of the White Revolution: land reform 'was purely a case of induced social change from above with minimal grass-roots input'.[79] However, it failed, as it claimed, to establish social justice and end the landowner–peasant economic relations, leading to landlessness and mass migration of the peasant class to urban centres.[80]

In contrast, the literature on land reform in the Kurdish region is extremely limited, although it has become a major topic for academic studies pertaining to Kurdistan, reflecting the growing number of Kurdish-Iranian academics in Iran's academic centres.[81] However, this study does not claim to fill the gap in this respect but attempts to contribute to studies on land reform in the Kurdish region by being concerned with methodology and highlighting other, understudied consequences of the reform. Studies on land reform in Kurdistan rightly identify the White Revolution, in general, and land reform, in particular, as major factors in both debilitating the hold of the *agha* class on Kurdish society and accelerating social change. Methodologically, however, they tend to remain within the confines of the dichotomy of traditional and modern, concentrating on the 'positive' impacts of the development plans. Nevertheless, one can acknowledge that recent historical research demonstrates more comprehensive discussions of the social consequences of the reform.[82]

The land reform, *Tahqiqat-e Eqtesadi* (Pe. Economic Research) informed its readers in 1963, was the result of 'debates [which had lasted] for almost two generations' across Iran.[83] In Kurdistan since the early 1950s, a new concept of *keshavarz* (farmer) to replace *ra'yat* (serf) had been cultivated by social and political activists.[84] To impact the life of the peasants, *Hezb-e Sa'adat-e Melli* (Pe. The National Prosperity Party), founded by Habibolla Mohit, a lawyer and a follower of Musaddeq, organized meetings and issued exclusive cards for farmers to allow them to benefit from available social provisions.[85] Against such backgrounds and in the absence of the *Majlis*, the Amini administration initiated the land reform in Maragheh in the northwest of Iran in March 1962 by 'bequeathing the peasants land deeds which had been obtained from previous landowners'.[86] The journal asserted that 'the biggest shortcoming of land reform [was] the lack of popular support' and thus warned that 'denting the power of big landowners might not lead to a profound transformation of agriculture in Iran nor the amelioration of the peasantry's living conditions'.[87] Although the contributors to the journal believed that such reforms would serve both *yeganegi-e melli* (Pe. national oneness) and economic growth necessary to tackle economic problems in 'backward societies', their articles reflected a concern with a critical reading of the economic needs of Iran, which, as demonstrated in the articles, contrasted the political ambition of the monarchy and reflected shared intellectual and popular expectations. On the other hand, as noted earlier, politically instigated reforms did not guarantee a radical transformation of the prevalent landowner–peasant relationship nor were they necessarily concerned with the provision of social needs or prepared for the consequences of land reform.

The appalling socio-economic condition in the rural areas, reproduced under the regime of the landowner class, demonstrated the magnitude of the problem which the land reform intended to address. In the early 1960s, the peasantry in Kurdistan was a poor social class, landless and deprived of educational and medical services. The village was largely disconnected from the city because of the lack of suitable roads or the absence of other means of communication. The rural-class structure and economy, discussed in Chapter 1, continued without significant changes, though peasantry and nomads were now more sedentarized. Rebellion against such conditions and the *agha* class was also a permanent aspect of life so much so that, in addition to individual subversion, collective defiance of the regime of the Kurdish *agha* has characterized Kurdish histories. One case in point, which demonstrated the depth of the social chasm, was the peasant uprising around Bukan in 1952–3, which was brutally quelled by the collective military forces of the government and the landowners in the aftermath of the Coup against Musaddeq.[88] Although there were exceptions on an individual level, the oppressive landowner class continued its luxurious lifestyle by exploiting impoverished peasant families in the most inhumane ways. Children grew up in sordid environments with no education and entered premature manhood as servants of the landowner household, shepherds or land labourers. Women, already buried under household tasks and childcare, contributed to the workforce needed on the land too. In villages, women were deprived of any medical help during menstruation or childbirth nor was there any medical advice on contraceptive methods. Even worse than women did in urban centres, the contraceptive prevalence rate was low, families were populated and immunization was unheard of. Moreover, the cultivation of the land and harvesting of the crops were carried out in unfavourable topography and without effective agricultural machinery. The mechanization of agriculture began in the 1970s; however, its pace and scope were slow and limited. In 1973–4, a decade after the inception of the White Revolution, from a total of 22,940 agricultural pieces of machinery in Iran, according to Plan and Budget Organization, the share of Kurdistan Province was 1,605, including 933 tractors and 205 Combine harvesters; two-thirds of such machinery were individually owned.[89] Even based on these statistics, the number of tractors covered one-tenth of the rural areas in Kurdistan at best, whereas combines, which began to increase towards the end of the 1970s, operated in less hilly areas close to main intercity roads with the effect that vast areas could not benefit from them.[90] The quantity becomes less impressive if we note that because of the absence of other job opportunities, most people were engaged in activities related to agriculture or livestock.

The land reform was supposed to transform the socio-economic condition of the village life by distributing the land and making farmers and their lives independent and prosperous. The Literacy and Medical Corps were other means to this end. The Land Reform Act (1962) triggered the first stage of the reform. It allowed the landowners to retain a village or one-eighth of a village in eight villages but sell the rest to the state. This enabled the state to sell or rent out the purchased lands to sharecroppers who worked on the same land while absentee landowners residing in the cities retained the ownership of both village and land. The second stage law (Esfand 1349/March 1971) demanded landowners either to rent out their lands or form agricultural units with farmers. The government was set to intervene to ensure the implementation of the next stages. Ostensibly, the landowners' defiance and, as scholars have argued, popular consternation pushed the government towards more radical solutions to abolish the peasant–landowner social relation.[91] Finally, the third stage from the end of the early 1970s onward was supposed to include more strict actions on behalf of the government. The different stages, therefore, were the manifestation of an uneven and prolonged process that continued to be affected by political crisis. For example, the replacement of Hasan Arsanjani, an ardent advocate of land reform in the early 1960s, 'set the land reform towards an unknown future',[92] while the concentration of power in the hand of the Shah increased as the modernization progressed. Land reform was not supposed to be an easy process since before its inception 65 per cent of the Iranian population lived in some 67,000 villages. Moreover, 37 families owned 19,000 villages or 39 per cent of all the villages; the rest was in the possessions of smaller landowners, who nonetheless owned a large number of villages.[93]

Parallel to the damage the land reform inflicted on the political and social status of the *agha* class and its liberating effect for the peasantry to move out of its oppressive regime, the peasantry faced modernization's new challenges. The scarcity of land or other sources of income forced thousands to migrate and seek work in expanding cities inside, but also increasingly outside, Kurdistan such as Tabriz and Tehran or in more southern or harbour cities on the shore of the Persian Gulf. As a significant consequence of this process, a new class of unskilled urban labourers and seasonal workers was formed.

The first challenge was urban life. New urban labourers usually resided with their families in poor city neighbourhoods, while seasonal workers left families most of the year and worked long hours in low-paid jobs such as building, catering and service industries. They found themselves in an unfamiliar environment, shared living space in squalid conditions with no access to social and medical services. Moreover, land reform induced the migration of the entire family to work in brick-oven factories, where child labour was also essential to the upkeep of the family and increased unskilled workers in Kurdish cities as low-paid labourers or porters. Luckier porters owned horse-carts; others relied on the strength of their shoulders. Moreover, housing became the most difficult issue for the migrants, who expanded the new class of wage workers because of little gains from the land reform – 'In 1351 [1972-3], 47 percent of farmers owned 3 hectares or did not own any land at all, while 33 percent owned 3 to 10 hectares', demonstrating an unimpressive distribution of lands.[94] On the other hand, unable to anticipate the outcomes, the land reform never included the provision of urban facilities to assist newcomers. Moreover, around the city of Kermanshah, more Kurdish (Shiʻa) Failis migrated to Iraq in search of income and ended up working in cleaning jobs or as shoeshine men.[95] Migration to search for work was not a new phenomenon. For example, seasonal workers had travelled to Sharazour, a Kurdish region in modern Iraq, to work for only three months a year, benefit from various bonuses and enjoy a familiar cultural environment. In comparison with the 1970s, they could transmit infectious diseases such as malaria but not sexually transmitted diseases, which many seasonal workers contracted in big urban centres of Iran.[96] The novelty of the era of the White Revolution was not only the scale and pervasiveness of migration but also the fact that it signified a social displacement of people on a more permanent basis. Resettlement in a new environment, now across Iran, carried with it estrangement from known cultural environments.

Furthermore, the land reform began to transform the rural-class structure. In addition to absentee landowners and the upper class (village headmen and landowner's bailiffs), the poor peasantry, divided into landless *rashaiy* and *jutbanda*, expanded with the effect that *rashaiy* provided a new labour force to the emerging wage labour class. Indeed, both inexorable urbanization and population increase across Iran exposed the scarcity of cultivated land in rural areas and attracted landless peasants into the urban workforce. As regards the social and political status of the Kurdish *agha*, the White Revolution effectively replaced the landowner with the state (represented by the gendarmerie force) as the sole authority in the village. However, the extent of the state's authority varied according to the accessibility or remoteness of an area and to social organizations. For example, in the northern Kurdish region powerful tribes managed to retain their power bases to a considerable extent. Therefore, when new forms of social bonds began to challenge tribal and conventional familial bonds, this proved to be a prolonged process. Moreover, during the 1979 Revolution the opportunistic class of the Kurdish *agha*, whose power had not been completely and permanently wiped out, began to claim the restitution of its lost lands. Before the revolution, the constant presence of the Shah's gendarmery force in the countryside had checked the *agha*'s political power. However, in the wake of the February 1979 uprising that terminated the Pahlavi state, the landowner class re-emerged in many parts of Kurdistan and organized mercenaries to reclaim their seized lands by force. For example, *Keyhan* reported in May 1979 that the representatives of Na'il Shekan village in the vicinity of the town of Diwandara had complained to Sanandaj City Council that 'some landowners under the leadership of 'Abbas Khan Mozafari had expelled many villagers from that village on the pretext that the downfall of the previous [Pahlavi] regime had invalidated its land reform'.[97] Therefore, this attested to the fact that the land reform had not completely diminished the economic and political power of the landowner class, which sought an opportunity to revive 'feudalism'.[98]

Infrastructural development

The constructions of new intercity roads, tunnels and bridges in the Kurdish region were defining moments in the transformation of the economy in the region. Beginning in the middle of the 1930s, these constructions gradually became the hallmarks of Kurdish cities and intercity roads.[99] For example, when 'Czechoslovakian Skoda built Saqqez Bridge between 1314 and 1317 (1935–8), it was both the dawn of motorized means of transportation for that city and a sign of more effective economic reforms'.[100] Two decades later, the city's Tobacco Factory was built in 1957. The factory was intended to regulate the production of tobacco concentrated in the region around the border. However, Saqqez had been selected for its relative distance from such a region. Silo, an agricultural storage or modern mill, followed in the 1970s. Mahabad and Sanandaj also acquired such production centres, which remained the only 'industrial' hallmarks of the Kurdish cities throughout the modernizing era of the White Revolution.

It can be surmised that infrastructural improvement was inspired by a mixture of economic and political motives on behalf of the state. In addition to the growing expectations and technological awareness of people amid the political and social transformation of the country, the state was economically motivated to connect the region effectively to an evolving economy. Political and military considerations in constructing factories or roads cannot be ruled out as it was evident in the construction of tobacco centres. As another example, according to contemporaries, during the construction of Sanandaj-Mariwan road, the constructors preferred to ignore recommendations by influential regional figures, who had suggested a shorter route, because 'it seemed that the state preferred to have continuous access to higher lands for military purposes'.[101] Moreover, other signs of political and military considerations included the construction of gendarmerie bases on intercity roads at intervals or in what was regarded to be strategic locations throughout the region and across the border. Usually as side effects, villages, located further away from intercity roads, benefited from roads, schools and medical centres provided they had contained a gendarmerie base. As was specifically the case with the Third Plan, Development programmes concentrated on the construction of main roads and not feeder roads.[102] Nevertheless, a few feeder roads such as Bukan city to Torjan (a prestigious village) and Khorkhora Road passed through several villages, hence primarily benefited from new means of transportation rather than social services. Therefore, roads in most regions initially followed the movement of the army. In the 1960s and 1970s, the military considerably contributed to connecting more villages to urban centres. Modernization entered the Kurdish village by following the military, and this led to the unplanned, spontaneous provision of welfare and technology, for example, electricity. The expansion of the state-led modernization into rural areas in Kurdistan took place in parallel with military expansion, and this is a crucial point that is ignored by social change studies of the modernization of rural life in this period. The extent (and the state) of the roads, the level of communications and transportations, the provision of electricity, let alone durables, almost matched the extension of military roads and cables. Even in prestigious locations, not all the residents benefited, for instance, from electricity, which was available to the gendarmery base and the *agha* household. Moreover, the absence of feeder roads restrained transportation, which had started to appear more frequently with the construction or improvement of main intercity roads, especially since the end of the 1950s. Iran witnessed more cars and trucks upon its occupation by the allied forces during the Second World War, but the impact of the Americans on the transport system was electrifying.[103] Many such vehicles scattered across Iran in the aftermath of the war, and the scarcity of cars in the following decades made their presence conspicuous. For example, obtained by their new owners, some American dodges or trucks continued to be used for transporting people across Iran, including in the Kurdish region well into the early 1980s. Nevertheless, by the mid-1970s both new roads, which connected village and city, and the expansion of money economy, which attracted countryside produce into city bazaars, increased the number of Jeeps or mini trucks in the countryside. Intercity buses and private cars also increased towards the end of the decade.

Before 1960 foreign construction companies undertook the construction of buildings owned by the government such as courts and various offices. The American firm MKO built army bases in cities while the Iranian-Italian COMSACS managed contracts, the construction of bridges and roads.[104] In addition to the extension of welfare services, new electric generators marked a crucial point in socio-economic development. Electricity's slow expansion since the early 1950s led to new generators by the 1970s; one of the pioneers of the introduction of electricity to Kurdistan during the Premiership of Muhammad Musaddeq was General Baharmast.[105] Electricity was not unheard of as a letter to the constitutional *Majlis* in 1910 demonstrates, in which two Kurdish *tujjars* or businessmen seek to obtain concessions to produce and expand electricity in Kurdistan.[106] It only took many more decades to introduce and expand, and, like hospitals, it awaited the expansion of the army. Nevertheless, the impact of electricity was revolutionary.

Despite military and political considerations, discussed earlier, economic motives remained prime reasons for infrastructural projects, which accelerated the pace of socio-economic change with the effect that in the long run, the state could not ignore the growing economic requirements of the region. Concerning rural areas, the movement of the military paved the way for modernization to reach villages on a limited scale.

Conclusion: Continuity and discontinuity

The White Revolution which intensified the Pahlavi modernization plans was born amid a political situation peculiar to Iran. The ideas already in circulation formed its tenets while political considerations, influenced by international and domestic economic and political developments, continued to shape its direction. In Kurdistan, land reform and infrastructural developments created a more dynamic economy, resulting in a fast pace of urbanization. The improvement of roads and the provision of social services took place as the *extension* of the state-led modernization, which was based on centralized development plans, thus lacking *extensive and deliberate plans to reform Iranian peripheral provinces*. Development planning in Iran matured into more comprehensive and elaborate planning by 1970, benefiting from massive oil revenue, statistical data, more sophisticated methodologies and technics, as well as economic units, for example, Economic Bureau. However, as contemporaries have noted, 'provincial development' remained an unknown concept throughout the White Revolution.[107] Analysed by contemporary economists cited in this chapter, the plans suffered from discrepancies between economic sectors too. Agriculture, on which the majority of the Kurdish population depended, did not experience growth, whereas the oil and service industries continued to have the highest growth rates. Crucially, the plans' objectives and concerns, for example, as regards transportation and roads, omitted a huge portion of the Kurdish region which required feeder roads to get connected to the mainstream of socio-economic transformation.

Undoubtedly the land reform was a defining moment in the transformation of socio-economic relations in the village: it damaged the oppressive regime of the Kurdish *agha* by diminishing their political and social powers. Along with the creation of more opportunities in life for the population, these were positive ramifications of land reform. However, both the 'positive' and 'negative' ramifications of modernization made sense in an ongoing institutional transformation of Kurdish society. From this perspective, modernization also revealed serious social challenges manifest in the following trends: unprecedented migration to urban centres; the expansion of seasonal workers and unskilled labour force geographically and numerically; inadequate social provisions or absolute lack of them; sustained city–village disparity; and, finally, the unpreparedness of reforms or development plans for unforeseen consequences of their actions. Moreover, 'industrialization' in Kurdistan was extremely limited to few production centres, confining its economy to its conventional bazaar and artisan manufacturing, though these were expanded while the construction boom absorbed a substantial portion of the labour force; the modern Kurdish working class began to form as a result of migration in search of income, urbanization and the expansion of the economy in urban centres. On the other hand, the expansion of the economy resulted in more infrastructural changes in the Kurdish region. However, political considerations also went into the construction of roads especially in the region across the border. The movement of the military in the countryside led to the construction of many important inter-village or city–countryside gravel roads with the effect that welfare services followed the military into the village. This meant that the introduction of social services was not according to any specific economic or social development plan. The spontaneous and irregular pattern of the expansion of such services further vindicates the point. According to oral history, villages located on the main roads, close to cities or with a gendarmery base could benefit from transportation, electricity or have access to medical centres, but this was extremely limited. However, the expanding population's awareness of welfare services, including healthcare, and technology such as new means of transportation and radio, were significant aspects of social change.[108]

Finally, the White Revolution, in general, and the land reform, in particular, triggered two crucial processes. First, it replaced the *agha* class with the state as the sole political body to have access to the means of control and violence, effectively restricting the direct access of the Kurdish *agha* to such sources. Previously, the state as an entity was either absent or an accomplice both in crimes committed by the landowner class and in the maintenance of its brutal regime. However, the stages of the land reform demonstrated a conservative approach to uprooting the regime of the *agha*. Second, the socio-economic consequences of the reforms along with urbanization and infrastructural improvements signified the emergence, or intensification, of a capitalist economy, symbolized by a money economy and a new class structure. As scholars have noted, the gradual replacement of a self-sufficient economy in the village by a money economy manifested the extension of a nascent capitalist economic system.[109] On the other hand, the transformation of the class structure led to the emergence of a new Kurdish labour class, whose existence owed itself to an expanding class of investors and owners of capital. Therefore, the class relation was going to be incorporated in a new framework of capitalist production that was not sustained by violence, predominantly characteristic of the *agha-jutiar* economic relation, but by a social contract. However, to assess the scope and pace of the institutional dimensions of change towards a framework incorporating capitalist production and industrialization, this modernizing process, as we noticed earlier, was both limited and prolonged.[110] Therefore, parallel to recognizing the crucial role of the intensifying state-led modernization in the 1960s and 1970s, it is significant to identify the social consequences of the modernizing reforms in Kurdistan in both rural and urban areas.

Chapter 3

THE SOCIAL CONSEQUENCES OF MODERNIZATION

Introduction

The previous chapter credited the White Revolution for intensifying, and in many ways triggering, the institutional transformation of Kurdish society. In this regard, the land reform and infrastructural developments were identified as parts of crucial mechanisms of the state-led modernization in that direction. These were, however, parts of a prolonged and uneven modernization with their social consequences, some aspects of which this chapter highlights. In addition to evaluating the social consequences of land reform and modernization, this chapter presents an interpretation of the following concurrent trends too: the transformation of the urban-class structure and the modernization of education and healthcare.

Social consequences of land reform and modernization

The land reform proved to be a prolonged and uneven process partly because of undesirable infrastructural conditions. In addition to the political factors involved in the introduction of the reform, its accomplishment was further paralysed by vast numbers of villages scattered in a geography that physically defied human movements. Therefore, the peasantry's gain from the deal depended on the location of the village and its approximation to services. Gradually, the migration of landless peasants or those with insufficient income to cities and towns increased. This was especially true in the case of those with no previous cultivating rights. This resulted in high rates of urban population increase and unbridled urbanization. Simultaneously, insufficient land in villages and low incomes forced a considerable number of village men to seek income in cities across Iran. Therefore, migration and seasonal labour were direct results of an inconsistent land reform that was unenthusiastically pursued by the state through various stages. On the other hand, as modernization accelerated across Iran with oil revenues soaring after 1973, work and life in urban centres became increasingly attractive. The urban and rural income gap was the primary motivating factor, while the availability of services and the prospect of a better life also prompted village proletariats, that is, landless peasants who only relied on their ability to engage in manual labour, to migrate to urban centres. According to a more contemporary assessment of migration to cities across Iran, the ratio of urban to rural income per head was estimated at 4.6 to 1 in 1959 and 4.7 to 1 in 1969, while official reports reveal that 'in 1972 the average income per day from agricultural work was only $1.40 for male and 74 cents for female laborers'.[1] Moreover, with a population of 33.5 million, Iran's 'urban growth rate in 1976 stood at 4.5 percent per year as against only two percent for rural areas'.[2]

Urbanization and modernization meant the transformation from a land-based to an urban-market economy, and this involved the two processes of stratification (in general a system of inequality based on class and status) and differentiation (specialization), setting up new institutions (e.g. alienable private property, contract, wage labour mediated by labour, capital, commodity and land markets), leading to a more complex division of labour. From this perspective, stratification and differentiation do not connote evolutionary progress of modernization as certain, but influential, modernization theorists argued.[3] For example, Marion J. Levy and Neil J. Smelser are among such theorists of the 1960s who, from a functionalist point of view, valued differentiation as positive and necessary for modernization.[4] From this perspective, 'effective differentiation' includes the displacement of ascriptive status ranking such as ethnicity, family, race and gender. Levy stresses a rationalizing modernization of society in which 'its members use inanimate sources of power and/or use tools to multiply the effects of their efforts'.[5] Based on this, Levy articulates a modernized society's characteristics which correspond to a highly specialized social unit.[6] Smelser, however, 'equates modernization with economic development', which he defines in terms of technological-scientific and mechanical and demographic (urbanization) shifts necessary for a transition from traditional to modern society.[7] Both arguments are for a highly differentiated society and define differentiation and stratification as evolutionary progress of modernization.

In contrast to such an evolutionary view of social change, this chapter argues that modernization in Kurdistan meant different things for different people. This is elaborated through the following four topics: *the unbridled growth of impoverished neighbourhoods; the expansion of seasonal workers; village population condemned to an undesirable rural life* and *urban unplanned growth*. These topics, therefore, reveal dire social consequences of the land reform and modernization for both the village and the city. While each theme, discussed only within the scope of this study, could individually constitute a further area of research in Kurdish and Iranian social change studies, collectively they illuminate a process which was far from a necessary or smooth 'transition' to a better, 'modern' way of life.

The unbridled growth of impoverished neighbourhoods

Development plans did not forestall the social consequences of their plans and, in the absence of adequate social services or a social security system, poor city neighbourhoods in the outskirts of cities and towns expanded amid sordid and degrading living conditions. The existing city neighbourhoods, the growth of which was negligible before 1960, did not perform much better as low incomes forced common tenancy of a house by several, usually large, families and restricted access to necessary services. The expansion of cities continued to outstrip services, including asphalt roads, electricity, sanitation, schools and health centres, whose provisions were hindered by lack of will, resources, trained staff and, especially as regards housing, legal procedures. The lowest layer of the rural population, that is, *rashaiy* or *qara* (Ku. landless peasants), spearheaded migration to such city neighbourhoods while at the same time the rural-class structure began to be defined not merely by its relation to land and the *agha* but by its relation to an expanding capitalist economy.

The state responded to urbanization by launching city projects which reflected growing pressures that stemmed from city expansion. As discussed in the previous chapter, the Plan Organization under Ebtehaj had envisaged city development plans by assigning provinces to different foreign firms. However, the provinces' financial contributions stipulated such plans. The economic plans, which followed and formulated economic directions of the Pahlavi modernization, totally disregarded specific plans for provinces, and its actions were mostly reactions to unplanned urbanization.

Urbanization and an expanding urban economy were characterized by growing bazaars that began to include both agricultural produce and factory pasteurized products, as well as small artisan shops. In addition to this, a construction boom created its marketplaces and the economy absorbed unskilled wage labourers who consisted of recently migrated or low-income city dwellers. This unskilled urban workforce included *fa'la*s (Ku. construction workers), cleaners and *hammal*s (porters). Daily wage labour and *hammali* (delivery) especially stood out. The luckiest of those in the latter job used horse-carts or *gari* (a four-wheeled, flat trolley) to deliver items, but the majority had to deliver usually heavy items long distances, on foot and with the loads tied to their back with a special coat in return for a trivial amount of money. Moreover, migration and urbanization considerably expanded the number of those engaging in other forms of daily wage labour such as bakery workers, who, poorly paid, worked long hours. Ironically, 'modernization' continued to sustain and even expand prominent forms of wage labour which, as C. J. Wills observed travelling in Iran between 1866 and 1881, characterized Iran's urban centres: 'These "hammals" bear gigantic burdens, and as in most Eastern towns there are no carriage-roads, they are of great use, and generally form a *distinct corporation*' (Italic added).[8] 'Minimum national wage', if not an unknown concept in Iran, was not at least in practice endorsed by any effective labour law.[9] This was partly because the dictatorial system restricted social activities effectively, and thus the working class expanded without representative bodies. According to contemporary observers, a form of social insurance was introduced in 1960–1 in the provincial city of Sanandaj for work centres with more than three employees.[10] Although this initiated plans to allow employees to benefit from a pension, it took a long time for social insurance to become widespread.[11]

Moreover, urbanization and modernization increased child labour (mostly young boys) in the forms of itinerant vendors of confectionary items, *shagerd* (assistant), an 'apprentice' who, for example, was employed by a tailor or an artisan for free in return for teaching him/her the skill, and shoeshine boys or girls. The growing city created a less restricted, but hostile, environment for young village migrants and provided young city dwellers with more opportunities to earn more, however in undesirable conditions. Urban poverty created an army of working children whose social and educational lives were negatively affected due to their families' low income and the lack of governmental services, including leisure and sports. In such families, women, helped by young girls, undertook domestic services for better-off families. As discussed in the previous chapter, new nomenclature epitomized these types of new impoverished neighbourhoods. Before the intensification of urbanization, when such neighbourhoods were mostly known by names rooted in clans or geography, the names Porters or Sweepers referred to 'modern' unskilled workers. Many such quarters were named after the name of a village or a region from which migration had originated. In the 1970s, there were also cases in which the city engulfed nearby villages.

Furthermore, a crucial consequence of urbanization was the emergence of categorization of rural migrants as *dehati* (villager) in contrast to *shari* (city dweller). In the past, communities had been defined according to their economic activities or ethnic traits, whereas modernization led to categorization based on modern concepts. Modernization's categorization of individuals developed a set of traits which became increasingly based on two concepts of *dwakawtu* (Ku. backward) and *peshkawtu* (Ku. advanced) with the effect that dress, accent, appearance, level of literacy and even diet were stereotyped. Moreover, verbal, and sometimes physical, abuse of those defined as *dehati* increased with the pace of modernization while *tahqir* (humiliation) in public spaces or schools, mostly in the forms of jokes or remarks, which had strong racial connotations, became part of life for many.[12]

The expansion of seasonal workers

Alongside the urban working class, the expansion of seasonal workers was another significant consequence of land reform and modernization. As touched upon previously, landless peasants had always exercised seasonal work by seeking employment in other villages or regions where their labour was in demand. Work in demand included a nine-month sheep tending season, tobacco farm assistant or servant of a landowner household. However, the land reform and the acceleration of modernization across Iran created a class of permanent seasonal workers who left the Kurdish region in search of work in expanding cities or in factories in other parts of Iran. Seasonal work became a permanent line of work that devoured an increasing number of free labourers. Confirmed by oral history, geographically, it expanded to cover all of Iran with its urbanizing cities and growing economy, creating seasonal workers who worked in factories and construction.[13] Therefore, new seasonal workers were distinguished from previous ones in many ways. Their numbers increased considerably; they travelled in search of work to remote cities and they worked and lived in an unsafe and culturally unknown environment.

Before the inexorable pace of modernization over the second half of the century, a poor Kurdish seasonal worker would generally work in a culturally familiar environment and for benevolent employers. This drastically changed when seasonal workers had to work in harsh conditions and live in groups in unfavourable circumstances. Moreover, although many travelled to cities in the neighbouring countries – Faili Kurds travelled as far as Baghdad[14] – seasonal workers were increasingly limited to Iran as the modernizing nation state's economy acquired its national shape.[15]

Seasonal work also had significant consequences for workers' families that were left behind. Because of the dearth of effective means of communication, families received remittances irregularly or had to wait until workers returned. As a result, they were dependent on relatives to survive. Moreover, the misery and hardship experienced by such families, including and perhaps especially by women whose spouses were away, are yet to be registered in history books or reflected in social studies. However, the collective memory is not devoid of such experiences.

Family migration and family as a unit of workforce

In the same way as seasonal workers, family migration was not unprecedented. As discussed in previous chapters, the landowner–peasant economy, governed by the oppressive regime of the Kurdish *agha*, more frequently than not compelled poor peasant families to migrate in search of a better life while subversives were expelled from the village forcefully. Nevertheless, the destination was rarely beyond a nearby village or a village or city in a nearby region; family migration was also caused by economic factors, for example, the loss of income, or political factors, for example, the pressure of the landowner or intruding tribes.[16]

In addition to family migration to reside in urban centres, modernization forced many other families to settle in production centres of which the brick-oven factory became well known for its harsh, inhuman conditions. Work in a brick-oven factory was based on a contract and, therefore, families and their children had to do heavy work to contribute to production in order to increase income. Because brick-oven factories were concentrated in the northern part of the Kurdish region, they embraced families more from that area, while people from the southern part were attracted to cities in the south of Iran or rice farms in the north. In a brick-oven factory, families' living space was part of the working environment, and therefore their lives were tightly shackled to the factory, deprived of education, healthcare and other social services. According to oral history, before the White Revolution, brick-oven factories did not attract anybody from the village.[17] When their number increased as the result of urbanization, more families left the village in favourable seasons to reside in such factories. In comparison to life in the village where a family could still live in relatively 'better' conditions, in the brick-oven factory they lived in squalid circumstances; were paid inadequately and most of the time with delay; and lived in remote places far away from available social services. In the absence of healthcare, sanitation and education, families experienced an unhealthy and meagre diet while sources of healthy protein or vitamin became luxury products for a labouring class which was also distinguished in this respect. The brick-oven factory was a direct product of the White Revolution's land reform and unbridled urbanization.

An undesirable rural life

Modernization allowed landless peasants to remain in the village either as free labourers working on the land or with the cattle. The sharecroppers, *jutbanda*, who stood just above this lower class, did slightly better as their land, though still insufficient, provided a degree of security.[18] It was small landowners rather than large ones that lost land as their power diminished.[19] Good quality lands remained in the possession of wealthier landowners.

If seasonal work and family migration in search of better income situated individuals in extremely unfavourable economic and cultural circumstances, this did not mean that life in the familiar environment of the village was more rewarding. The continuity of harsh socio-economic conditions after the introduction of land reform was still prevalent. City–village disparity, discussed in the previous chapter, epitomized this continuity in many ways. Even as late as 1978 optimistic assessments of Iran's economic performance and its future planning attested to 'the existing gap between rural and urban areas (in physical facilities, income level, educational and employment opportunities, cultural advancement and political participation)', a problem supposed to be dealt with in the Sixth Plan (1978–83).[20] The population movement, the construction of roads and provision of services to some extent undoubtedly helped connect rural areas to urban centres, which were experiencing a faster pace of social change. However, the best part of the Kurdish rural area was either disconnected or loosely linked to the process of change. This was because the White Revolution was an urban phenomenon, prioritizing projects that would create an advancing image of Iran. Regions close to main roads began to acquire rudimentary levels of some social services. However, to get access to higher levels of healthcare or educational services individuals had to travel to cities to see doctors or reside in cities to continue their education. Travelling to see doctors was both difficult and expensive and residing in cities to continue education meant that young boys had to rent their accommodation in groups and work to survive. Because of their regionality, it was especially this group that was the target of verbal and physical abuse.

Undeniably, the land reform as the centrepiece of the White Revolution marked the effective beginning of the end of both the Kurdish *agha* class and tribalism. However, this was a prolonged process that outlasted the Pahlavi regime itself. Indeed, connecting the village to the city as the centre of the process of change became an irreversible process from the early 1960s onwards. Nevertheless, state-led modernization was accountable for the continuity of the miserable village life, the rural-urban development gap and the absence of specific development plans for the Kurdish region, in general, and its rural areas, in particular. Therefore, up till the political upheaval of the end of the 1970s, the socio-economic condition of the village continued to experience only limited change. Indeed, the continuity of the undesirable village life was an accompanying feature of modernizations in all countries of the region – a universal phenomenon, reflected in literary works of Gholamhossein Saʿedi, ʿAli Ashraf Darwishyan, Hanan Al-Shaykh, Yusuf Edris, Yashar Kemal and Mahmud Tahir Lashin and formed the themes of many movies shown on television or in rapidly popularizing cinema.[21] In Iran, however, widespread awareness of shocking rural conditions came with the 1979 Revolution.

Cities

Modern Kurdish cities began to grow based on no specific plans. This illuminates a significant failure because, as discussed previously, there were sophisticated minds and state organizations that designed comprehensive development plans which benefited from huge oil revenues. It was not necessarily the question of resources as much as the question of policy: the economic plans were centralizing and lacked specific provincial plans. Cities were abandoned to deal with modernization and face its reverberations which originated from the centre. A realistic expectation of non-centralized, provincial-oriented economic plans in the context of Iran in the 1950s, 1960s and 1970s is corroborated by increasingly upbeat attitudes of both the monarch and more sophisticated development plans. Therefore, the unplanned expansions of economy and society, specifically in the Kurdish region, signify a multilayered social change affected by political consideration and the nature of the state.

The economy in conventional trade expanded but did not lead to the emergence of production centres, except for tobacco factories and Silos, nor to a coordinated economic system to utilize the regional potential and benefit from the expansion of the economy across Iran. The unrestrained expansion of the city and economy amid infrastructural developments engaged the population of rural areas in city markets by bringing to city markets mostly homemade dairy products, while the emergence of pasteurized products created competition for the local economy. As a result, city markets swelled with increased contributions from the countryside. However, the existing economic patterns of bazaar and craft production continued to dominate city life.

Furthermore, as another significant aspect of urbanization, the growth of cities outstripped social services. Defined as an establishment responsible for conducting urban affairs, an elected municipality was a modern notion, and although its introduction originated in the expansion of modern bureaucracy in Iran since the Constitutional Revolution, it was in the 1960s and 1970s that it began to exert more influence as a new urban institution across Iran.[22] In 1968–9 the new municipality law (qanoun-e shahrdari), passed in 1956 and amended in 1966, was finally implemented and Tehran's was 'the first council to convene'.[23] However, the implementation of the law had no implications for Kurdish cities, and this seems to be the case across Iran. A *sharadar* (Ku. City Councillor), imported from outside the region, was appointed by an *ostandar* (provincial governor) or by a *farmandar* (regional governor) who were also non-natives.[24] New municipalities gradually replaced the conventional community councils which consisted of reliable and respected men of the community. Throughout the 1970s, parks and asphalt roads were created, and electricity and sanitation reached more homes. Nevertheless, a neighbourhood continued to rely on wells, public baths and mosques' toilets. It was inner parts of a city rather than the poor, shapeless districts surrounding the city that benefited from the new city council. Therefore, modernization created, in the same way as it had sustained the city–village disparity, an urban disparity between a city's neighbourhoods. The absence of a social welfare system, assumed by the new municipality's law to be the task of the new city council, allowed the continuation of formidable hurdles for the amelioration of living standards which, as mentioned earlier, correlated highly with the level of income eked out by individual efforts in unfavourable socio-economic conditions.

Amid the expansion of the economy and public sector, both the level of income and the type of employment were crucial factors affecting the transformation of the urban-class structure. The expansion of trade enriched both non-bazaari and bazaari merchants and enabled them to invest and expand trade. In addition to the capital invested in the bazaar, construction contractors accumulated capital in the booming construction economy. On the other hand, the nature of construction as labour-intensive rather than a capital intensive economy led to employing an army of unskilled or semi-skilled free-moving labourers who became an important part of the new Kurdish working class. The socio-economic impact of the construction industry was massive, creating a wide network of other trades around it. However, the expanding economy remained within the existing modes of trade and did not enter a phase of 'industrialization' to promote the industrial potential of the region. Moreover, the level of income determined the level of access to technological or cultural products.

Simultaneously, the expansion of the public sector created new employment, distinguished not only by the provision of regular salaries but also by its access to cultural innovations. Public education and healthcare stand out as two prominent public areas. Working in education or healthcare increased family incomes and transformed the family culturally too. In this way increased income and access to the means of cultural consumption and production distinguished another section of society from those whose low income restricted their access especially to technological but also to cultural products. Therefore, a Kurdish 'middle class' emerged as a result of the expansion of the economy and public sector. Whereas many could be identified as *sarmayedar* (one with capital) towards the end of the 1970s, a 'capitalist class' engaged in the organization of an industrial economic system did not exist. With the same token, 'bourgeoisie' developed as a notion referring to a cultural way of life rather than a specific class. However, the middle class in question was divided into lower and upper levels, distinguished by their possession of alienable or inalienable wealth and income and benefiting from different levels of materialistic well-being and cultural capital. Women's place in both private and public spheres functioned as another significant distinction for the 'middle class' wherein women had potentially more access to socio-economic or cultural innovations and worked to gain a degree of economic independence, becoming empowered in the process. This new image of Kurdish womanhood applied to the new generation of women that emerged from the 1960s across Iran. Nevertheless, the modernizing institutions, especially education, affected (mostly urban) women in low-income families, by enabling them to enter employment.

Education

As discussed in Chapter 2, modern Iran witnessed the emergence of an educated, urban generation in Kurdistan increasingly independent of its tribal society. This process intensified between the 1950s and the 1970s. Although this generation was the product of modern education, they played a crucial role in expanding modern education into urban, but especially, rural centres and can be credited for attempting to promote social, cultural and political awareness in urban and rural populations. For modern intellectuals, education was the new nation's vehicle of progress and aimed to eradicate illiteracy in Iran. As Taqizadeh claimed (see Chapter 1), it was a 'sacred goal' which had been pursued by intellectuals since the Constitutional Revolution. Although eradicating illiteracy was a monumental task for the modern nation state of Iran, the result was by no means negligible by the end of the 1970s.[25] However, there are two points to be made. First, the expansion of modern education, like many other modernizing institutions, took place in a changing sociopolitical context in which not only the state but an educated generation was needed for its expansion. Modern education was not essentially a 'humanitarian' effort to help lift 'traditional' societies out of poverty, but it was crucial to the future prosperity of the imagined 'nation' in the way the state desired. Second, the new state was ethnically a homogenizing polity, and its educational policies were aimed at Persianization of the culture. Therefore, resistance against the nationalization of education was also reflected in the efforts of the Kurdish educated urban groups who were involved in expanding literacy and imparting social and historical awareness to the people. These two points enable us, on the one hand, to identify more contributors in the struggle to eradicate illiteracy since the Constitutional Revolution, and on the other hand, to promote a critical reading of the state's modern education that distinguishes literacy as the ability to rote skills such as reading, writing and arithmetic, and literacy as the ability to acquire knowledge critically. By the 1970s, Iran's education system had become an instrument to form the 'new Iranian', as the state became more authoritarian and was inspired by more radical nationalist agendas.

Education: 1920–60

A considerable number of Kurdistan Province's Education Office documents, which had been abandoned in cellars or awaited shredding, were saved for posterity by tenacious efforts of Sayyed Abdolhamid Hayrat Sajjadi. Published in Persian under the title *The History of Education in Kurdistan (1941-1979)*, the book provides important data, which along with information published by the

Education Ministry's journal of *Amuzesh wa Parvaresh* (Pe. education), form valuable source materials for further analysis of education in this period in Iran, in general, and in the Kurdish region, in particular. Distinguished also for its inclusion of female teachers and headteachers, who formed a crucial part of the education system throughout the Kurdish region, the documents in *The History* identify fifty educational centres in the province between 1941 and 1946, many of which are in rural areas, attesting to continuous educational efforts since the early century.[26] However, the number is higher if we add schools in the Kurdish cities excluded from the province because of Iran's administrative divisions. The share of the provincial city of Sanandaj was fourteen which increased to more than sixty in two decades.[27] As Table 5 shows, bigger cities also acquired secondary schools.[28] By the mid-1950s the growth was more impressive as the number of both primary and secondary schools, the number of students and the proportion of girls in education had grown considerably since late 1930;[29] this included an increase in the number of female teachers and headteachers (see Table 6). Therefore, although efforts to expand modern education by the 1940s had been impressive, the period in the aftermath of the Second World War stands out because of a profound change in the educational structure of Kurdish society.

However, the performance of growing Kurdish cities was average or below average compared to educational statistics for all provinces in this period.[30] Constant administrative divisions, the exclusion of the Kurdish cities allocated to other provinces, and statistical methods, which served to create an image of constant and satisfying growth of modern education, hindered educational statistics.[31] In this regard, documents in Sajjadi's book cast a better light on the state of education in Kurdish cities.[32] Quantitative changes did not conceal educational deficiencies regarding facilities and trained teachers.[33]

Furthermore, parallel to impressive quantitative changes, the perception of education and its role continued to transform throughout the Pahlavi era. This was reflected in the Education Ministry's journal of education, *Ta'lim va Tarbiyat*, an Arabic-derived title, published ever since 1925 to promulgate modern education. As part of the process of linguistic simplification and purification in Iran, the term was replaced by 'amuzesh va parvaresh', a more Persian-derived term, in 1938 as a result of an intellectual and governmental attempt to create new vocabularies compatible with the image of the new state. Although political crises and the lack of enthusiasm interrupted its publication – it was postponed for five years from March 1929 – its first issues contained enlightening, educational articles and educational statistics.[34] By 1938, these aspects had already been diminished as eulogizing articles on the Shah and the crown prince, Muhammad Reza, along with their photographs, emerged more frequently. Moreover, although the school curriculum became more cohesive and began to contain a variety of scientific subjects, patriotism along with kingship and a homogenizing, national Iranian history was increasingly emphasized. The most effective instruments to inculcate such ideas were the Persian language and Persian literature; all other languages and works of literature in Iran were neglected in favour of Persian studies. As a result of the changing political contexts, the journal and its diverse contributors

Table 5 Primary and Secondary Schools in Some Kurdish Cities (1955)

City	Schools				Students				Teachers	
	Primary		Secondary		Primary		Secondary		Primary	Secondary
	Public	Private	Public	Private	Public	Private	Public	Private		
Sanandaj	68	2	5	1	4,629	296	708	22	255	42
Saqqez	26	-	3	-	1,554	-	233	-	87	16
Mahabad	58	-	5	-	3,359	-	595	-		
					Boys: 2,657		Boys: 488			
					Girls: 702		Girls: 107			

In 1955, Sanandaj and Saqqez were parts of the Kermanshah Province, while Mahabad had been allocated to the Rezayie Province. Based on the number of students in Mahabad, the ratio of girls to boys is 1 to 3.

Source: Amuzesh wa Parvaresh, No. 3, Mehr 1335 (September 1955); Amuzesh wa Parvaresh, No. 4, Dey 1335 (December 1957).

Table 6 Education Centres and the Number of Female Teachers in the Kurdistan Province

All educational centres: 1320-5 (1941-6)	Educational centres in Sanandaj 1941-6	Educational centres in Sanandaj 1352-3 (1973-4)
50	14	62
Female headteachers in Sanandaj 1973-4	Female teachers in nine primary schools in Sanandaj 1349-50 (1970-1)	
27	82	

Source: Sayyed Abdolhamid Heyrat Sajjadi, Pishineye Amuzesh wa Parvaresh in Kurdistan (the history of education in Kurdistan) (Sanandaj: Kurdistan Publications, 2004), 330 and 343-6.

vacillated between an educational, critical journal and one under the shadow of the ruling Shah. In the aftermath of the abdication of Reza Shah in 1941, the Education Ministry issued a new law for universal and compulsory education. It lamented that despite 'thirty-five years since the Constitution's [introduction of] compulsory education, unfortunately [universal and compulsory education] has remained a dream'.[35] Even by the end of the 1950s, reporting to UNESCO's international congress, a contributor warned that 'no country was supposed to use schools as means to promulgate radical nationalism'.[36] Made possible by its various contributors, *Amuzesh va Parvaresh* published articles that presented critical assessments of Iran's educational methods. As an illustration of this, the ineffectiveness of both one-way teacher-student teaching (*naqli*) and the method of learning by heart (*hefzi*) were addressed.[37] Equally interesting, poverty was linked to learning at schools;[38] and a history of education in Iran drew attention to the continuance of corporal punishment and detrimental educational environments in the previous fifty years.[39] Furthermore, research conducted to assess education in rural areas featured in many issues of the journal,[40] while the publication of educational books, including comparative studies, increased.[41]

The existence of such critical assessments of the educational system demonstrated the presence of a diverse, educated generation determined to affect social change. *Amuzesh va Parvaresh* remained a battleground for the clash of dictatorial and democratic educational ideas. However, the journal and its contributors generally maintained a philosophical and historical approach to education, hinged on the Persian language and literature, with the effect that the conspicuous dearth of other works of literature lingered on while the curriculum continued to ignore the cultural diversity of Iran.[42] Language had become an indispensable component alongside historiography to reinforce a national image of Iran. As a result, the promotion of Persian was even more consciously pursued from the 1950s onwards. For example, in one of its issues towards the late 1950s, the journal lamented the deterioration of the quality of the 'sweet' Persian language and listed several requirements to tackle that overriding problem, one of which was 'the prevention of teaching foreign languages (*zabanhaye biganeh*) [i.e. other Iranian languages spoken in Iran] in kindergartens and primary schools'.[43]

A decade later, despite educational and critical articles, the journal continued to identify itself increasingly along national lines. A contributor to one of its 1965 issues stated that

> Another big goal of the educators [in teaching Persian] is a national goal. In this age especially when our country has entered a new historical epoch, this goal should be seen as an overriding goal in [teaching] the Persian language. Because in the current age, the biggest wish of humanity is to achieve a high status [. . .] [and] therefore from plurality to unity or from nationalism to the oneness of humanity and brotherhood of nations is [generally] considered the best logical and scientific way [to achieve that status].[44]

Such intensified linguistic efforts and radicalized perceptions were clear manifestations of an intimate relationship between an inexorable state-led modernization and the process of nation-building. Moreover, by extolling the ancient, pre-Islamic Iran, the journal also became a platform to reinvent ancient traditions such as *Mehregan*, *Nowruz* and *Sadeh*, a mythical ancient Iranian fire festival, to 'safeguard *qaumiyat* and *melliyat* [Pe. ethnicity and nationality]' of Iran.[45] The journal reflected the way modern education in Iran was expanding; however, by the middle of the 1970s, it was the development of the mass media, especially television and cinema, which elevated Persian to an unprecedented cultural status.

In contrast to significant educational progress in urban centres, the advance of literacy in peripheral, and dominantly rural, regions like Kurdistan was curtailed by weak infrastructure, the remoteness of the village and also by educational decrees which stipulated the existence of 'enough' students to form primary and secondary schools.[46] Moreover, the absence of an adequate number of teacher training colleges in Kurdish cities except for Sanandaj, let alone universities and other institutions of higher education, affected education in Kurdistan negatively. This remained the case towards the end of the 1970s.

Table 7 Primary and Secondary Schools in Iran (1955)

Primary schools		**Girls**		**Boys**
Public	6,245	221,723		528,734
Private	359	25,296		45,584
Secondary school		**Public**	**Private**	**Total**
Girls		153	35	*188*
Boys		466	72	*726*
Students	Girls	25,706	8,520	*142,751*
	Boys	89,814	18,711	

Source: *Amuzesh wa Parvaresh*, Vol. 28, No. 1, Farvardin 1335 (March–April 1956).

Education: 1963–79

The availability of more precise educational statistics distinguished the 1960s and 1970s. According to later statistics, in 1966 from a school-age (seven+ years) population of less than 19 million only 29.4 per cent were literate.[47] In urban areas, where more people lived, this number was almost 60 per cent; and there were twice as many literate men as women.[48] Therefore, in the early 1960s illiteracy still constituted a major issue for Iran. Under pressure to tackle this, the state began to present new methods and invest more in education with the effect that educational conditions improved every year. For example, in 1968 the rate of literacy rose to 33.4 per cent among a school-age population of almost twenty-two million, rising again in 1972 to 36.7 per cent among a growing school-age (six+ years) population of more than twenty-two million in 1972.[49]

The educational image of the Kurdish region changed radically in this period when the number of both primary and secondary schools increased and more people attended schools. Mixed secondary schools had been established in bigger Kurdish cities by the end of the 1960s, though in smaller towns schools either came late or were only available to boys. Except for establishing teacher or nurse training colleges in the provincial centres, founding universities were not on the agenda and school graduates had to travel to cities outside of their region, usually to Tehran or Tabriz to acquire higher education. Furthermore, parallel to both infrastructural improvements and new educational policies, more villages acquired teachers who in many cases began teaching in the absence of school facilities. New educational methods and investments were outcomes of both the pressure from below and the authority of the state which embraced a set of reforms incorporated into the White Revolution. Therefore, the interaction of many forces led to the intensification of educational reforms that took place in a changing sociopolitical context.

One of the most significant educational developments in Iran was the introduction of the Literacy Corps at the end of 1962. Explaining the new Literacy Corps in a speech in 1963, the Minister of Education, Parviz Khanlari, informed his audience that despite educational achievements, from a population of '20 or 21 million only a few were literate nineteen years after the passing of the Compulsory [and Free] Education Law'.[50] The Shah too, agreeing with this bleak picture, claimed that 80 per cent of the population was illiterate.[51] 'Even by the end of the [current] twenty-year plan', Khanlari maintained, 'there will still be twelve million illiterates in Iran.'[52] Therefore, he argued, it was for this reason that the Literacy Corps was presented as an effective alternative to such a plan. It had been formed in the previous autumn, and, like many other ideas, it had been initiated before the announcement of the Shah's White Revolution. However, it was hailed as the achievement of the monarch. While the ideas had been hatched in intellectual circles by likes of Khanlari for whom this was a new dawn in the battle against illiteracy, *Amuzesh va Parvaresh* embellished its first page with the message of the Shah who announced the start of a 'sacred battle' and a 'national holy war' to eradicate illiteracy, thus expropriating the idea as his and labelling the action as his '*fatwa*' or decree.[53]

The Literacy Corps consisted of new school graduates who were assigned to villages across Iran, and their tasks also included advising on other issues such as health and infrastructure.[54] According to contemporary observers, in the early 1960s, the Literacy Corps consisted of mostly Persian-speaking young graduates who were scattered across the Kurdish region.[55] Their impact cannot be disputed; however, the number of villages, the poor quality of roads and lack of facilities restrained the impact of education on rural areas. Moreover, linguistic barriers and in most cases probably the lack of motivation among the corps hindered the expansion of modern education,[56] whereas undertaking other tasks, for example, providing advice on social or health issues, depended on individuals' political and social proclivities or dispositions and was not necessarily part of the job.[57] According to oral history, the way individuals' intellectual dispositions and practice were shaped was conditioned on their contact with the literature of the time, which included examples of similar actions in other parts of the region, for example, the writings of Nayef Hawatmeh, the Marxist Palestinian leader, and with ideas which encouraged closer contact with the masses.[58]

In parallel to the Literacy Corps, some native teachers were allocated to villages to teach and gain experience before being employed in urban schools. Upon graduation from a teacher training college, a graduate had to undertake a five-year teaching job in a village.[59] Villages were not popular career destinations for teachers. However, inspired by progressive and philanthropic ideals of the time, 'teaching in a village became a vogue for the educated, urban generation' in a changing political context.[60] For the growing popularity of such very ideas (see the next chapter) many chose to teach 'as a way to promote social and political awareness of *toodeha* [the masses]'.[61] Indeed, the increase in the number of social and political activists and the formation of what is assumed to be a network of such activists proved to be indispensable for the transformation of the educational image of Kurdish society. A successful doctor rising from a poor background in the city of Baneh recalls:

> My education could have been terminated after 6 years if it was not for a group of political and social activists in my home town. For example, Hashim Karimi, 'Abdulla Eqdami and Muhammad Qaderyan were educated individuals who were influenced by Kurdish cultural products and movements, valued education, and imparted social, ethnic and political ideas of the time. In the absence of state institutions in this regard, they encouraged me to continue studying and although I suffered from the lack of adequate income and had to work at the same time, I nonetheless continued my education and, after passing *Konkur* (Iranian university entrance exam), I was among the 220 students admitted to Tehran University's Medical Faculty in 1969.[62]

Therefore, both the expansion of literacy and the increase in the number of people in higher education were owed to the intersection of many factors, namely the authority of the state to establish new educational institutions and the existence of a new educated, urban generation, shaped in a rapidly changing world. This generation exposed the limit of the state-led modernization and the vitality of non-state agents of change as regards the expansion of modern education, a crucial point entirely ignored in modernization theories (see diagrams in Chapter 1). Max Weber explains such actions on behalf of individuals as 'value-oriented' – a type of social action 'determined by a conscious belief in the value for its own sake of some ethical, aesthetic, religious, or other form of behavior'.[63] However, in contrast to Weber's observation that action of this kind occurred 'for the most part only to a relatively slight extent', across Iran in general and in the period under discussion, 'value-oriented' actions characterized such a generation who contributed immensely to social change.[64] In a progressive perception of history, which guided activists during these decades, education was indeed an indispensable social value to fight for. It was through access to education that many were able to rise from poor socio-economic conditions.[65]

Another aspect of modern education, which exposed the limits of state action, was its unequal and prolonged nature. The following data elucidates this point: in April 1963 there were only thirty-two Literacy Corps in Kurdistan.[66] Teacher training included women too, though their number was still low, and in 1963 from fourteen applicants nine were admitted.[67] According to Muhammad Sadeq Sheikhestani, the incumbent deputy director of the Statistical Centre of Iran, 'in the academic year 1341-2 [1962–3] from 1,720,000 primary school students across Iran only 39 percent (apart from [those taught by] the Literacy Corps) [were] village students, while three-fourth of the population live[d] in rural areas'.[68] In the same academic year, *Amuzesh va Parvaresh* informed its readers that the number of primary students across Iran was increasing with different paces in different regions, 'leading to a considerable disparity between provinces'. As an illustration of this, in 1964 from the above total number of primary school students, the Fars Province's share was 14.5 per cent while the Kurdistan Province's share was 4 per cent.[69] Since the latter did not include all Kurdish cities, the share of the Kurdish region was probably slightly higher.[70] Educational disparities surrounding gender were other aspects of education. In the same year, across Iran the share of girls was 30 per cent, and, based on the difficulties of modern education to reach the peripheral regions in general and the countryside in particular, and also affected by cultural barriers, the number of girls in education, especially in rural areas, remained much lower than boys.[71]

According to statistics, the number of primary and secondary schools began to increase throughout the 1960s. In 1964 there were 420 primary schools against 18 secondary schools in the Kurdistan Province.[72] A yearly increase in the number of students was recorded in the next issues of *Amuzesh va Parvaresh* which continued its publication regularly, although the appearance of the images of the Shah, his patriarchal messages, as well as eulogizing pieces on the monarch (on his new calendar and performed reinvented traditions) increased to the detriment of intellectual and educational articles of the journal's earlier periods. Diverse both in the subject and in philosophical persuasion, one interesting aspect of the journal had been to recognize the individual efforts of men as well as women in the struggle against illiteracy. For example, 'Aziz Al-Muluk Ma'refat (Mo'temedi) was a Kurdish teacher from Sanandaj, whose teaching career and efforts to build schools for girls earned her, like many other pioneers across Iran, a deserved reputation among her contemporaries.[73] She taught in Sanandaj and founded *Namus* (honour) School for Girls in Hamadan before accepting a headteacher role in Kermanshah's Shahdokht Primary School for Girls. She then continued working in education after her retirement in 1963 and was assigned the role of *bazras* (Pe. inspector) in Tehran.[74] The name *Namus*, which has protectionist connotations concerning women, perfectly reflected the existing gender order of the society in which a brave individual like her not only had to fight illiteracy but also appease a hostile, patriarchal environment. Such individuals set the stage for a later, more educated urban generation, including women, that became a distinguishing feature of the era of the White Revolution.

According to official statistics, throughout the 1970s the number of primary and secondary schools in Kurdish urban areas continued to rise with the effect that between 1966 and 1974 the number of elementary schools increased from 393 to 597 schools.[75] Without specifying their urban or rural locations, available statistics claimed that these numbers for Literacy Corps elementary schools were 330 and 609, respectively;[76] enrolment in such schools increased from 8,000 to 15,000 pupils in this decade.[77] This data, whether inflated or even complete, generally illustrates a picture that demonstrates both the impressive growth of modern schools and the rate of literacy. Official statistics claimed that while in March 1966 only 52 children attended kindergartens in the Kurdistan Province, this number rose to 793 in March 1974.[78]

Nevertheless, the expansion of modern education did not include universities, the absence of which outlasted the Pahlavi rule itself. This was caused not only by the shortage of staff and a high rate of illiteracy but also by the state's lack of will and plans. Therefore, in pursuit of higher education, school graduates continued to enrol in universities outside Kurdistan. As their number grew in the 1960s and 1970s, this resulted especially in the formation of more networks of Kurdish social and political activists (see the next chapter).

Finally, at the end of 1965 the role of television in education was discussed in *Amuzesh va Parvaresh* in search of more effective, coordinated educational methods by rather ambiguously comparing 'centralised methods' used in France and Switzerland with 'decentralised methods' used in England.[79] This demonstrated the increasing significance of television in people's lives in Iran. However, despite such intellectual and educational debates, television became an effective tool for the concentration of political power and the homogenization of culture by the mid-1970s (Table 12).

Healthcare

This section discusses several important themes as regards modern healthcare such as the impact of modern healthcare on Kurdish society; the role of the state but also its limits and shortcomings; and the role of non-state agents of change.

Figure 3 ʿAziz Muluk Maʿrefat (Moʿtamedi).*Source*: Amuzesh wa Parvaresh, Vol. 37. Nos. 7 & 8 (1346 (1967)), 116. The text in the background reads, 'Lady Maʿrefat in a Struggle against Illiteracy Class in Tehran Laleh Primary School'.

Table 8 Educational Institutions in the Kurdistan Province

Institutions	1346–7 (1967–8)	Enrolment	1352–3 (1973–4)	Enrolment
Elementary schools	393	27,000	597	47,000
Literary corps elementary school	330	8,000	609	15,000
Secondary school	22	6,000	22	8,000
Technical and vocational schools	1	75	6	682
Normal and teaching training schools	4	23	3	455
University	0	0	0	0

Source: Plan and Budget Organization, *Statistical Yearbook of Iran 1352 [March 1973 – March 1974]*.

The expansion of healthcare institutions in Kurdish urban centres was another significant aspect of social change in the era of the White Revolution. By the end of the 1970s, more people had access to medical treatments such as immunization, medical information and advice. Parallel to this, the number of nurses and (foreign or native) doctors increased. As was the case with the expansion of literacy and schools, healthcare went through a prolonged and uneven process of change, but at a much faster pace and with considerable quantitative results. Healthcare was an urban phenomenon that needed time to become an ingrained institution in a society that was mainly rural and had continued to suffer from the absence of social services. Later, improved statistical data demonstrates the appalling medical conditions faced by earlier (mostly rural) populations and reveals a slow expansion of medical services. Therefore, with a growing awareness of medical issues, this process gradually engaged the educated generation.

Modern healthcare advanced throughout the 1970s amid unhealthy environments and prevalent diseases, especially in rural areas. Urban centres benefited more from sanitation, hygienization and the expansion of health centres, though not all the neighbourhoods were affected equally. Most villages continued to live in an unhealthy environment. In the second half of the century, health conditions in the Kurdish region were still appalling. This applied more acutely to peripheral regions and rural areas across Iran. In the 1950s or 1960s, there were no health centres in rural areas in the Kurdish region while its towns and cities only had limited access to health and medical services. Death rates and infant mortality were high while ratios of physicians and hospital beds to population demonstrated the scarcity of doctors and hospitals.[80] As the next two figures demonstrate, by the mid-1970s these conditions improved considerably in comparison with earlier periods.[81] The movement to ameliorate these conditions continued to face serious obstacles in a situation in which 'many villagers never benefit[ed] from medical science from cradle to grave'.[82] According to oral history, across the rural areas in the Kurdish region 'lice, swollen eyes, coughing, sloughy wounds, and leprosy in many villages, were prevalent'.[83] People affected by leprosy faced extra challenges to make a living, and though they were not completely excluded from the community life and were helped by co-villagers, they nonetheless experienced social isolation. Moreover, the region was still characterized by the absence of *hamam* (bathhouse/room) and toilets. For example, 'except in a landowner's house, in 1973 there were no private or public toilet to be used by people in Jalalvand and Osmanvand regions in the vicinity of Kermanshah' while people continued to rely on other unhygienic ways.[84] Common characteristics of Kurdish villages included the dearth of electricity, potable water and sanitary sewers – there were usually no suitable toilets or baths – which kept the level of disease high. Moreover, animal manure was shaped into *koshkalan* (Ku. dried dungs heaped upon each other), located in front of the house to be used as fuel, becoming a haven for disease-transmitting insects; domestic animals were kept in *gawr* (Ku. stable) which was a part of the inner space of the house. Immunization was unknown and, consequently, measles and chickenpox were endemic and continued to kill or infect individuals' lungs and brains or affect eyesight; the death toll was tens or hundreds of people annually.[85] Moreover, contact with animals and animal waste kept tetanus disease high while unhygienic washing materials spread microbes. Moreover, the lack of durables such as refrigerators and freezers left people with no way to store food.

In urban centres, too, 'low standards of sanitation and contact with hazards of waste contributed to the spread of cholera and typhoid, usually leading to an epidemic in summers'.[86] A shocking aspect of life in urban areas in the 1960s was the absence of a sanitary sewer system. Within cities 'open channels carried sewage through the residential areas, ending up in nearby lands under cultivation'.[87] Cholera was a lethal disease, while people still died of rabies.[88] Public awareness of health issues was at its lowest level while doctors and pharmacies with an adequate supply of medicine were rare, and advanced laboratories were unheard of. At the same time, people did not necessarily trust modern medical practices and therefore continued to use conventional methods.[89] These conditions in more populous cities

Table 9 Iran's Healthcare Indicators for 1923 and 1976

Indicator	1302 (1923)	1355 (1976)
Crude death rate (per 1,000)	22	8.5
Infant mortality (per 1,000 live births)	250	40
Child mortality (0–5 age; APTA)	50%	25%
Death from communicable diseases (APTA)	60%	10%
Death from smallpox (in non-pandemic years)	270	none
Cases of malaria (annual in Iran)	1 MM	12,000
Sanitary water supply coverage:		
Country	none	50%
Urban	none	85%
Ratio of physician/population	1/11,000 (Tehran)	1/2,150 (country)
Ration of hospital beds/population	1/11,000 (Iran)	1.5/1,000 (country)
APTA = as per cent of total age		

Source: Quoted in Mohammad Ali Faghih, 'Behdārī'.

Table 10 Healthcare Facilities in Iran (1978)

Hospitals	503
Hospital beds	48,850
Rural health units	1,550
Health corps units	450
Urban dispensaries	2,245
Health centres	564
Mother and child health centres	150
Diagnostic laboratories	638
School health units (covering an estimated 5 million pupils)	151

Source: quoted in Mohammad Ali Faghih, "Behdārī".

were only slightly better. People continued to use public baths, mostly *khazena* (pool), washing in a shared pool, although in most cases new public baths with shower rooms replaced them by the end of the 1970s. Private baths in households were a new urban concept only used by the wealthy. However, visiting public baths on days of celebration also carried with it some cultural meanings. For example, the act of visiting public baths as a family on New Year's Eve or religious days was a custom to welcome such important days (Tables 9 and 10).

Healthcare: Its pace and scope of change

The health conditions, discussed earlier, were radically transformed throughout the 1970s but more in Kurdish urban rather than in rural areas. This was another factor that further consolidated the disparity between city and village. Despite the emergence of a more organized and effective healthcare system, including its various training organizations, it was outstripped by the health-related demands of a rising population. The states' shortcomings in this regard emanated from the late emergence of effective methods to expand the healthcare system. The introduction of the concept of such a system was one of the basic objectives of Iran's Fifth Development Plan (1973–), which was followed by a social security system (bime-ye ejtemaʿi), introduced in 1975. Accordingly, in addition to a central apparatus, which included many directories, the Ministry of Health introduced various departments to improve healthcare at a peripheral level. For example, general departments of health (edara-ye koll-e behdasht), departments of health headed by county health commissioners and district health centres headed by medical officers were assigned to function in Iran's twenty-three provinces. This took place in the mid-1970s; however, merely increasing institutions did not necessarily yield quick results. Health conditions in many Kurdish rural areas at the end of the 1970s were either as terrible as or minimally better than what they had been twenty years ago. The shortage of trained medical staff, slow infrastructural improvements and difficult access to villages were formidable hurdles for the expansion of modern healthcare. This is in addition to the religious and cultural resistance of people to modern healthcare, which resulted from a lack of awareness and misperceptions of new scientific advances. Even on this front, 'the task fell on the shoulders of the recent school graduates who enthusiastically imparted medical knowledge to people'.[90] Crucial, however, was the direction of centre- and urban-centred development plans, which generally lacked the will and initiatives for the peripheries and rural regions. This was partly, but significantly, compensated by a healthcare movement in Iran that promoted the idea and pushed for more reforms.

Indeed, the transformation of healthcare in Iran in the 1960s and 1970s originated from 'a new and dynamic health movement' which gained momentum in the early years of the second half of the century. The movement was characterized by an increasing number of individuals, who in the capacity of social activists contributed to the promotion of health awareness and was embodied in public and private associations like the Iranian Nurses Association (founded Khordad 1334/1955) and Persian journals such as *Health for All* and *Health Today*, published throughout the 1950s.[91] This was extended to privately funded organizations to provide maternity care in rural areas.[92] The movement was inspired and supported by an active generation of individuals epitomized by poet Sohrab Sepehri or children's book writer and illustrator Muhammad Zaman Zamani.[93] Usually overshadowed by elitist or political historiographies, this generation had its history and continued to include many other literary figures, teachers and doctors, who, carrying a *revolutionary* zeal, were committed to social change to improve the life of Iranians.[94]

Hospitals and medical services in Kurdistan

According to statistics published in March 1974, there were 9 hospitals, including 1 run by 'foreign mission', with 359 beds in the Kurdistan Province.[95] Along with most provinces orbiting the centre, there were no specialized hospitals or children hospitals.[96] Plan and Budget Organization's 1974 *Statistical Yearbook* listed 66 unspecified clinics, 10 ambulances and 26 pharmacies for the province where around 100 children were claimed to have received support from the Pahlavi charity.[97] Mostly general practitioners and some general surgeons, the number of doctors did not reach 100. The considerable rise in the number of medical staff across Iran did not mean that they were distributed equally over provinces. The number of people employed in healthcare across Iran rose from 34,000 in 1966 to 79,710 in 1978.[98] As the next figure shows, healthcare in Iran at the end of the 1970s could not be compared with earlier decades. According to contemporaries, a gradual change in health conditions in the Kurdish region became more tangible since the early 1960s. By 1970 there were more medical centres in urban areas, immunization had become available and sanitation improved with the effect that cities began to acquire covered carriage systems for transporting sewage; there were more toilets, cleaner public baths and piped potable water. However, hygienization depended on planned urbanization, the availability of services such as electricity, roads and transportation. These elements improved slowly and remained vulnerable in the face of harsh climates. For example, in winter and spring roads were blocked or flooded, interrupting transportation and the supply of fuel.[99] As more roads were built more villages benefited from piped potable water, fertilization and exterminators for the application of chemicals to eliminate vermin and insects.

The Health Corps, included in the principles of the White Revolution, was not a royal innovation but emerged from the health movements and aimed to address the medical and living conditions in rural areas more effectively. It consisted of young men and women, whose educational level was high school diploma or above, and were trained for a few months before being dispatched to rural areas to work on rudimentary health and sanitation projects as part of their military service. There were also mobile units, including medical women, who supplied free contraceptives, an important medical development in rural areas since the end of the 1960s, and provided advice on menstruation and pregnancy.[100] These units visited villages that had access to roads and transportation but excluded a considerable number of inaccessible villages. Nevertheless, female nurses and teachers were crucial to the improvement of women's living conditions. In the 1970s the risk of miscarriage or death during childbirth was still high. By the middle of the 1970s, the number of infectious diseases had decreased because of the availability of immunization. However, this was primarily an urban phenomenon, leaving the rural areas and the majority of the population struggling with poor standards of hygiene and without healthcare.

Many reasons explained this gradual hygienization and continuation of gruesome conditions in both Kurdish rural areas and poor city neighbourhoods. According to contemporary observers, the state-led economic development was influenced by political considerations with the effect that, for example, the budgetary share of hygiene in comparison to the military was much lower. Although statistics refer to an institutional transformation of healthcare in Iran by the end of the 1970s, from a population of almost 30 million, the number of students attending medical schools (daneshkade-ye Pezeshki) across Iran was only 500–600 per year, indicating the low number of trained medical staff.[101] Moreover, the state concentrated on the centre and did not follow specific economic plans to boost peripheral regions' economic potential, as was the case not only in Kurdistan or Baluchistan but also in Khuzistan despite its oil and gas mines. As another study on the subject argues,

> Despite these advances, the development of health care in Iran was hampered by a lack of central planning and organization. Services provided by state and municipal organizations, on the one hand, and private groups, on the other, at times overlapped, causing wasteful duplication, while at the same time, because of maldistribution of services in terms of quantity and quality, segments of the population and some geographical areas could not be served properly.[102]

There were also cultural barriers to the expansion of healthcare. Modern healthcare not only had to transform living conditions but also the perception of people who trusted conventional methods. Religious authorities like prominent *sheikhs* who had vested interest in maintaining conventional or religious methods continued to consolidate their authority on people's mind by ridiculing and demonizing new scientific knowledge. The absence of a tenacious effort on behalf of the state, except for its military presence, to expand knowledge and services meant that religious authorities continued to keep their hold on the society, especially in rural communities. This uneven modernization of healthcare in Iran is best seen in the horrific health conditions which were still common in most rural areas in the Kurdish region in the late 1970s. The revolutionary upheavals at the end of the decade exposed the quality of life in villages when contacts increased and more educated individuals, including doctors and nurses, visited the countryside. Their testimonies demonstrate how villages (many only 10 to 20 kilometres away from cities) were still deprived of electricity or potable water, or people used the same hot water pool for washing;[103] in other villages open sewers passed through houses and into the nearby river while, shockingly, people used the same river, that had absorbed sewage of upper villages on its way, for drinking and cooking.[104] The presence of this new revolutionary generation in rural areas was an unprecedented event that exerted a profound impact on the social awareness of the people.

Utopias of social welfare

As was the case with the concepts of *behdasht* (health), hygienization and healthcare institutions, 'social welfare' was a latecomer too, prioritized in Iran's Fourth Development Plan (1968–73). Evaluating a request for social welfare expertise by Iran's Plan and Budget Organization, the Middle East Department of Britain's Ministry of Overseas Development noted that this ambitious plan included 'social insurance, family and child welfare, Youth Development, Community Development, Industrial Welfare, Rehabilitation of handicapped groups,

Research and Training'.[105] It was no secret that Iran was conspicuously devoid of expertise, trained personnel and relevant institutions and that this deficiency was the reason behind the organization's request made in 1969 for social welfare experts.[106] Although the request was initially regarded as both an indication of Iran's seriousness 'about its plans for the development of social welfare' and an opportunity to invest in 'a well-developed and progressive outfit', the final reply states that 'the Iran request in present circumstances is a dubious one and need not be followed up'.[107] The main reason for this was the department's dissatisfaction with an old-fashioned, nineteenth-century perception of welfare as 'soup kitchen and crutches for cripples'.[108] Therefore, as the ministry's representative in Iran, J. H. O'Regan, stated later, it was better to 'concentrate on those tasks which are either in our interests to pursue, or which are likely to make a reasonable impact on Iran's development (in the wider sense of the term) or both'.[109] Mrs Behaqi, who supervised the organization's social welfare plan, desperately searched for expertise to teach new modules related to social welfare in Tehran and Shiraz universities.[110] The organization found itself in such a desperate situation that it even welcomed experts with lower degrees to teach or work as development officers.[111] Therefore, while the welfare system was at best unorganized and ineffective, both a faulty conception of welfare and desperate requests for experts revealed the grim state of 'welfare' in Iran at the end of the 1960s.

The principles of the White Revolution included social policies, including, by the end of 1975, policies regarding free education, including free meals 'for the needy', 'from kindergarten through the eighth grade', and free secondary and university education in return for undertaking public services. In addition to the expansion of health centres and hospitals, the Lion and Sun Society (the equivalent of the Red Cross) was assigned the task of providing healthcare to the underprivileged while other state organizations affiliated with various ministries were supposed to cover people and regions not covered by the national health plan; more emphasis was put on medical units for the rural areas. However, as regards social welfare projects, dreadful social conditions continued. Social projects envisioned in the Fourth Plan became utopian projects which, with more promises made by the mid-1970s, continued to excite some economists who, based on Iran's unprecedented economic growth during the early 1970s, believed 'there were bright prospects for a resurgence of another Great Civilization'.[112]

During the 1970s the Kurdish rural region remained outside any social welfare. There are no reliable statistics on or any indication of the existence of any such projects by contemporaries. Simultaneously, the impoverishing impact of the unplanned urbanization and population growth revealed the dearth of social services in urban centres. For example, modernization exposed on a wider scale those with physical or learning difficulties, as well as those in need of mental healthcare. Social problems emerged in many forms, and the state at best responded to only some aspects of them. For example, in some cities, city councils set up *parvareshgah* (Pe. Orphanage) to protect orphaned children who were born out of marriage or abandoned by the side of a road. They came to be called *parvareshgahi* (Pe. raised in an orphanage), and the law for the protection of infants without guardians allowed the adoption of these children by Iranians.[113] Being raised in such an institution had both cultural and social consequences. Children born outside marriage were perceived as *na-shar'i* or illegitimate; *parvareshgahi* was a new category that connoted a lower social status of those either born outside marriage or not living in a family. Moreover, there were limited centres for the protection of people affected by lethal or life-changing diseases such as tuberculosis and leprosy. Leprosy patients were completely unprotected in the Kurdish rural areas and isolated in the cities. Infectious diseases were still lethal during the 1970s. For example, according to a medical college student, in the mid-1970s a high percentage of patients who admitted to his university hospital in Tehran died.[114]

In fact, the notion of 'people in need' was itself dubious, confirmed by the extension of the categorization of people to those who looked or acted 'differently'. Many city neighbourhoods were characterized by individuals, many of whom adults, who suffered from Down syndrome or speaking disabilities, but instead of their needs being recognized, they faced continuous violence in the form of derogatory names, insults, intimidation and staring. There were no institutions available to take such individuals under their protection. Moreover, physical disabilities determined the social status of individuals identified as '*goj*' (Ku. 'deformed'), maintaining a feeling of shame in them, social isolation and deprivation. Individuals affected by such conditions were deprived of education, while in most cases they also had to work in unfavourable circumstances. Categorization and the continuation of ingrained cultural attitudes, the lack of education, health and social services were not peculiar to Iranian societies. They were universal issues. However, a decade after the introduction of the relevant projects in the development plans, such individuals continued to rely on family and relatives rather than state institutions, which were either absent or inadequate.

Conclusion

This chapter analyses the social consequences of land reform and modernization, which in the Kurdish region were followed by the migration of poor peasants to cities and by unbridled urbanization. Insofar as the land reform is concerned, its uneven and inconsistent nature failed in ameliorating life in rural areas, still characterized by appalling conditions at the end of the 1970s. Moreover, although it dealt the landowner class a mighty blow, this class remained wealthy and powerful and, for this reason, a form of authority (sometimes military power) was consistently needed to ensure its acquiescence. That is why once the central authority was weakened amid the popular revolution in 1978–9, in many regions the Kurdish *agha* class re-emerged to demand the restitution of their lost lands. However, both the regime of the Kurdish *agha* and tribalism were effectively weakened because of the *combined* effects of land reform and the socio-economic transformation of Iran.

Modernization also significantly affected the class structure of Kurdish society. A socio-economic structure based on oppressive landowner–peasant economic relations was crumbling in the face of capitalist social relations. Identified with the left across Iran, according to Sami Zubaida, the class structure can be critically assessed from the economically powerful bourgeoisie to the poorest.[115] However, underdevelopment in the Kurdish region precluded the creation of a class structure including a dependent or national bourgeoisie; instead, bazaar merchants and investors in the construction industry remained prominent. Nevertheless, a (lower) middle class emerged as the number of educational and healthcare professionals and other government employees increased. This began to become evident in the expansions of what are classically called the petty bourgeoisie and the intelligentsia. The peasantry's structure was profoundly altered by land reforms, migration and landlessness; many peasants had already joined an expanding working class, comprised of casual workers (porters, city pedlars, bazaar vendors), semi-skilled construction wage labourers, seasonal workers, child labourers and the marginal urban poor or lumpenproletariat. The result was a widening income gap between various social groups. Furthermore, the unpreparedness of the development plans to face the consequences of modernization and the dearth of social services created impoverished city neighbourhoods, which were made up of the lower strata of the village population. Moreover, the expansion of Kurdish cities and the search for income by the new free-moving labour class increased the number of urban wage labourers, who simultaneously faced both educational and healthcare deprivation and were exposed to social categorization.

The middle class was distinguished by higher income and employment in the public sector, which bestowed on them a higher social status; they had more access to healthcare, new means of communication, that is, radio and television, books and magazines, while their offspring could experience a relatively comfortable childhood. In short, these emerging classes were discernible by (1) level of income and (2) access to services, technologies and cultural capital. Moreover, in the making of a modern Kurdish working class the emergence of a new class of seasonal workers and family migration, which marked two significant consequences of land reform and modernization, is significant. In all cases, individuals were exposed to exploitation in the absence of any labour laws, exacerbated by undesirable social and cultural environments; children and women were particularly vulnerable in this environment. Concurrently, village life remained devoid of social services still until the end of the 1970s, while the unequal expansion of modern education, *behdasht* and social services consolidated the existing gap between city and village.

Meanwhile, the intensification of modernization led to more radical approaches in economic planning. Finding its rationale in an uneven economic development or existing regional gaps, the aborted Sixth Plan (1978–83), which 'modelled after France's *aménagement de territoire* [spatial planning]', meant to achieve 'closer national integration – geographic, socioeconomic and cultural'; and 'aimed at a *holistic* development of various regions and ultimately the entire *nation*' (emphasis added).[116] Moreover, economic development plans were affected by both political considerations and a nationalist vigour to 'catch up with [Western] Europe' economically, as well as socially within twenty-five years, as the monarch claimed in 1975, lest the oil resources run out.[117] This holistic approach was pursued not merely in economic spheres but also in sociocultural realms. As noted earlier, based on a homogenized Persian culture, Iran's modern education became increasingly an institution to foster a new, uncritical 'Iranian'.

Finally, dictatorship alongside intellectual and ideological radicalization widened the gap between the state and what is assumed to be Iran's *generations for change*. Excluding others and ignoring advice in the last two decades of his reign, the Shah eventually became the embodiment of the state, whereas, as the product of both modern education and the ideas of the time, the generations of social activists and intellectuals acquired an increased role in social change, determined to move towards a socioculturally progressive and democratic modernity. Even before the Shah was proven to be 'not a man of crisis', as the American ambassador noted during the political upheavals of 1978–9, one is tempted to say that he had already failed these generations by his authoritative role in the mismanagement of the modernization process, providing indirectly the 'objective conditions' for the intellectual ascendancy of an authenticity searching nativism instead.[118]

Chapter 4

THE POLITICAL AND CULTURAL CONSEQUENCES OF MODERNIZATION

Introduction

The intensification of the processes of socio-economic and political modernization in the era of the White Revolution resulted in significant political and cultural changes which conditioned the Kurds' resistance against homogenization and marked the origins of modern trends in Kurdish politics. In the new age of visual means of communication, the era reshaped cultural encounters in the multicultural nation state of Iran.

Politically, the dual process increased political centralization and effectively obstructed political participation. The state was eventually mutated into an omnipotent and omnipresent force and prevented any form of dissent through a standing army and, in some cases, explicit militarization. However, the state's politics of cultural exclusion and homogenization reinforced *Kurdayeti* in many forms. Consequently, ideologically embedded in an Iranian and worldwide context, networks of political and social urban activists emerged, leading to the formation of the nuclei of modern Kurdish political parties. The state justified suppression by reinforcing the assumption that *armed* struggle was an intrinsic characteristic of Kurdish opposition, undermining the existing non-violent political, social, cultural and literary movements. That said, the political history of the era is more complicated and is distinguished for the prevalence of non-violent forms of opposition and, interestingly, a critique of armed struggle, which new Iranian organizations such as Fedayyan and Mojahedeen perceived 'as both strategy and tactic'.[1]

Insofar as cultural consequences of modernization are concerned, this chapter focuses on 'Westernization' and the establishment of the cultural hegemony of the Persian language and culture. This is for two reasons. First, these two aspects provide specific perspectives to deal with cultural modernization in multicultural Iran. 'Westernization' here refers to new cultural products and ways of life originating from Western Europe and the United States, which either were embraced or elicited resistance. Second, an analysis of these two aspects enables us to identify other mechanisms of cultural encounters in a historically multicultural entity. In contrast to the mechanisms of cultural encounters in a colonial context, this includes the centralization of power and the cultural hegemony of the 'superior' culture. Of course, the post-colonial era witnessed the reproduction of the colonizer's cultural superiority over the natives and the spread of economic corporations, which compensated for the colonizer's physical absence or military and political rule. However, the distinctive elements of foreign/native always remained. In the case of the *modern* encounter of Persian and Kurdish cultures, the meaning of this distinction was different from a colonial encounter, which was deeply rooted in race and conquest. Within multicultural Iran, modern cultural encounters began to take place between cultures with intimate relations with each other, resulting in the hegemony of one over others. This is explained by analysing the process in which Persian cultural hegemony, defined and (re)introduced as *Iranian*, was realized and ensured its superiority over others in modern Iran. Moreover, in this process, the new audio and visual means of communication were as essential as modern education. Also for this reason, the era of the White Revolution is distinguished, to borrow from John Thompson, for the *mediasation* of culture, that is, 'the rapid proliferation of institutions of mass communication and the growth of networks of transmission through which commodified symbolic forms were made available to an ever-expanding domain of recipients'.[2] Therefore, as regards the cultural transformation of Iran, it is precisely for achieving Persian cultural hegemony that the era of the White Revolution sets itself apart from the preceding eras.

Modernization and the political situation in Kurdistan

The modernization of Iran continued to transform the political structure of Kurdistan. By the second half of the century, tribal local powers, mainly under duress, had submitted to the authority of the state. By the early 1970s, nobody could cast doubt on the existence of an omnipotent state, recognized by its military prowess and intelligence agencies and characterized by an expanding bureaucratic administration. However, since the experience of the Kurdistan Republic of 1946, the oppressive machinery of the state had remained on standby for quelling any possible re-emergence of Kurdish opposition, which nevertheless re-emerged, were quelled and against all odds rose again to challenge political power. On the other hand, political centralization effectively undermined political participation with the effect that the electoral process for the parliament became meaningless while the parliament itself became all but a rubber stamp. Therefore, these circumstances, affected by modern education, resulted in new networks of Kurdish political activists and, subsequently, the formation of the nuclei of modern Kurdish political parties. Iran continued to constitute the framework for political activism, while the organizational structure was not limited to the Kurdish region and ideological bearings reflected wider regional and international contexts. This situation was a direct result of the socio-economic and political modernization of Iran. Indeed, when new Kurdish political parties emerged amid the 1979 Revolution, it was no coincidence that their political programmes were explicitly articulated within the framework of modern Iran. To elaborate these claims, the following two sections present an overview of the political situation from the fall of the Kurdish Republic until the end of the 1970s. This arbitrary periodization is based on moments when changes are visible regarding the formation and political orientations of Kurdish opposition.

1946–68: The formative years of the Kurdish modern opposition

This period begins with the suppression of the Kurdish Republic and ends with the quelling of what is known in Kurdish collective memory as *the rebellion of 1968–9*. In the post-Republic era, the political structure of Kurdistan continued to be shaped by political considerations of the state because of the threat of Kurdish opposition. Political suppression and incarceration of activists persisted, but, despite this, clandestine political activities also continued. Although the idea of armed struggle, with its universal appeal in the context of the concurrent Kurdish movement in Iraq, was going to become attractive, Kurdish political activism was recognized by clandestine, political and other non-violent methods, devoid of any specific plan for armed struggle. Even in the 1960s, when because of changing circumstances a group of activists based in Iraqi Kurdistan carried arms to protect themselves against capture and detention, the main concern remained the reorganization of non-violent forms of dissent inside Iran. Nevertheless, 1968 and 1969 are significant years in Kurdish collective memory in Iran. During these years, Kurdish opposition met the aggressive reaction of SAVAK (Sazman-e Amniyat Va Etelaat-e Keshvar), Iran's fearsome intelligence service, and the Iranian army. This culminated in a dangerous situation in 1968 when the army succeeded in quelling an important section of the opposition, which moved as armed groups mainly in the northern part of the Kurdish region and made contact with the population and their sympathizers. As a result, the myth of *shorresh-i 46-47* (Ku. The rebellion of 1968–9) was born.

Political activities in this period had their origins in the quasi-autonomous situation of the early 1940s which culminated in the Republic. Converged effectively in the following decades, political activities concentrated in the northern areas of the Kurdish region, whereas political and cultural activism in the southern parts, which remained under the state control during these years, continued to be reshaped as socio-economic and political modernizations of Iran persisted. Dispersion and prolonged incarcerations followed the demise of the Republic, symbolized by forced exile and Ghani Blouryan's and 'Aziz Yousefi's prison years.[3] However, the remnants of *Kumita-i Lawan-i Dimukrat* or the Republic's Democratic Party of Iranian Kurdistan's (DPIK) Youth Organization matured to form the backbone of a new reinvigorated group, reinforced later by many others in the 1950s and 1960s, including university students. In these years, DPIK owed its nominal existence to a few individuals and was mostly regarded as a regional branch of the Tudeh (masses) Party of Iran until after the 1953 coup against Muhammad Musaddeq. Although for many DPIK members the Tudeh Party maintained its ideological and organizational significance, the expansion from the early 1960s to the 1970s was concurrent with DPIK's growing organizational independence and the demise of the influence of the Tudeh Party.[4]

The Iraqi Revolution of 1958 and the waves of arrests in Iranian Kurdistan in 1959 and 1963, which forced many to flee to Iraqi Kurdistan, were two important developments in the revival of Kurdish opposition.[5] According to prominent members of DPIK, in 1959 500 activists were either arrested or fled to Iraqi Kurdistan; this was repeated in 1963.[6] According to Sa'id Kawa Kwestani, who became a central figure in the reorganization of the party in the early 1960s, the Iraqi Revolution of 1958 reinvigorated Kurdish dissent after it had experienced serious setbacks during the 1953 coup, which was followed by the quelling of the peasant uprising in Iranian Kurdistan.[7] However, this revival led to new waves of arrests and imprisonments as a result of which a considerable number of political activists escaped to Iraqi Kurdistan.[8]

The Iraqi Revolution had strengthened the Kurdish movement in Iraq under Mustafa Barzani, subsequently creating a space for a group of Kurdish-Iranian activists, among them Ahmad Eshaqi (known as Ahmad Tawfiq), to try to rebuild DPIK in the early 1960s.[9] Attached closely to Barzani, the arbitrary measures of Tawfiq shrank the size of this group in Iraqi Kurdistan and disillusioned others. Finally, in the aftermath of the party's rather impromptu Second Congress in 1963, Tawfiq became increasingly isolated and then disappeared 'mysteriously' in the areas under the Barzani's control – he had allegedly met Iraqi officials secretly in Baghdad, and this 'betrayal' apparently sealed his unfortunate fate. Simultaneously, other members followed a different, more democratic path in a new international context. One member later described his colleagues' ideological and political outlooks:

> These individuals were left-wing *runak-biran* [Ku. enlightened; roshan-fekran in Persian]. In those days [the 1960s] it was the left-wing forces that led and pioneered anti-imperialist and emancipatory movements in East Asia, Africa, and Latin America. We might not have matched such groups in theoretical capacity, but we passionately felt attached to the path [they followed].[10]

Attempts to rebuild the party and expand political activities continued in trying circumstances but with determination. Distancing themselves gradually from Tawfiq, the majority of this group, reinforced by a new wave of sympathizers, who had fled the political suppression of 1963, organized in the form of small, armed groups which led excursions to the Kurdish region in Iran in order to reorganize cells and inspire political actions. This continued until 1968 and led to military clashes with the gendarmerie on many occasions. In a delicate situation, the shah's dictatorship installed brutal political repression in the aftermath of the political instability of the early 1960s as a response to the Kurdish movement in Iraq, which had given Kurdish activists in Iran motivation to expand their activities. Inevitably, the political activities of this group based in Iraqi Kurdistan, and their attempts to maintain the organizational structure of the party in Iranian Kurdistan involved armed excursions. However, they lacked any plan for pursuing a guerrilla war. Instead, they argued that they had to be armed to protect themselves and avoid capture. In contrast to the prevalent popular and academic assumptions that this group's primary objective was to organize the armed struggle, oral accounts and published memoirs present a more complex picture.[11] The concept of 'armed struggle' indeed constituted this generation's ideological bearings, and this is vividly reflected in Esmail Sharifzada's letter to Karim Hesami, written towards the end of the 1960s, in which he points out that 'today a revolutionary storm has engulfed the country [Iran] and people have concluded that the only way to freedom is to take up arms'.[12] However, this statement refers more to a new opportunity to expand and continue the struggle rather than a collective and planned action in that direction. Moreover, the letter did not necessarily represent the group, the main aim of which was to reorganize the party cells and maintain political opposition. As Muhammad Khezri recalls, when

> Suleiman Mu'eini and other members undertook an excursion [inside Iranian Kurdistan] [...] the purpose of their expedition was not to instigate a [armed] rebellion [...] because they had a good understanding of the situation which was unfavourable. They had to move back to Iran to avoid detention and extradition to Iran [by the Barzanis].[13]

The absence of both a collective plan and intention to embark on armed struggle is confirmed by Sa'id Kawa Kwestani who was a central figure in the Committee for the Reorganization of the DPIK in the early 1960s. Based on Kwestani's autobiography, one can infer that for many years the main aims of their group were to reorganize the party and its cells in Iranian Kurdistan and resume political activities. Therefore, armed struggle as such never appears to gain any pivotal role in the group's activism or political programme; firearms were carried merely for protection and used in self-defence.[14]

Furthermore, unlike the Iranian Fedayyan, who, believing that the small engine of the revolutionaries could stimulate the big engine of the working class or the general public, attacked a gendarmerie in Siyahkal in northern Iran in February 1971, this Kurdish group never intended to carry out any *planned* armed activity. Indeed, except for eulogizing the clashes, Kurdish texts never refer to any premeditated actions. Of course, dictatorship and the militarization of Kurdistan, in addition to the existence of other Kurdish movements in the neighbouring countries, strengthened inclination towards armed struggle as a form of resistance, as there has always been a correlation between militarization and armed struggle in modern Kurdish histories. Therefore, armed struggle was an attractive idea, but its practice was stipulated by circumstances; it was never planned as 'strategy or tactic'. As another illustration of this, when armed groups appeared more frequently in Iranian Kurdistan, Esmail Sharifzada appealed in another letter to Kurdish activists studying in universities across Tehran to join them;[15] they rejected the appeal. The group and their associates inside

Iran were aware of the obstacles to expanding their overt political activities or transforming it into an organized armed struggle. For example, the population remained merely sympathetic because the fear of arrest, torture and execution was widespread. Jeldiyan detention centre, or the 'slaughterhouse of Jeldiyan' as it was known in those years, became notorious for its brutal treatment of detained Kurdish political activists.[16] Therefore, on the one hand, rather than eluding to a plan, the evidence refers to the popularity of armed struggle especially in a new worldwide context, for example, in the wake of the Cuban Revolution and because of the Vietnam War. On the other hand, based on oral history, the complexity of this issue simultaneously defies the notion of the Kurdish opposition's intrinsic proclivity to guerrilla warfare and undermines the state's pretext of armed rebellion to suppress Kurdish political and cultural resistance in any forms. The state was especially sensitive to this situation, as it had experienced a formidable Kurdish peasant uprising in 1952–3 and had to intervene on behalf of the threatened Kurdish *agha* class; as comrades in arms, they brutally suppressed the uprising.[17]

Moreover, the political situation of the end of the 1960s increased pressure on the Kurdish activists who were based in free zones under Barzani in Iraqi Kurdistan. The amiable relationship between the Kurdish movement in Iraq and the Iranian government, which was engaged in hostility with part of the Arab world, exacerbated the situation, effectively restraining the group's activity with the effect that the Barzani movement detained and extradited some members of the group to SAVAK. Suleiman Mu'eini came to symbolize the Barzani movement's acts of detention and extradition. He was allegedly assassinated by those associated with the movement in May 1968, and his body was surrendered to Iranian authorities and publicly displayed.[18] The expansion of this group and its political activities forced the Iranian government to militarize especially the northern areas of the Kurdish region and deploy more troops to guard the border with Iraqi Kurdistan. Astonishingly, this was followed by the Iranian army's encroachment onto Iraqi Kurdistan to arrest the activists.[19] The 'Rebellion of 1968-9' took form in such circumstances rather spontaneously.[20]

At the same time, the Union of Kurdish Students in Tehran crystallized the characteristics of the Kurdish political movement of the 1960s. In fact, it was both the other pole of the group described earlier and a centre for Kurdish opposition. The Union was historically significant for two reasons: first, it reflected the reorganization of Kurdish political activities around an urbanized, educated generation; second, it embodied an intellectual transformation in a broader context of the popularity of anti-imperialist, left-wing and revolutionary ideas, leading to an explicit critique of armed struggle in favour of social revolution in the 1970s. However, the members of the Union faced political repression amid political instability in June 1963 with the effect that many of its members were detained when security forces raided Tehran University in Amirabad, while some others fled to join the group already in Iraqi Kurdistan.[21] This marked practically the end of the Union.[22] However, upon their release from prison a year or so later, many of the members resumed their political activities. According to a contemporary observer, 'this was the time when in the middle of the 1960s left-wing and socialist ideas attracted more students in Tehran and Tabriz universities' as new centres of intellectual activities.[23] For example, students' social perception was effectively shaped by Dr Amirhosain Aryanpur's sociology class at Tehran University.[24] Furthermore, the political developments, for example, the Arab-Israeli war of 1967, shaped political outlooks. By then, Marxist and socialist ideas alongside *Kurdayeti* became guiding principles for a growing population of Kurdish university students, inspiring the remnants of the Union to contemplate organizational and political actions.[25] This was especially the case in the wake of the quelling of the group, although, for example, Kurdish activists from Tehran had pondered to join them when DPIK members had begun to appear more frequently in northern regions of Iranian Kurdistan between 1968 and 1969. However, they were discouraged by internal disagreements and ultimately by the news of the rebels' capture or death.[26] The deaths of Esmail Sharifzada, Mala Awara, Mina Sham and Mu'eini brothers, Suleiman and Abdulla, terminated the rebellion. However, for the Kurds, they became legends, connected past and present and inspired future generations. The termination of the rebellion was meant to be the start of a new era for Kurdish political activism in Iran.

1968–79: The expansion of the urban, educated generation and intellectual transformations

The legacy of the political activism of the 1960s, symbolized by the rebellion, lived on, but a new era had begun around a critique of armed struggle too. The political activism of the post-1968 era is distinguished by two groups of political activists. The first group, which was still influenced by left-wing ideas, included those who were committed to rebuilding and re-organizing DPIK, and its prominent members lived in exile.[27] Inspired by the movement and with their main bases in universities, the second group committed themselves to Marxism and social revolution. In fact, with more ideological and cultural connections with the outside world, the modernization of Iran had created new possibilities for political action, this time around quite different organizational and political ideas: Marxism and the need for a communist party to prepare subjective conditions for the overthrow of capitalism and building of socialism by a (social) revolution, objective conditions of which, they believed, had become ripe.[28] Revolutions, anti-colonial struggles and progressive movements around the world enhanced the credibility of such ideas, whereas the structural transformation of Kurdish society from a landowner–peasant economy or 'feudalism' into a capitalist-worker economic system 'necessitated' new theoretical and practical approaches. While the second group of activists shared Marxist and socialist ideas with other left-wing forces such as Fedayyan, they differed from them by their explicit refutation of Fedayyans' *mash-e cheriki* or guerrilla policy. Lastly, although unlike the rest of Iran the growing modern Kurdish opposition was mainly dominated by leftist and secular ideas, 'Westernization' of Iran also had its political implications for religion in the

Sunni dominated Kurdish region. This came to be embodied in the political life of Ahmad Muftizada (see Modernization and Secularization).

Concerning political participation, as modernization and urbanization accelerated, giving form to new political and cultural desires, no means of political participation in Kurdistan was promoted. In contrast, during the 1970s, the state became increasingly personified in the shah who stopped listening to critiques or proposals while more capable individuals were sidelined in favour of uncritical acolytes, thus undermining collective efforts to modernize Iran more democratically. For example, uncritical Amir Abbas Hovaida replaced Mansour, assassinated in 1965, as prime minister, while Abdulla Entezam, the chairman of National Iranian Oil Company, 'who appreciated different opinions [and] a wise administrator [. . .] of which there were too few in Iran', was dismissed in the aftermath of June 1963 religious uprising[29] – he had advised in the presence of the shah that 'the will of people ought to be respected'.[30] Ideologically, based on historical myths, an exclusively radicalized national perception of 'Iran' was being promoted by grand gestures such as the outrageously expensive 2,500 Celebration of the Iranian monarchy in 1971. This, in turn, encouraged further linguistic purification in favour of Persian, leading to the sudden change of the calendar in the mid-1970s to reflect a historical monarchy. Thus, the cult of personality was complete, and the shah had become *saye-ye Khoda* or God's shadow on earth.[31]

As a result, nascent political participation of the Constitutional years, noted in Chapter 1, continued to regress, shaping the Kurdish society of the 1970s in which people were, to benefit from Henry Tudor's insight on another topic, 'either excluded from politics altogether or who find their participation so regulated as to be ineffective'.[32] The election of ineffective Kurdish members of *Majlis* (Iran's Parliament) exemplified precisely such a situation. This was accompanied by coercion via both constant surveillance and detentions by SAVAK and the presence of the army and gendarmerie bases in cities and the countryside, respectively.

In brief, the Kurdish opposition until 1979 included various groups whose political orientations were influenced by past events and current social changes with intellectual implications. Parallel with attempts to reorganize DPIK, a new group, the core of which came from Tehran and Tabriz universities, formed a new circle in 1968–9 which became the nucleus of the later influential Revolutionary Organization of the Toilers of Iranian Kurdistan, popularly known as Komala (Ku. organization). This was followed throughout the 1970s by new networks of political and social activists who were influenced by past events and ongoing ideological transformations. Such networks were significant both politically and historically because, in the aftermath of the 1979 February uprising, both the new DPIK and Komala emerged as the most influential *modern* political parties in Iranian Kurdistan; structurally, they were the amalgamation of such networks. For this reason, they became rapidly popular within a short time span. This was especially the case with the latter (Figures 4 and 5).

4. The Political and Cultural Consequences of Modernization   111

Figure 4 The Iranian army displays Sulaiman Muʻeini's body, 1968. Addressing Sulaiman Muʻeini, the text reads, 'this is the outcome of treason'. *Source*: Author's collection. Sulaiman Muʻeini, a well-known figure in Mahabad 1933–68, who studied in Mahabad, Tehran and Tabriz. *Source*: Author's collection.

Figure 5 Kurdish university students in the 1960s. By the 1960s, the intellectual centre of modern Kurdish opposition moved to new Iranian universities. Kurdish university students at the University of Tehran, March 1964. Esmail Sharifzada (back row, right); the poet Swara Ilkhanizada (fourth from right); and (second from right) Amir Hassanpour (1943–2017), who became a renowned professor of Kurdish studies.*Source*: Courtesy of Kurdipedia.

Cultural consequences of modernization

'Westernization' and the establishment of Persian cultural hegemony, that is, the consensual acceptance of Persian language and culture as superior to other cultures in Iran, were two significant consequences of the state-led modernization in the era of the White Revolution. While the focus is not 'Westernization', this chapter discusses how the era's cultural transformation reshaped the cultural positions of communities, in this case Persian and Kurdish, in modern times. New cultural positions were a consequence of modern education, the proliferation of the new audiovisual means of communication and an exclusive literature, all accompanied by new cultural critiques from different perspectives. An analysis of these themes is preceded by exploring the topic of cultural encounters in modern Iran, which provides both a historical context and a conceptual framework. The chapter is finalized by discussing the following themes: 'modernisation and secularisation', intellectual transformations and cultural resistance.

Persian and Kurdish modern cultural encounters

There are abundant analyses of cultural encounters taken place between in many ways fundamentally distinct cultures such as between Europeans and Native Americans or the British and Indians. However, cultural encounters *within* Iran do not conveniently fit the framework provided by such analyses and present their own challenges. A closer analogy to Persian and Kurdish cultural encounters is Ireland. Scholars of Irish historiography and cultural studies warn that a homogenizing and monolithic approach to Irish, including Northern Ireland, history and culture is misleading, and they draw attention to the misconception that 'Ireland's position was or is exactly the same as that of all Britain's African, Asian or Caribbean colonies'.[33] Therefore, Ireland is not to be seen simply as a 'colony'; indeed, it seems there is an ongoing debate about to what degree the British Empire perceived 'Irish questions as colonial'.[34] Therefore, as Stephen Howe gives a detailed account of these debates, themes of Irishness versus Englishness, language, race and culture continue to form historiographical and cultural debates.[35] However, there are many aspects of the cultural encounters between the British Empire and Ireland which distinguish this relationship from the one between Kurdish and Persian cultures in modern times. First and foremost, a colonial context formed British and Irish cultural encounters on a massive scale, followed by the issue of race, empire and nationalism, the colonialist structure of imagery. Moreover, unlike the case of the Kurds, Ireland became a state in a 'post-colonial' world, probably a former partner and/or victim of empire but undoubtedly a new partner of Europe. If the analogy is closer in terms of language, cultural nationalism and cultural hegemony, both a colonial or imperial context and the existence of an Irish state indicate more differences than similarities. Finally, it is important to avoid the widespread application of post-colonial theories to analyse, for example, Ireland history and culture or cultural encounters within a nation state such as Iran, without taking into account such entities' historical and cultural formations.[36] This is also significant for envisaging the kind of resistance to hegemony in such entities and to enable, as Bill Ashcroft rightly argues, the subaltern 'to speak *out* of otherness to speak *as* the other' by engaging with the dominant culture to contest it, to change it, to make the voice of subculture heard.[37]

Mechanisms of cultural encounters in colonial contexts are identified as conquests and direct colonization.[38] However, mechanisms of cultural encounters differ in non-colonial, multicultural contexts in which one culture assumes cultural hegemony over others. Finding themselves in a new historical context in modern Iran, the Persian and Kurdish cultures had historically lived in close geographical and cultural proximity prior to the formation of the modern Iranian nation state which institutionally and politically endorsed the Persian culture and language. This was followed by the proliferation of new audio and visual means of communication in the second half of the twentieth century, which effectively transformed (pre-modern) political–cultural authority of Persian into a cultural hegemony. While they were linguistically familial and culturally resembled one another, these two peoples' cultural practices in many ways were based on common historical and mythological origins. Therefore, this compels us to explain a situation in which a culture's more distinctive characteristics (e.g. language, custom and religion) assume superiority over its surrounding cultures with which it shares cultural resources. In our case, the Persian culture used its administrative experience and cultural prestige to assume cultural hegemony with the proliferation of both institutionalized and centralized means of communication.

The following discussion elaborates on the above claims by benefiting from Raymond Williams's theory of communication as a means for cultural formation and production. First, his idea of 'complexity of hegemony' advances the Gramscian perception of hegemony which 'is not to be understood at the level of mere opinion or mere manipulation. It is a whole body of practices and expectations; our assignments of energy, our ordinary understanding of the nature of man and of his world.'[39] Second, he highlights a 'central system of practices, meaning and values, which we can properly call dominant and effective'.[40] Additionally, crucial to this study is Williams's notion of 'residual' culture, that is, some cultural and social forms that continue to live despite the cultural hegemony of the other, and 'emergent' culture, that is, the creation of new cultural meanings, values and practices which explicitly defies the hegemonic culture.[41] This leads the study to the notions of 'residual-incorporated' and 'residual not incorporated', and 'emergent-incorporated' and 'emergent not incorporated'.[42] Based on these notions, it becomes understandable why residual Kurdish cultural forms, for example, music and clothing, are incorporated into the dominant culture but emergent cultural forms, for example, in literature and education, are suppressed by it. Therefore, to elucidate such aspects, Williams's theory of culture becomes immensely useful to understand the dynamics of Kurdish and Persian cultural encounters.

Furthermore, post-colonial theories and subaltern studies provide valuable cultural insights for evaluating cultural encounters within Iran. However, as argued throughout this chapter, Kurdish and Persian cultural encounters in modern times, in general, and in the age of visualization of media, in particular, did not take place in a *colonial* context nor did these cultures perceive each other as alien. In addition to this, the Kurds have been partners in empire-building, and later also in nation-building, though they did not reap the main benefit of such processes. Therefore, it is necessary to identify other mechanisms of establishing cultural hegemony beyond colonial conquest.

In the history of Iran, the main mechanism of cultural encounters was the exertion of political and military dominance of successive ruling dynasties of Iran on Kurdish ruling families, Emirates or principalities, which also preserved distinct cultural characteristics of their Kurdish subjects. This situation changed during the middle of the nineteenth century when the process of the modernization of state and society also meant the transformation of the Kurds into modern *aqaliat-e qaumi* (Pe. ethnic minority), a modern subaltern position. Since the expansion of the Islamic civilization in the seventh century, ruling families of Iran were comprised of dynasties with Arabic, Persian and Turkish origins until the modern Iranian nation state made the Persian community the core-ethnocultural community of modern Iran. Historically, Persian had been a lingua franca and cultural practices overlapped without categorizing people as minority or majority. There were forms of cultural domination of course, but the age was distinguished by multilingualism.

In contrast to the mechanism of conquest or the presence of the state in pre-modern times, the mechanism of *modern* cultural encounters sustained relations of domination through cultural hegemony. Simply put, this refers to a situation in which the ruling culture is incarnated in *unmanned* technical means and, as set out by Foucault, this power becomes non-corporeal, that is, it does not engage in a physical confrontation. Although the modern Iranian nation state had been promoting the Persian language and culture since its formation, the political and military prowess of the state ensured that non-Persian cultural practices were curbed or incorporated into the 'main' culture. For example, as discussed throughout the book, the Kurdish language under Reza Shah was banned and cultural practices were restricted through the coercive force of the gendarmerie. The heavy presence of the state was needed to implement the Pahlavi dress code and for the surveillance of individuals engaged in oppositional actions. The corporeal presence of the state diminished as its favoured cultural practices, for example, the dress codes for teachers in schools and civil servants became norms. In this regard, the socio-economic transformation of Iran was crucial. By the early 1940s, there was already an expanding educated urban generation, which had emerged as a result of modern education, urbanization and the expansion of the economy. However, the state still needed its heavy presence to provide political authority for the cultural practices it favoured. The state's non-corporeal presence permeated widely as modern education expanded and publications reached more people. Moreover, in the second half of the century, the state's authority was substituted for the Kurdish *agha* or the landowner class, facilitating more direct access of the state and its modernizing institutions into the rural areas. Despite being sluggish, such changes were considerable. For example, modern education was socially significant as a mode of cultural incorporation of others and its institutions, defined by Williams 'as the main agencies of the transmission of an effective dominant culture' were recognized as an effective and necessary way towards cultural homogenization in Iran[43] – literacy was achieved through Persian. However, because of its novelty and uneven expansion, modern education could not have achieved a hegemonic scale with the same speed as the new visual means of communication would later obtain. As noted in the previous chapter, in the early 1960s, 70 to 80 per cent of Iran's twenty to twenty-one million population was still illiterate, a fact disadvantageous to Persian cultural hegemony – thus inspiring the idea of the Literacy Corps. Therefore, cultural hegemony stipulated the transition from corporeal to non-corporeal cultural power, which truly took off with the proliferation of the technical and visual means of communication in the 1960s and particularly in the 1970s, creating conditions for Persian culture to achieve such an unprecedented hegemonic status. In Gramscian terms, hegemony refers to the maintenance of authority through consent or the acceptance of 'the norm' through consent rather than coercion. In this process, hegemonic ideas and practices, that is, those supported and propagated by the ruling or superior culture, become common sense or norms, while other cultures were simultaneously condemned to the margin. Raymond Williams elaborates this Gramscian perception of hegemony by applying 'a central, effective and dominant system of meanings and values which are not merely abstract but which are organized and lived'.[44] He maintains,

> That is why hegemony is not to be understood at the level of mere opinion or mere manipulation. It is a whole body of practices and expectations; our assignments of energy, our ordinary understanding of the nature of man and of his world. [. . .] It thus constitutes a sense of reality for most people in the society. A sense of absolute because experienced reality beyond which it is very difficult for most members of the society to move, in most areas of their lives.[45]

Therefore, the era of the White Revolution becomes culturally significant for its mediatization of culture and creating the conditions to constitute a 'reality' sensed by all. Crucially, this process simultaneously reproduces conditions for cultural resistance to defy the hegemonic culture. However, considering Williams, this is a complex process for two reasons. First, the hegemonic culture develops capacities to tolerate and incorporate difference and opposition. Nevertheless, once cultural hegemony is established coercion does not disappear but remains to be applied when the dominant system is *challenged* by an alternative. Until then, one can defy dominant ideas but still be incorporated in the dominant system, which, as noted earlier, does not amount to mere ideas but organized meanings and values. Moreover, some modes of opposition become incorporated so that 'whatever the degree of internal conflicts and internal variations, they do not go in practice beyond the central effective and dominant definitions'.[46] This was the case with the Kurdish university students and academics in the 1960s and 1970s whose literary writings, valuable as they were, did not challenge the boundaries of the dominant culture (see Cultural critiques and the new communicative phenomena). This was one reason why the hegemonic culture tolerated such practices. Second, different views of the world may be expressed while a hegemonic perception, which is cultivated through modern education and ostensibly disseminates objective knowledge, continues to nurture those who have expressed doubt. This has a bearing on internal variations in reaction to events and their impact on one's understanding of the world. For example, as post-colonial studies reveal, individuals may criticize the harsh conditions of colonization but continue to hold a racial conception of the world, relying on a binary opposition of primitive versus developed to explain historical phenomena. Again, while an argument for the superiority of the Medes over the Achaemenes in ancient Iran is permitted, the representation of the Medes as the origin of a 'Kurdish nation' by Kurdish national historiography will evoke a fierce reaction from the dominant culture. 'Kurdistan Province', though as an act of re-division of the Kurdish region in the west of Iran is formed and tolerated by the modern state as an act of sustaining the perception of the Kurds as an inextricable component of Iran and Iranian identity. However, the idea of 'Kurdistan' as an independent entity challenges the effective dominant system. This provokes coercion, explaining the continuous corporeal presence of the state. Kurdish cultural practices during the Pahlavi era were tolerated to the extent that they did not pose any threat to what was deemed the *official*, which safeguarded 'national unity'. So long as these variations are incorporated, they pose no danger to the dominant system. Ultimately, 'the dominant culture itself changes, not in central formation, but in many of its articulated features.'[47] In fact, in modern society, it always needs to change to remain dominant. This situation changes when different views began to defy the effective dominant culture and mutate into an alternative.

Finally, in the specific historical and social contexts of this era, especially throughout the 1970s, the institutionalization and management of new means of communication, especially television, cinema and radio, took place in a two-pronged process. First, Iranian cultures increasingly became targets of 'Westernization' and new ideas, though there were different cultural reactions. For example, unlike the centre, nativism as a movement for cultural purity and a reaction to 'Westernization' did not become very relevant to the Kurds for various religious, ethnic, historical and political reasons. The second process pertains not only to the way that 'Westernization' was mediated by the Persian cultural medium and hence restricted understanding because of linguistic barriers but also to the way that new means of communication proved to be effective tools to serve homogenization of culture based on *Persian* culture. This resulted simultaneously in the institutionalization of the Persian language and culture as *the* norm, 'mainstream' or 'official' (*rasmi*), and in the marginalization of Kurdish culture, which was defined as *mahalli* (Pe. local). Nativism's and others' cultural criticism of *hojum-e farhangi-ye Gharb* (the cultural onslaught of the West) led to a more conscious emphasis on the 'local' languages and culture in Iran to preserve Iranian culture. This changed the position of Persian from 'the national language of Iran', a perception promoted after the First World War and during the reign of Reza Shah, into the *official* language of Iran. Both the terms 'local' and 'official', the latter increasingly since the 1940s, had been in use; however, the new position of Persian was achieved by a process which degraded other languages and groups into subcultures and engrained a superior 'official' culture and inferior 'local' cultures. On the other hand, the emergence and proliferation of the new *visual* means of communication, for example, television and cinema, in addition to the existing audio means of communication, were crucial cultural developments for both the 'Westernization' of culture and the establishment of Persian cultural hegemony. As Pierre Bourdieu argues, culture as a symbolic system or structure, that is, instruments of knowledge and communication can exercise a structuring or symbolic power needed to construct reality, relies on corresponding social conditions and relations of power to produce and perpetuate meanings that serve indirectly or directly the interest of the dominant groups or classes.[48] From this perspective, the era of the White Revolution profoundly impacted the existing social conditions and relations of power, the result of which was, in Gramscian sense, the cultural hegemony of the Persian language and culture over non-Persian-speaking peoples in Iran. As such, the dominant culture contributed to the legitimation of the established order by establishing distinctions (hierarchies) and legitimating these distinctions. The dominant culture produces this ideological effect by concealing the function of division beneath the function of communication: the culture which unifies (the medium of communication) is also the culture which separates (the instrument of distinction) and which legitimates distinctions by forcing all other cultures (designated as sub-cultures) to define themselves by their distance from the dominant culture.[49]

At the same time, as the symbolic system presents itself as a classification system that generates meaning through binary oppositions, the enduring bipolarity of Persian as *mainstream* or *official* and other cultures within Iran as *local* not only distinguishes the era in question.[50] As the product of the era, this mainstream–local binary concealed both the homogenizing nature of this enterprise and its marginalizing effect on other cultures. As an illustration of this, the new monopolized means of communication realized cultural consent by making Persian the normal medium of communication, the normal educational means for social and economic success, and the normal way of achieving, in Bourdieu's terms, various forms of cultural capital and intellectual prosperity for individuals.[51] All this took place to the detriment of other cultures in Iran. Indeed, it is this duality that continues to characterize modern Iran.

Cultural critiques and the new communicative phenomena

Both in perception and cultural and economic practices, the state's nationalism throughout the era of the White Revolution radicalized towards creating its perceived monolithic Iranian civilization. Technical modernization exposed Iranians to a Westernized way of life and world view, which enjoyed a worldwide cultural superiority. However, within Persian culture, the state's Westernizing modernization evoked ideological reactions from an increasingly politicized Islam, which claimed to defend religion and cultural purity, and from socialist ideology, which criticized social inequality. Cultural critics were not necessarily concerned with cultural homogenization even when their critiques of modernization and capitalism expanded to include other ethnic communities. Nevertheless, exemplified by the works of many prominent critics and writers, the critiques included an emphasis on 'local' cultures, from a nativist perspective, also to preserve cultural purity and, from a socialist world view, mainly to achieve more cultural rights for the non-Persian communities.

Reza Barahani's *Tarikh-e Mozakkar* (Pe. Masculine History) written towards the end of the 1960s, perfectly reflects the existence of the widespread literary discussions of the time around the positions of Persian and other languages in Iran. Although he mainly attempted to raise cultural awareness and his stance on 'Westernization' was quite different, for example, from that of Ale Ahmad, Barahani drew attention to 'the relationship between Persian language and local languages' because the latter, according to him, also formed part of Iranian identity.[52] The renowned cultural critic claimed that 'the official language of Iran is Persian, which is right and justified. If someone denies this, you can have him hanged. But you cannot deny the local languages of Azerbaijan, Kurdistan, Gilan, and Mazandaran.'[53] Barahani was mainly concerned with a relentless 'Westernization' of culture in general, which also tended to harm local music and languages. He made a mockery of the education system by saying that 'from the very first moment the pupil wants to become an American'.[54] Discussing non-Persian-speaking students, he then reminds his readers that 'this [Persian] language which is compulsory is not the pupil's mother tongue language but an additional language, an official and state language, which must be learnt by the pupil'.[55] Criticism of the inferior position of 'local' languages, that is, mother tongues, surfaced in the works of other intellectuals and writers. For example, Jalal Ale Ahmad, a renowned Iranian writer who popularized the concept of 'Westoxication', was also concerned with the state's homogenizing language policies which, according to him, had no regard for local languages.[56]

During the decades in question, Samad Behrangi (1939-67), famous for his children's literature, 'played a role in giving a voice to Azeris. Dedicated to preserving Azeri culture, he struggled with Pahlavi authorities to publish poems and tales translated from Azeri to Persian.'[57] In this sense, Behrangi's dedication to Azari culture is another example of the literature's emphasis on the 'local' cultures, revealing how the terms 'local' and 'official' began to be increasingly used in the context of the intensifying modernization. However, representing socialist literature, the output of Behrangi did not surpass the duality of official and local and instead remained confined to the boundaries of class and class disparity.[58] Language was not discussed in relation to the cultural transformation Iran was experiencing at the time; for Behrangi language only reflected reality: 'language is connected to reality (*Nezam-e hastiy* [Pe. the order of existence]) through ideas.'[59] Therefore, in the age of grand narratives, including the socialist outlook with the singularity of 'class' as the primary conceptual and organizational category, Behrangi was not attracted to nativism or the issue of cultural purity but was concerned with criticizing social injustice through his pedagogical literature. The emphasis on the 'local' cultures, however, did not lead to a critic of the new hegemonic position of Persian in relation to other cultures and languages within Iran.

The conspicuous absence of studies on cultural encounters *within* Iran was another aspect of the contemporary literary journals such as those published by various universities' faculties of literature between 1960 and 1979. For example, a glance at the journal of the University of Tehran's Faculty of Literature, *Nashriye-ye Daneshkade-ye Adabiyat-e Tehran*, and those of Tabriz and Mashhad, reveals two prevalent trends of the time. First, Iranian (culture and language) and Persian are used interchangeably with the effect that the latter is consistently confirmed as Iran's core linguistic and cultural element around which other Iranian cultures orbit. In a speech on the preservation of the Persian language in the summer of 1959, Saʿid Nafisi (1895-1966), an internationally renowned literary figure for his immense contribution to Persian literature and a prolific writer, stressed how language (in this case Persian) was the most important tool for any modern nation, urging everyone to regard its 'preservation and expansion as their most important national duty'.[60] The second trend bears on the absence of 'Kurdish literature' (and other non-Persian works of literature) as a field of study or as a literary subject, a trend vividly represented by contemporary literary journals. For instance, throughout the 1960s and 1970s, Tehran University's journal discussed the Kurdish language to a very limited extent, mostly in conjunction with *gouyesh-haye Irani* (Pe. Iranian dialects).[61] While researchers were willing to warn against the threat of the extinction of the dialects, they did not forget to emphasize, for example, that 'among Iranian languages, the Persian language has a sublime status (*maqam-e arjomand*). This great language represents a brilliant civilisation and in its own right is unique in the world.'[62]

However, culture as a source of domination also shapes the cultural resistance of the unprivileged. The systematic promotion of Persian's cultural supremacy was paralleled by the promotion of Kurdish literature by the notable contribution of several Kurdish students or scholars of Kurdish literature, for example, Qadir Fattahi Qazi, 'Ubeidulla Ayyubiyan and 'Abdulhamid Huseini. This group admirably continued to write interesting articles on Kurdish folklore, epics, poetry and culture for Tabriz University's Faculty of Literature during the period. Ayyubiyan provided across many issues of the journal a translated version of Ahmad Khani's *Mam u Zin* (Mam and Zin), classifying it as *chryka* or, according to him, an epic story.[63] This remained, however, an example of residual, tolerated culture, and not emergent culture, because the *Mam u Zin* of the mid-seventeenth century is written in Kurdish and distinguishes the Kurds as a people with a distinct history and language. This means that Khani's story was, to borrow from Berger, nationally inflicted, which increasingly became a characteristic of early modern history-writing.[64] Other topics discussed by articles included a Kurdish calendar, which was presented in conjunction with, and not in contrast to, an Iranian calendar (see Figure 6).[65] Along with the work of several other contributors, this

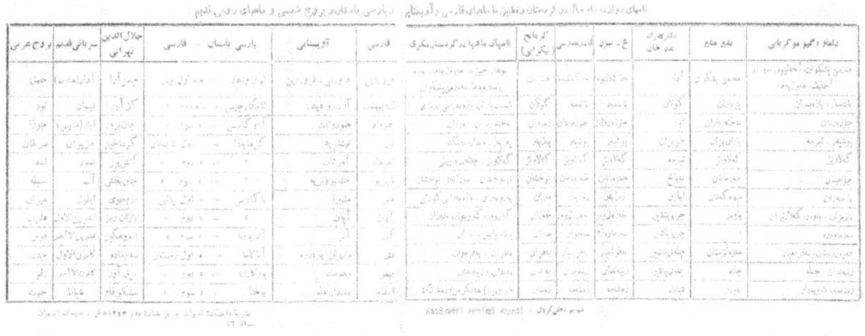

Figure 6 'Ubeidulla Ayyubiyan's Kurdish Calendar. In this calendar, Ayyubiyan presents the names of the months in ancient languages of Avesta, ancient Persian, Syriac, Arabic and modern Kurdish and Persian. Different Kurdish names of the months in this calendar are proposed by six Kurdish authors of whom E. Bizhan's proposed names (the forth column from the right) have become established Kurdish (Sorani) names of the months. *Source*: The Journal of Tabriz University's Faculty of Literature, No. 2, 1964.

group's contribution to such literary journals continued throughout the 1970s. Yet however concerted their efforts were to draw literary attention to Kurdish literature and culture, their works remained limited in scope and reach, lacked institutional support and, thematically, did not transcend an aesthetic analysis of Kurdish literature; they were residual and mostly introductions to Kurdish literature.[66]

Meanwhile, the efforts of the literary journals of the era of the White Revolution to promote Persian intensified. In addition to *Sokhan* (Pe. Speech), which claimed to be a literary, scientific and social monthly journal, *Rahnemay-e Ketab* (Pe. Book Guide) was a monthly journal of language and literature, which published research on Iranology and included book review, run by prominent literary figures such as Iraj Afshar. In addition to various literary and intellectual journals, a state-sponsored or 'royalist' trend also existed, which promoted the modern Iranian nation and state. This trend was represented, for example, by the monthly journal of *Gowhar* (Pe. Essence) dedicated to the literature, art, history and culture of Iran, published by *Bonyad-e Nikukariy* (Pe. The Centre for Charity) since winter 1973; and *Barresihay-e Tarikhi* (Pe. Historical Analyses), published interestingly by the army's higher command, *Setad-e Bozorg Arteshdaran*, since the summer of 1966. Therefore, developing a core cultural and linguistic position counter to other cultures in Iran, Persian literature was institutionally elevated. This was achieved not only through modern, including higher, education but also with the support of the new means of communication. Prior to the foundation of radio broadcasting, Nafisi informed others in September 1939 that

> [I] had been assigned by the Commission of Radio to collect articles on the history and geography of Iran. [. . .] Because radio was one of the means to disseminate and propagate language and culture and an important factor in introducing Persian literature [. . .] since its inception, I have regarded radio as a target of [my] scientific and cultural services.[67]

Moreover, in a couple of years, Nafisi started his *Az Yaddashtha-ye Yek Ostad* (Pe. Notes from a Master) radio programme and then contributed to another programme called *Marzha-ye Danesh* (Pe. the Boundaries of Knowledge).

Despite differences, a common characteristic of these critiques and publications was their emphasis on the significance of the Persian language and 'Iranian' (Persian) culture in conspicuous exclusion of studies of other languages and cultures in modern Iran. Their literary attitudes were at best sympathetic but also culturally incorporative; that is, Kurdish literature was allowed to be practised to the extent that it did not challenge the status of Persian literature. There were no rigid literary or institutional instructions to prevent the practice of Kurdish literature but rather boundaries shaped and reshaped by hegemony. Moreover, Persian literature continued to be more widespread and incorporative, producing knowledge to represent Persian's national and official status, whereas Kurdish literature was devoid of such a strategy and platform. Subsequently what is Kurdish was represented by an exclusive literature, revealing that the scope of the practice of Kurdish literature remained within the boundaries of hegemonic culture, on the one hand, and was determined consensually rather than coercively, on the other, because Persian was increasingly perceived as superior, thereby reducing other kinds of literature to the less literary statuses of *mahalli* or 'local' and of *guyesh* or 'dialect'. Based on the contents of various journals published by Iranian universities' faculties of literature, Kurdish literature found itself effectively in the shadow of Persian literature, whereas sympathetic attitudes towards Kurdish literature were either promotive or conservative – 'Kurdish literature' was a phrase used mainly by the Kurdish students of literature and not by, for example, those in charge of the influential literary journals or responsible for the educational curriculum. The literature, including the literary journals published by the universities, considered comparative or cross-cultural analysis outside the purview of their programmes and publications. In this context, an Iranian national narrative, which continued to use 'Iranian' and 'Persian' interchangeably, shaped the Persian literary giants' literary works.[68] Therefore, the hegemony of Persian culture created a condition where, to borrow from Raymond Williams, 'residual' (Kurdish) cultural forms faced massive barriers to become 'emergent', that is, to create new forms to challenge that which was accepted as the norm.[69]

However, the second Pahlavi era was distinguished for modern education and the mediatization of culture which, along with other aspects of change and transformation, facilitated Kurdish cultural resistance on many levels (see Cultural resistance). Subsequently, despite the residual or emergent qualities of different literary and cultural endeavours, resistance was also a significant factor for the increasing stress on 'local' languages and cultures by the Iranian cultural critics of the 1960s and 1970s. On the other hand, regarding emergent cultural production, state oppression was not the only or probably the most important barrier anymore. Massive barriers were invisible cultural perceptions, informed by the idea of the superiority of Persian culture which protected it against counterhegemonic attempts. As a hegemonic culture, however, it was not regarded as alien but a familiar/partner culture in relation to which, to borrow from Homi K. Bhabha, 'in-between' spaces had continued to produce hybridity and blur cultural boundaries for centuries;[70] indeed, whenever the two met 'things did not fall apart', as it was the case, Chinua Achebe's *Things Fall Apart* so forcefully reminds us, between Europe and Africa. In the context of intensified cultural transformation, the new means of communication significantly changed this situation in multicultural Iran in favour of one culture.

The proliferation of the audio and visual means of communication

The era is also distinguished for the proliferation of the audio and visual means of communication which, as a characteristic of modern culture, transformed cultural encounters in modern Iran. The new means of communication, especially television and cinema, were a result of the intensification of modernization. In this respect, John Thompson's analysis of the phenomenon provides great methodological insights. According to Thompson, new means of mass communication serve to 'reorganise and reconstitute social interaction', and this is precisely the significance of the deployment of technical media.⁷¹ He explains it as a site for the operation of ideology in modern societies and defines 'ideological phenomena as meaningful symbolic forms in so far as they serve [. . .] to establish and sustain relations of domination'.⁷² However, while this approach rightly invites extensive studies on the relation between ideology and mass communication in Kurdish-Iranian society, I focus on the way the framework for social interaction was transformed, for example, when radio and then especially television and cinema were institutionalized and spread in Iran in the second half of the twentieth century. Furthermore, Thompson formulates his thesis of 'the mediasation of culture' in contrast to the theses of secularization and rationalization of social life because, according to him, it is the mediasation of culture 'which provides the principal frame of reference' to analyse ideology in modern societies.⁷³ The proliferation of new means of communication involves the transformation of individuals' social interaction, their perceptions of the world and the reorganization of the relationship between the state and society. Benefiting from new means of communication, the era of the White Revolution transformed cultural encounters of Iranians with the outside world but just as crucially it transformed cultural encounters between various culturally distinct communities within Iran, resulting in the establishment of Persian cultural hegemony. This thesis of cultural encounters in multicultural Iran is based on the establishment of the cultural hegemony of one community over many other communities that shared historical interactions and geographical proximity. It addresses cultural encounters which are not necessarily colonial or imperial. Cultural critics of colonialism or 'Westernization' of culture, for example, in Iran during the White Revolution, shed light on cultural encounters in direct or indirect colonial contexts where 'cultural/historical/racial difference' is fixed by the discourse of colonialism;⁷⁴ or where 'nativism' is revoked in the wake of the cultural onslaught of the alien.⁷⁵ Simultaneously, cultural critics have been concerned with the role of culture in the formation of the modern nation.⁷⁶ That said, the question of cultural encounters in the Middle East between *related* cultures has been largely overlooked by cultural and post-colonial studies which nevertheless provide a repository for a variety of critical practices which are methodologically significant for a study of cultural encounters in the nation state of Iran.⁷⁷ Studies on themes such as representation, power and knowledge, cultural production, resistance and diaspora provide theoretical foundations for cultural studies in Iran because there are similarities between colonial and non-colonial contexts, for example, in forms of control, legitimizing ideologies or forms of resistance (see Table 11).⁷⁸ However, such a study requires to go beyond, for example, post-colonial studies and focus on a multicultural, non-colonial context to present more productive analyses of cultural encounters of interrelated cultures within a nation state in the age of visual media and avoid clichés. A close analogy to Kurdish and Persian cultural encounter is perhaps that between Ireland and the British Empire. However, an assessment of this example highlights more differences than similarities with the nature of cultural encounters within Iran.

In addition to the state's political authority and modern education, the new means of communication constituted the mechanisms needed to ensure

Table 11 Cultural Encounters in Colonial and Nation State Contexts: Similarities and Differences

A colonial context		A multicultural, nation state context (Iran)
Conquest	Mechanisms of (modern) cultural encounters	Modern education
Maintaining the colonizer's presence		Written modes of communication
		Audio and visual means of communication
		Physical presence of the state
Economic (natural resources, market, free labour)	Motivation	Political: the integrity of the state
		National: safeguarding the superiority of the core-ethnocultural group
Maintaining the empire's international and regional positions		Territorial
Institutional and administrative control	Forms of control	Institutional and administrative control
Exclusion		Exclusion
Coercion		Coercion
Exploitation (Congo; the New World)		Militarization
Militarization		Psychological pressure, for example, by linking political demands to foreign desires
The Civilizing Mission	Legitimizing ideologies	Discourses of national unity and territorial integrity
Rejuvenation of stagnant cultures		
Neo-colonialism		Safeguarding the monarchy/Islam
		Reading others into the national
		Mainstream versus local (culture)
Racial superiority	Elements of cultural superiority	Persian linguistic and literary superiority
Scientific superiority		Monarchical and imperial pedigree
Intellectual/philosophical superiority		Political centralization
Technological superiority		Monopolization of education and new means of communication
		Monopolization of the idea of 'nation', for example, the idea of 'Iran', to serve the core-ethnocultural community
		Marginalization of other cultures
		Restricting others' access to cultural capital
Resistance to imperialism as culturally and 'racially' an alien force	Forms of resistance	Resistance to an exclusive state
Nationalism		Nationalism
Non-violent/non-cooperation resistance		Armed struggle
		Cross-ethnic revolutionary activism
War of independence		Literary resistance
International alliance		The practice and production of culture, for example, music
Literary resistance		
The practice of culture		
Industrialization to maximize economic exploitation and facilitate effective colonial administration (e.g. railway; factories)	Economic attitudes	Economic deprivation to prevent economic empowerment (e.g. Iranian Kurdistan, 1921–present)
Destruction of the native economy (e.g. spinning and weaving in India)		Unequal modernization and the absence of planned, regional development programmes
Consumerism		Unequal distribution of cultural capital, hindering cultural production

Table 11 (Continued)

A colonial context		A multicultural, nation state context (Iran)
Post-colonial state Indirect colonization (neo-colonialism) through economic, cultural and political means Maintaining scientific and technological superiorities Imposed colonial relationships transform into new conditions such as neo-coloniality or dependency	Post-colonial conditions/ globalization-localization	Increased demands for structural, educational and administrative reforms (e.g. today's Iran) and for cultural rights Local autonomy State-led modernization simultaneously strengthens the historical, socio-economic and cultural bonds and creates new ones between culturally distinct societies

Persian cultural hegemony. In an age of widespread illiteracy, the introduction of radio and, crucially, the *visualization* of broadcasting added a different dimension to culture in general and modern cultural encounters in particular. A significant effect of this process was the transformation of the framework for social interaction. Giving primacy to these modes of communication does not imply that the written modes such as the journals published during the era were insignificant. However, the written mode cannot be placed in a simplified cause and effect relationship with the establishment of the cultural hegemony of Persian because, first and foremost, they reflected a hegemonic process of which they were crucial parts. In contrast, audio and visual media, although, according to Williams, described misleadingly as 'mass' communication, enabled the 'transmission [of cultural products] to *individual* homes',[79] thus obviating the need for both the corporeal presence of the producer and the literacy skills of the receiver as a prerequisite.

Historically, the outbreak of the Second World War coincided with an increase in both radio sets and radio broadcasting in Iran. In addition to audio and written modes, visual modes of communication such as television and cinema, and the number of consumers, had considerably increased by the middle of the 1970s. In 1973 there were 424 cinemas in Iranian urban centres.[80] According to Amanat, '*filmfarsi* competed with foreign imports, both Hollywood and Indian productions, in offering entertainment and moral messages customized for Iranian popular tastes'.[81] In 1965 more than two million viewers saw *Ganj-e Qarun* (Qarun's treasure) movie.[82] Prior to this, the most important development had been the addition of radio in 1935 to the existing oral and written modes of communication. As discussed in the previous chapters, linguistic homogenization had effectively restrained publications in Kurdish. However, pervasive illiteracy across Iran meant that only a limited number of people could benefit from the written modes. Therefore, radio compensated not only for this deficiency but also connected the individual to the outside world, and the radio set became a luxury in both urban and rural areas. However, modernization sustained the technological chasm between the two areas in the Kurdish region with the effect that most of the rural population remained effectively deprived of not only television, cinema and telephone but also written modes of communication, even into the 1970s.

In 1977, according to Jahangir Amuzegar, a contemporary economist,

> Radio Iran covers 85 per cent of the population [and] Recent technological breakthroughs in transistorizing communications devices have been directly instrumental in bringing radio to most remote towns and villages. There are now more than three million receivers in the country, serving an audience of about 29 million.[83]

Amuzegar highlights as a positive development the key cultural role of radio when its use achieved such an unprecedented scale:

> As a result of the widespread popularity of radio in Iran, it has come to be increasingly utilized for public education. [. . .] More important, it has played a key role in preserving and promoting traditional Iranian music and culture. In the meantime, by using Western programs, it has also been instrumental in funnelling *Western knowhow* and technology to Iranian society.[84]

Indeed, the role of radio in public education was seminal. For example, according to contemporary observers, in the early 1960s, 'all available radio broadcasting was instrumental in promoting public knowledge on matters concerning, for example, agriculture, animal husbandry, and hygiene'.[85]

Radio broadcasting included Kurdish radio stations, for example, Radio Sanandaj, which had been founded in the early 1960s, culminating in the foundation of Radio Kermanshah which engaged with Kurdish poetry, music and theatre.[86] According to another account, with a critical view of Westernization, 'between 1335 and 1350 [1956 and 1971], Radio Sanandaj functioned satisfactorily until the quality of its programmes began to decline because of widespread decadence across Iran'.[87] Although the latter account engages with 'decadence' to undermine the modernization efforts, retrospectively it highlights the religious criticism of modernization.

Kurdish radio programmes were the outcomes of two concurrent processes: first, Kurdish cultural activists' continuous endeavours to benefit from the new means of communication; second, the state's policy to exploit such means to maintain its authority. Whatever the aim of the state, new means of communication, such as radio, satisfied cultural needs to some extent and encouraged poets and writers to benefit.[88] As an illustration of this, the aim of Radio Kurdish Kermanshah, which had taken over Radio Tehran's Kurdish programme,

> was [to promote the Kurdish movement in] Iraqi Kurdistan [in the 1960s] because of the ongoing conflict between Iran and Iraq. However, the literary individuals, who were employed [to run the programme], aimed at promoting Kurdish culture and language instead. The poet, Swara Ilkhanizada was an

example. Teahouses in Kurdish cities were packed with people who had come to listen to the radio.[89]

The revolutionizing effect of the emergence and the expansion of visual transmitting technology should not undermine the role radio played as an audio means of communication before and after the emergence of the visual means of communications for two reasons. First, when expanded, radio also revolutionized communication in a society that was characterized by widespread illiteracy and a predominantly rural population. Before the introduction of radio, itinerant literary figures like Qane', encountered in Chapter 1, travelled and spread knowledge eliciting their recipients' responses in many ways. For example, more interested in oral and written skills, people became more aware of the world, presumably affecting their social interaction.[90] Second, the availability of Kurdish broadcasting in neighbouring Iraq naturally attracted attention from Iranian Kurds partly for their limited knowledge of Persian and partly as they looked elsewhere for cultural resources. This enhanced the Kurds' interest in *Kurdish* culture and their desire for news about the Kurdish movement in that country too. The relatively free practice of the Kurdish language in modern Iraq, allowed for political reasons, discussed in Chapter 1, and probably the desires of successive Iraqi governments to appeal to Iranian Kurds, made Radio Kurdish Baghdad very popular. According to several oral history accounts, Radio Baghdad broadcast the works of prominent poets such as Goran, and this had cultural impacts on the listeners, who also reacted to broadcasts of political writings, news from Vietnam, China and Cuba, and even to obituaries. An example of this was (Radio Baghdad's) commemoration of Che Guevara after he had been captured and then executed (in Bolivia) in 1967.[91]

Moreover, using Kurdish as a political tool in the tension between Iran and the Arab world, Radio Cairo also broadcast in Kurdish memorably the song *Azhdahak* along with other Kurdish songs by the famous Kurdish singer, Salih Dilan.[92] Written modes too fell victim to this tension. In retaliation, the Iranian government founded the *Kurdistan* newspaper (1959–63) in Tehran, targeting Kurds in Iraq, which mirrored regional clashes of interest.[93] However, Kurdish literary activists used the paper to promote Kurdish culture by publishing Kurdish poems and articles, in the same way, for example, that Amir Hassanpour, the future professor of Kurdish language and history, participated in Swara Ilkhanizada's regular series *Tapo w Boomalell* (The shadow and the misty land) on Tehran Kurdish Radio.[94] Simultaneously, Radio Kurdish Kermanshah increased interest in Kurdish literature, for example, through *Karwan-i She'r w Musiqa* (Ku. the Caravan of Poetry and Music), a programme broadcast at the end of the 1960s.[95]

Therefore, although indirectly promoted by the state, radio broadcasting in Kurdish in Iran played a crucial role in advancing *Kurdayeti*. Individuals began to interact, albeit in one-way communication, regardless of time and space. Although the implications of this new form of interaction were manifold, radio primarily transformed the recipients' perceptions of the world. Furthermore, seasonal workers brought radio sets back connecting the village to the outside world by increasing the availability of technology.[96] The state utilized radio to exert political influence and pursue its homogenizing policies. However, this elicited cultural resistance to preserve Kurdish culture and language and thus radio promoted Kurdish identity, too.

Television and cinema

Television stations were first established in Iran as private ventures. The Iranian government granted concessions to private companies which established the first television broadcasting systems in Tehran in 1958 and Abadan in 1960. State-owned organizations followed suit, leading to the centralization of television broadcasting by the early 1970s:[97]

> In 1966 the state owned National Iranian TV was inaugurated. Later on, the government purchased the two private stations [. . .] and established the Iran National Iranian Radio Organization, an independent agency to the government. In 1971 the two independent radio and television organizations were merged into one administrative unit called the National Iranian Radio Television Organization (NIRT), to speed up and facilitate balanced expansion of the mass communications networks in the country.[98]

The number of major television production and transmission centres increased to fifteen by 1976. Of these, two were stationed in Tehran and the rest were stationed in provincial centres or cities, including one in each of the predominantly or partly Kurdish cities of Sanandaj, Mahabad and Kermanshah.[99] These three stations proved to be more imitative than original because they had limited hours and programmes in local languages, and their programmes were no match for those which were broadcast by the main stations in Tehran.[100] NIRT had impressive coverage for its three main programmes of Nationwide, Second Programme and International by 1976, as Amuzegar rightly predicted:

> At the end of 1976 the International Program broadcast eight hours per day. The Nationwide program covered 10 per cent [of the population]. Late in 1976, also, color television broadcast was introduced on regular channels. By the end of the Fifth Plan [in 1978], the Nationwide Program will cover 80 per cent of the population, and the Second Program will reach 50 per cent of the people.[101]

Television programmes quickly became popular. They mainly consisted of 'Western classical music, biographies of important personalities and popular American and British series dubbed in Persian, as well as several indigenous series'.[102] At the same time, a new industry evolved and expanded the market for television sets. 'The estimated number of television receivers in March 1976 was over 1,000,000 of which half a million sets were in Tehran.'[103] Television revolutionized social interactions differently from radio, consuming messages and their content visually and more profoundly. As scholars have noted, television replaced the traditional (Persian) *naqqal* or (Kurdish) *bait-bezh* (storyteller) of teahouses.[104] In the Kurdish region radio had already replaced *bait-bezh* and, according to Amir Hassanpour, threatened Kurdish folklore more widely.¹⁰⁵ According to a survey conducted in 1974, the most popular programmes were either foreign series or, what some would call, 'Westernised' local series.¹⁰⁶ 'Westernised' was a vague term that was used to describe films and television series the content of which created tensions with religious or nativist views, but also engaged the population with new ideas. By 1979 more people acquired TV, and it became very influential in 'implementing the state's cultural policy [of Westernization]'.¹⁰⁷ Even though it was the capital and other urban centres which primarily benefited from the availability of television, and regardless of their limited availability per household, television exerted a great psychological effect on individuals' minds. Unmatched by any other means of communication in terms of the speed and range of impact, television reoriented social focus and made people regulate their social lives around the new programmes or series.

Indeed, because of the novelty of television, its visual effectiveness and the state's centralization of radio and television broadcasting, powerful narratives shaped perceptions, determined cultural practices and blocked other narratives from forming and emerging. For example, while favourable images of the United States and its history were (re)produced in many ways, including through television series and movies, no critical knowledge of that country's formation or the lives of its indigenous and black population were provided. Instead, *sorkh-pust*s (Pe. 'redskins'), a new term to describe Native Americans, was juxtaposed with stereotypical cowboys. As a result, an inferior image of the former, against a progressive image of the latter, was institutionalized. As Barahani observed at the time, 'America has managed to project such an [inferior] image of the natives that it encouraged the natives to support America and oppose themselves'.¹⁰⁸ Similarly, movies telling the stories of Europe's colonization of Africa and India depicted the conquerors as the missionaries of civilization in the 'remote' places of the world, where the natives presumably struggled to come to terms with the new age. Indeed, the greatest success of such movies took place in the colonized world or rapidly Westernizing non-Western countries.¹⁰⁹ The crucial aspect of this production of knowledge was the link between culture and power, which produced narratives to maintain the cultural superiority of the powerful by confirming that superiority.¹¹⁰ Television had the primary role in the 'Westernisation' of Iranian culture(s) through, at the same time, undermining critical reading of the world and shunning worldwide intellectual debates.

Meanwhile, Iran was rapidly acquiring greater intellectual and literary capacities in relevant spheres because of ongoing literary and intellectual transformations. In addition to journals, translation of foreign novels increased, as did the number of new male and female writers.¹¹¹ This was matched by an increase in public interest in reading. A significant embodiment of this period was the formation of *Kanun-e Nevisandegan-e Iran* (Centre for Iranian Writers) in 1968, which was suppressed after only two years.¹¹² As Hassan ʿAbedini's study of story-writing in Iran reveals, this literary transformation 'was a result of social transformation [and] the emergence of intellectual groups amid the obstruction of political and social activities';[113] following a process since the coup of 1953, Iran had eventually become an outright dictatorship by 1970.[114] Becoming more prominent intellectual trends, nativism and Marxism reflected the socio-economic, political and cultural aspects of modernization in a context in which the new means of communication continued to reshape cultural encounters. Nativism was a diverse intellectual trend that advocated a return to 'cultural purity'. Literary works, with different conclusions and which remained either unpublished or suppressed by the state, vigorously criticized the 'Westernisation' of culture. For instance, Barahani's *Tarikh-e Mozakkar* to a great extent registered the intensity of 'Westernisation' in urban centres, along with its effects on various layers of the population.[115] Likewise, though coming to more radical conclusions, Jalal Ale Ahmad's *Gharbzadegi* (Pe. Westoxication) could only be written in a climate of intensive 'Westernization' that Iran had begun to experience especially since 1960. These works, especially the latter, had their origins in the works of some other intellectuals such as Fakhreddin Shademan (1907–67) and Ahmad Fardid (1904–94) who is believed to have invented the term *gharbzadegi* and reflected a growing form of reactionary nativism to safeguard 'cultural purity'. While Shademan and Fardid had formulated its historical and philosophical foundations, it was due to Ale Ahmad's work, as Mehrzad Boroujerdi argues, that the concept became a discourse to oppose the West's cultural onslaught.[116] According to Dariush Ashuri, a well-known literary critique, 'we were preoccupied with this discourse [of Westernization] [. . .] and obsessed with the search for the lost East'.[117] Moreover, in the sphere of more explicit political opposition with a violent undertone, Ali Shari'ati, an ideologue of the Islamic Revolution, symbolized the return to cultural roots through more explicit political opposition. Alternatively, a secular, left-wing discourse had been forming by other literary groups, including those publishing literary journals and members of the Centre for Iranian Writers who defied the shah's dictatorship and preserved a kind of Iranian 'Enlightenment thought'.[118] Additionally, social and political activists attempted to interpret social change, dictatorship and advancing capitalist imperialism by social theories dominated by Marxism. Indeed, while counter-narratives' access to new means of communication was regularly blocked, publishers circumvented censorship. Therefore, book publication increased, while other modes of communication, for example, cassette, emerged. It was no coincidence that the 1979 Revolution was also characterized by an explosion of book publishing, 'unprecedented in the history of Iran, around one hundred million books were published in 1979'.[119]

Therefore, the proliferation of the new means of communication was significant for the cultural transformation Iran experienced during the era. In many ways, the establishment or consolidation of Persian cultural hegemony owes itself to the phenomenon, while the centrality of the dominant discourses continued despite facing conscientious critiques. Moreover, regarding the production of nomenclature, modern cultural encounters popularized new terms, for example, *sorkh-pust*s, as well as the conceptions accompanying them, in the dominant culture's language – no equivalent Kurdish term was needed.

The Pahlavis' unequal cultural modernization

The cultural consequences of the modernization of Iran also included the enrichment of cultural resources to transform perceptions and promote cultural awareness. As argued above, the contribution of a new educated generation across Iran to this transformation, especially since the Second World War, was integral. This was reflected by a multifaceted culture of change represented by a wide range of journals and the cultural products of academics, writers and activists, some in ministerial posts. However, the state's distribution of cultural resources remained unequal because the White Revolution's unequal modernization was not confined to socio-economic spheres. This seemed to benefit the preservation of the targeted non-Persian cultures, which had come into a new way of contact with a hegemonic culture. In reality, however, while the expansion of modern education in Kurdish rural areas was limited and written modes of communication faced the formidable barrier of widespread illiteracy, the enrichment of cultural resources in Iran could have benefited all Iranian cultures because it involved new ideas and literary forms which would defy conventional ways of life. The inferior social status of women was a case in point. This becomes more evident when one considers the state's inability to deal with aspects of customs or traditions, which as cultural fetters continued to bind many layers of Kurdish society to undesirable ways of life. Therefore, a major shortcoming of the state-led modernization was its failure to provide an equal distribution of new means of communication and establish cultural venues and centres such as theatre, library and other centres related to the promotion of *Farhang wa Honar* (Pe. Culture and Art). But individuals did not necessarily receive transmitted 'message' passively. Interaction with audio and visual means of communication and transmitted ideas, as argued in this chapter, transformed the framework of social interaction. Eventually, it was a specific culture and language that succeeded in monopolizing cultural resources and means of communication with the institutionalized and political endorsement of the state. Therefore, the state's unequal distribution of cultural resources constituted another complementing aspect of cultural encounters. At the same time, the provision of Kurdish cultural resources was restrained with the effect that the level of the existing literary works or radio and television services in Kurdish was no match for those in Persian broadcast on a massive scale.

City–village disparity extended to cultural realms too. As discussed in the previous chapter, the village was by and large left out of technological modernization. Although the state replaced the landowner class as the sole political authority, it did not become the provider of technological needs nor, in this case, of cultural needs of the population in rural areas. Except for radio, which became gradually available in limited numbers, the Kurdish village was deprived of visual or written means of communication, let alone cinema, until the end of the 1970s. Concurrently, homogenizing educational and media policies stipulated Persian linguistic skills for individuals to become educated, gain more economic prosperity and benefit from various cultural modes of communication and entertainment. Moreover, both widespread rural illiteracy and the 'remoteness' of the village, an image sustained by the unavailability of transportation and roads for innumerable villages, aggravated the situation by restricting effective access to cultural resources. Although the content was not necessarily objective, as illustrated earlier, being deprived of new ways to engage with cultural activities and encountering a different language debilitated individuals' intellectual capacities. Nevertheless, the promotion of cultural awareness or initiating positive social change in rural areas was not the aim of the state. Except for its unsteady land reform and limited attempts to expand modern education and healthcare, throughout the 1970s, there was no organized attempt by the state to promote cultural awareness in the rural areas. This was mainly because of the absence of provincial development programmes in the state's successive development plans, which were primarily urban-oriented and aimed to project a progressive, 'Western' image of Iran. Indeed, the national image of Iran invited culturally homogenizing policies enforced through education and, later more effectively, visual means of communication, which demonstrates the vitality of the new means of communication for the assertion of Persian cultural hegemony in modern, mediasized Iran.

The village's deprivation of new cultural means was mainly due to the state's indifference to motivating cultural change and its obsession with security and superficial aspects of development and Persianisation, which had many consequences for rural communities. Most importantly, social institutions, which were based on patriarchal or unequal class relations, continued unchallenged; such relations of power were reproduced at the expense of less-privileged groups within the village population, most notably among women and the lower strata. Moreover, with the intensification of modernization between 1960 and 1979, people from rural communities, in general, found themselves caught up with modernization's unfavourable social and economic consequences which forced them to engage in migration, seasonal work, and menial urban labour and embrace urban poverty (see the previous chapters). With no technology available for rural women in particular, they continued to be exploited within an oppressive, gendered social order while their access to social, educational and medical advice was barred by powerful religious and social institutions. The only effective link between the rural areas and the process of cultural change was established by urban social and political activists who, as teachers or medics, went the extra mile to engage more actively with the rural population, imparting new ideas which defied such relations of power. According to oral history, discussed in more detail in the previous chapters, although the state paved the way for modern education and healthcare to spread in rural areas, it was mostly teachers, adhering to the humanitarian ideas of the time that walked this extra mile. In contrast, the state did not intend to impose extra humanitarian tasks on the Literacy Corps except for the urge to spread literacy. Indeed, the expansion of modern education and healthcare in Kurdish rural areas was limited. The effect of this was that, by the end of the 1970s, rural areas had not fundamentally changed in two decades. It is precisely in such circumstances that the role of non-state agents of change in the promotion of social and cultural awareness of people must be recognized.

The growing cultural chasm between Kurdish urban and rural areas was evident, for example, in the institutions of marriage and family. At the end of the 1970s, the village society was still characterized by customs of *zhn ba zhn*, literary meaning woman for woman or exchange marriage, and 'engagement from birth'. In the former, a family would agree to marry their daughter only in return for a girl from the proposing family to get married to one of their sons. In this exchange, the other couple had to marry against their will. The latter custom allowed the engagement of girls and boys from birth. These customs corresponded either to the existing patriarchal system or served the economic needs of a household. In contrast, throughout the 1970s Kurdish urban centres witnessed the emergence of a new generation of educated women who also entered employment on a wide scale (see Chapter 5).[120] This was a result of a change in the perception of individuals, and the availability of cultural resources, something which conspicuously remained absent in Kurdish rural areas. Undoubtedly, the return of seasonal workers or students to the village brought back new ideas. However, the absence of the new means of communication, among many other things, restricted the scope and pace of cultural change in rural areas. In cultural terms, too, the White Revolution remained an urban phenomenon.

Modernization, the expansion of the economy and modern education intertwined with the proliferation of written, audio and visual means of communication (see Table 12), which, along with cultural resources, were concentrated in the capital and its surrounding cities. The quantities for cinemas, theatres or libraries did not witness any significant change by the end of the 1970s. The first cinemas in Kurdish cities were technologically rudimentary. However, bigger cities distinguished themselves for their cinemas, which became more popular throughout the 1970s. This concentration applied to radio and television broadcasting, too, with the additional problem of the scarcity of programmes in Kurdish, which could not match Persian programmes in length or quality. One significant cultural effect of this was that Kurdish broadcasting was too paralysed to compete with a powerful, homogenizing Persian. Table 12 demonstrates the near non-existence of publications in Kurdish in terms of written modes of communications such as newspapers and magazines. Moreover, the decrease in the publication of such modes across Iran corresponded to the ascendancy of dictatorship and the increase in censorship – in official statistics total numbers for 1964 and 1973 are 207 and 195 respectively, indicating a downward trend in publication. In contrast to political upheavals during which a degree of freedom was allowed to Kurdish publications of many forms, the era of the White Revolution imposed a strict surveillance regime, while the state's oppressive apparatus became more sensitive to Kurdish cultural activities. As a result, literary works, such as Hemin's *Tarik w Run*, were published outside Iran and distributed clandestinely along with other Kurdish publications. This was the case across Iran, where the number of books and interest in reading had increased, especially among university students, but censorship affected the publication and distribution of books that were labelled as subversive.[121] In almost all cases the reason for the

Table 12 Radio Broadcasting, Cinema, Theatre, Library, Newspapers and Magazines, 1972–3

Radio broadcasting in Kurdistan (hours)

Radio	Total (hours)	Iranian music	Local music	Foreign music	Literacy, science	Religious programmes	Plays	Varieties	News
Voice of Iran	8,760	2,916	234	1,395	699	286	286	1,150	1,796
Sanandaj	5,715	655	810	186	1,234	582	203	875	1,170
Kermanshah	7,116	690	386	267	3,437	562	357	650	767
Marivan	525	150	150	0	60	45	60	20	40
Mahabad	6,176	980	815	150	1,600	310	335	47	1,939

Cinema by administrative divisions

	1972	1973
Total	418	424
Markazi		
Tehran	121	122
Other Cities	18	17
Kurdistan Province	6	6

Theatre and attendance

	1972			1973		
City	Theatres	Seats	Attendance	Theatres	Seats	Attendance
Total	13	4,856	374,000	14	5,450	325,420
Tehran	7	2,435	29,000	8	3,030	31,420
Sanandaj	1	350	35,000	1	350	15,000

Public libraries

	Libraries	Books
Total	308	1,035,658
Tehran	13	171,000
Central Province excl. Tehran	17	63,000
Kurdistan	8	22,262

Newspapers, weekly and monthly magazines, 1973

Administrative divisions	Total	Newspaper	Weekly magazines	Monthly magazines
	195	39	31	57
	(1964=207)			
	(1964=207)			
	(1964=207)			
Central	134	26	29	55
Kurdistan	1	0	0	0
	(1945=3)			

Source: Plan and Budget Organization, *Statistical Yearbook of Iran 1352 [March 1973 - March 1974]* (Iran: Statistical Centre of Iran, 1975), pp. 141–5.

detention of Kurdish individuals by SAVAK in the 1970s related to possessing Kurdish publications, some mere poetry, which were deemed revolutionary.

During the era of the White Revolution, the new theatre in bigger Kurdish cities emerged to some extent. Despite admirable individual endeavours, the lack of state support and the increasing dictatorship of the 1970s hindered theatre's artistic advance. The history of modern theatrical activities went back to the early 1940s.[122] Historically, celebrations of important days such as Nowruz were accompanied by theatrical performances such as *Miri Nowrozi* (Ku. the Nowruz Prince) who symbolically ruled over a town or village and replaced their rulers during Nowruz.[123] As Ayyubiyan noted in the early 1960s,

> Those National celebrations (*Jashnhay-e melli*) in Kurdistan, and especially in Mahabad, are celebrated with utmost enthusiasm. The residents of Mahabad give national and local (*mahalli*) flavour to religious days and celebrate them more enthusiastically than other Muslims do. For example, [on such days] they visit each other and celebrate the day by special ceremonies. [. . .] There is no custom of *marsi-ye khaniy* (lamentation ceremony) in Mahabad.[124]

Such non-religious dramatic performances provided conditions for the advancement of artistic activities, especially the new theatre. However, political oppression remained a constant obstacle. For example, 'by 1936, the celebration of *Miri Nowrozi* had declined until suddenly it was celebrated magnificently in 1945 [. . .] *Miri Nowrozi* ruled Mahabad for fifteen days without causing any disorder whatsoever.'[125] However, the decline of *Miri Nowroz* celebrations continued until it was eventually replaced by similar performances, which amounted to short, amusing plays, while the threat of political reprisals and lack of state support remained constant obstacles.

Meanwhile, new theatrical performances increased with the expansion of modern education.[126] According to oral accounts, Saqqez city epitomized the way theatrical production increased by secondary school students and other educational or military individuals. The latter, for example, used opportunities such as the state's celebration of twenty-eight Mordad (the coup against Musaddeq, 19 August 1953), twenty-one Azar (the enthronement of Reza Shah on 12 September 1925) or six Bahman (the referendum day for the White Revolution, 26 January 1963) to perform plays of different types.[127] Introducing branches of *Farhang wa Honar* in 1971 to bigger cities in the Kurdistan Province boosted theatrical activities by organizing music and theatre groups, while 'some experts [in theatre] were dispatched by Iran's Centre for Theatre to train young enthusiasts'.[128] Plays such as *Jan Nesar* (the self-sacrificing man) written by Bizhan Mufid was performed. A notable aspect of theatre in Kurdish cities was the emergence of young artists who pursued theatre as a distinct artistic field, composed plays and performed them with the least financial support and in poor facilities.[129]

This trend reveals that modern theatre in Kurdistan developed spontaneously, without effective state support but because of individual endeavours by those who were determined to expand it. While Persian cultural hegemony and a more oppressive Pahlavi state of the 1970s hindered the Kurdish theatre, other individuals across Iran contributed to the growth of theatre in Kurdish cities. Taking into account the dearth of adequate research on Kurdish theatre, evidence and oral history allude more to the perception of theatre as a kind of modern art, which indeed was a modern tool of expression, rather than a site of at least explicit cultural resistance. The plays limited their themes to include social issues and folklore while this scarcity was compensated for by performing plays written by prominent Iranian playwrights. Theatre in Kurdistan became very politicized during the 1979 Revolution (Figure 7).

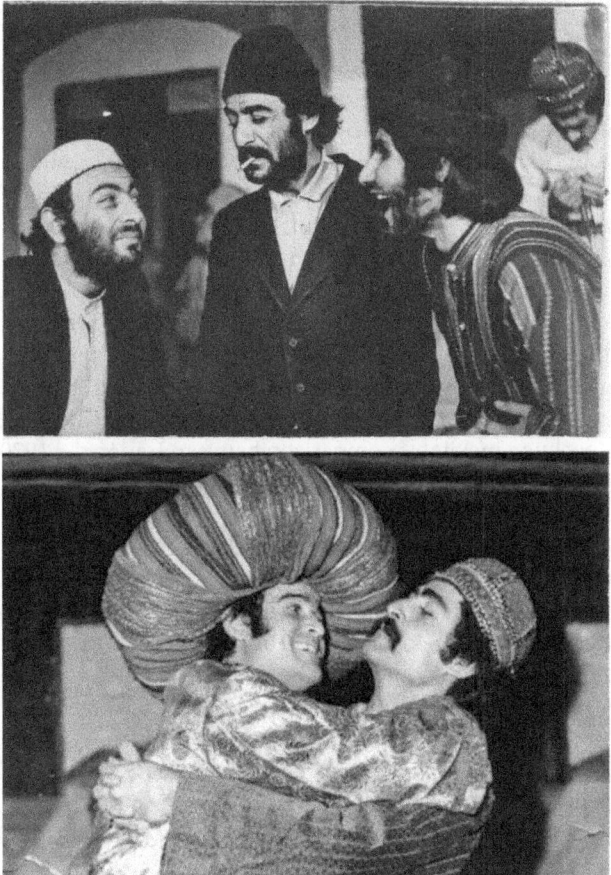

Figure 7 Theatre in Kurdistan. Theatre in Kurdistan in the middle of the 1970s. Scenes from Shahid-e Zende (The living martyr), 1977. In the picture above perform Ja'far Ja'fardust, Amjad Alimuradi, and Ebrahim Weisiyan who with many others were active in Saqqez, Mahabad and Sanandaj. *Source*: Courtesy of Nasrin Alimuradi.

Modernization and secularization

Oral history confirms a popular perception of the era of the White Revolution as a 'secularizing' age in which supposedly the religious way of life diminished and a new secular generation emerged. This new generation was increasingly characterized by possessing education and adhering to a 'modern', progressive world view. This view of the era is generally evidenced by many factors, for example, the emergence of educated women and their increasing presence in the public sphere, and by ongoing cultural transformations reflected by visual means of communication. The economic and political stability of the early 1970s seems to be another crucial factor that suggests the rise of secularity in the era in which a religious image of Iran was effectively being replaced by a 'secular' state. Indeed, the Pahlavi state was preoccupied with attempts to redefine Iran's international place among 'world civilizations' through appealing to pre-Islamic Iran in expensive celebrations, for example, the extravagant 2,500th Celebration of 'Iranian Monarchy' in 1971. At the same time, the cultural transformations strengthened that secular image, especially now that it was characterized by famous female singers.

This view, however, is a symptom of the modernization thesis. According to Nikki Keddie, the thesis 'correlates modernization with secularization and generally measures secularization primarily through declining church membership and declared religious beliefs'.[130] She argues that the secularization thesis 'asserts that the social significance of religion diminishes in response to' modernization. From this perspective, social and cultural transformation should be seen neither as the secularization of society nor as a natural consequence of modernization. This idea of 'becoming modern' underlines a popular perception of 'modern' as advanced or civilized in contrast to 'traditional', that is, backward. Therefore, the dichotomy of modern and traditional reproduces the popular misconception of 'secularism'.

Simultaneously, an inevitable comparison between Iran in the 1970s and earlier Iran (or what came to replace the Pahlavi state after 1979) strengthens the popular perception. However, this popular perception loses ground if one focuses on the Pahlavi state and its policies. When considering the Pahlavi state, it is clear that authoritarianism and Westernized modernization sowed the seeds of, or at least contributed immensely to, the rise of, political Islam which aimed at the seizure of political power in Iran. Admittedly, the growth of political Islam was not an inevitable outcome of modernization. Contingencies and external factors, undoubtedly, play their role in history. However, to understand the ascendancy of a social force over others, one should recognize, to borrow from Gramsci, 'the preceding cultural period',[131] which, especially in this case, resulted in the cultural and political hegemony of the religious opposition. The ascendancy of nativism or political Islam in Iran seriously defies the perception of the Pahlavi era as a secularizing age.

In fact, during the White Revolution, the Islamic movement became increasingly revolutionary and politicized. This process had started in the early 1940s, as shown by the leadership of the militant activists, who deployed 'clandestine political journalism and organisation while using religious sermons as a political platform ... [and] the cooperation between the militant clerics and petty-bourgeois intellectuals'.[132] Moreover, Islamic associations across Iran grew and the number of trained *mujtahids* or interpreters of the shari'a increased,[133] adding to the already considerable number of religious functionaries, major and minor mosques, seminaries and religious schools, all of which were financially sanctioned by *vaqfs* (the offices of religious endowments), as well as religious taxes.[134] Moreover, the dissemination of radical ideas took place through a network of mosques and religious associations, by which activists spread political tapes, including the speeches of Ayatullah Khumeini,[135] who embodied this movement and organized meetings in the *Hossainya*s, congregation halls for Shi'a commemoration ceremonies.

This image of the growth of religious opposition does not fully apply to Kurdistan, which both adhered to a different branch of Islam and engaged in *Kurdayeti*'s cultural resistance against ethnic and cultural oppression. The dissimilarity results from the following religious and cultural reasons. The Westernizing modernization of Iran was threatening the religious, hegemonizing/hegemonic side of Persian culture, which was bound to a Shi'a Islam represented by an authoritative, hierarchical religious establishment. At least an effective part of this establishment was politically inspired by the modernization of Iran as a result of which it experienced a fundamental intellectual break with the past by committing itself to political action to seize power. At the same time, the scale of cultural transformation in central Iran and its major urban centres was more profound than elsewhere, for example, in the Kurdish region. Therefore, *Kurdayeti*'s major cultural and religious components functioned as effective barriers to the possible impact of the politicized religious movement in Iran. As noted earlier, the new educated generation in Kurdistan, which represented cultural, social and political activities, inclined towards a socialist or progressive world view that was preoccupied with social inequalities. In the political sphere, this world view historically became the foundation on which organizational and practical cooperation between Kurdish activists and others in Iran took place. In contrast, organizational or practical unity based on religion has been almost non-existent in Kurdistan.

That said, the above assessment does not imply the complete absence of a religious movement in Kurdistan in the era of the White Revolution. Overlooked by studies of or memoirs on the period in question, modernization stimulated a political and religious trend, which came to be embodied by Ahmad Muftizada (1933–93) who eventually came to represent a religious *Kurdayeti* in 1979. He was born into a *mufti* family, and the title is believed to have been designated by Naser Adin Shah, the Qajar ruler.[136] The *mufti*'s role offered religious prestige to the *mufti* and his descendants in attracting the support of followers. Ahmad Muftizada's grandfather and father resided in Sanandaj, presiding over the religious duties of the population. By the time he was born, the *mufti* role had to a great extent been institutionalized. In the early 1960s, Ahmad followed his father to Tehran University's School of Theology where the latter taught and, when he fell ill, Ahmad began to teach. Among other Sunni teachers, there was Hajj Abdul

Rahman Agha Muhtadi, a former minister of the Kurdistan Republic of 1946 and from a famous landowner family, who exerted a profound impact on the current generation of Kurdish students.[137] Ahmad Muftizada became a regular guest in Rahman Muhtadi's residence in Tehran where regular meetings on Kurdish culture and literature were held. He became the theology teacher's son-in-law in the early 1970s after he became an activist for Kurdish political, cultural and religious rights.

Ahmad Muftizada's political activities went back at least to the early 1960s when he was detained with other Kurdish activists for a short period. In these years he distanced himself from the *mufti* institution because it was 'deriving its legitimacy from the King'.[138] However, there seemed to be intellectual reasons too. He was influenced by Sayyed Qutb, the Egyptian political Islamist, and by the Muslim Brotherhood while he argued for 'scientific' aspects of the Qur'an, and also came to support a Wahhabi interpretation of Sunnism.[139] For such reasons, 'he ceased to be a Mullah, replaced his clerical dress for men's suits, and led a simple life'.[140] By the middle of the 1970s, according to oral history, Muftizada had distanced himself from other Kurdish activists who inclined explicitly to the left and became more outspoken against the Pahlavi regime. This is exemplified by his speech at Swara Ilkhanizada's funeral in 1976, related through his wife's family.[141] This is also illustrated in his contribution to public debates in which on one occasion he censured a prominent Baha'i in Iran – in the eyes of adherents of other religious schools in Iran, the Pahlavi regime favoured the Baha'is in detriment to others.[142]

Furthermore, intellectually and practically, his social location was also important for him as a religious thinker. Sanandaj, the provincial centre, was a city which more than any other Kurdish city was affected by cultural transformations through television and radio. Indeed, a crucial technological development, which made Muftizada a household name in Sanandaj, was the city's part-time television channel in the Kurdish language. In the holy month of Ramadan in 1976 when a programme on religious matters was to be broadcast in the evening, 'there was no question about who would be the most appropriate individual to present on the show' which continued for the entire month of Ramadan.[143]

On the other hand, Muftizada's idea of *Maktab-i Qur'an* (Ku. Qur'anic School), materialized in 1979, was formed in the context of the modernization of Iran. It was the result of his religious thinking which placed the holy book in the centre of the religious interpretation of social life. By the middle of the 1970s, he had become a critic of the clergy, of superficial ways of interpreting the Qur'an and the Prophet's sayings, and a religion, which had become, in his view, 'empty' for people.[144] The Islamism of Ali Shari'ati and the political and religious ideas of Mehdi Bazargan, a prominent liberal and religious figure, contained attractive elements for Muftizada.[145]

Moreover, although religious practices declined as a new educated, urban generation increasingly characterized Kurdish society, the Pahlavi's 'secularism' did not satiate the spiritual needs of people, whose older generation continued to embrace religious practices. Generally, the decrease in the number of religious schools and sects, and the gradual out-fashioning of various religious methods of healing, all went against the place of religion in society. In urban centres, where religious beliefs had shown signs of decline – this was seen in adopting new customs and ways of life – the population was gradually attracted to religious practices which included hajj pilgrimage and conducting rituals and ceremonies. This happened during the same period that technological novelties of television and cinema, and modern education were in full swing.

Therefore, the popular perception of the era of the White Revolution as secularizing emanates from a flawed understanding of secularism and survives because of superficial analysis of the era in this regard. Insofar as Kurdish society is concerned, the Westernizing modernization of Iran also sowed the seed of modern religious *Kurdayeti* embodied by likes of Muftizada, whose political stance responded to ethnic and religious prejudices against the Kurds, while his religious thinking was a critique of not only the institutional inferiority of the Sunni religion but also a transforming society.

Cultural resistance

The resistance of marginalized identities against a homogenizing identity reshaped modern cultural encounters within Iran. Insofar as the Kurds are concerned, while the process of socio-economic modernization of Iran succeeded in incorporating Kurdish society into modern Iran by strengthening existing bonds and creating new ties, political modernization encountered resistance. *Kurdayeti*, as resistance to homogenization, continued to rely on Kurdish cultural forms to preserve the main components of Kurdish identity. A dynamic modern *Kurdayeti*, encouraged by ongoing ideological transformations, is thus directly related to the political modernization of Iran based on the centralization of power and cultural homogenization.

A crucial aspect of cultural resistance was both intentional or organizational and unintentional use of Kurdish in cultural activities, which defied Persian cultural hegemony. At an organizational level, cultural activities since the early 1960s were organized by Kurdish university students. The Union for Kurdish Students organized meetings, distributed published books and celebrated specific days such as the formation of the Kurdish Republic of 1946.[146] These activities included lexicographical efforts and regular literary meetings. These organized cultural practices were inevitably linked to political activities, leading to establishing connections with the Iranian left, which subsequently shaped the students' socialist world view.[147] At a more popular level, teachers and other social and cultural activists played significant roles in cultural resistance. Affected by a culture of change across Iran, the new educated generation disseminated Kurdish cultural forms, too. They benefited hugely from Kurdish music and poetry, now transmitted by various radio stations.[148] At the same time, an ongoing intellectual transformation closely corresponded to the current socio-economic transformation, which made new socialist ideas very attractive. It was for this reason that, for example, Aryanpur's sociology class was packed, and Kurdish teachers or cultural activists across the Kurdish region established libraries and bookshops.[149] As a significant impact of this process, the ability of people to read and write in Kurdish increased. This was especially the case with those engaged with Kurdish literature because political oppression effectively suppressed the wider population from gaining Kurdish literary skills. The popular awareness of Kurdish culture, literature or history was limited. Indeed, the combination of the state's increasing dictatorship and Persian cultural hegemony significantly restricted access to knowledge. The process of Persian cultural hegemony crucially popularized the idea of 'Persian culture as a more advanced culture'.[150] Many trends illustrate this. For example, using conventional religious names for children declined while choosing Persian names increased considerably, and growing cities such as the provincial city of Sanandaj became more 'Persianised' in lifestyle and language. 'Persianised' also connoted 'Westernized', and it was no surprise that the cleric Ahmad Muftizada emerged to represent an Islamic *Kurdayeti* in Sanandaj during the 1979 Revolution.

Music, a stronghold of Kurdish identity, had gained more significance in the cultural resistance, so did the reinvented traditions such as the celebration of *Nowruz*, defined (exclusively) as a *Kurdish* new year. In the context of homogenization, such practices quickly became politicized. The expansion of Kurdish customs and traditions indicated their paradoxical growth as distinct cultural traits in relation to the increasing socio-economic integration of Kurdish society. Nevertheless, because the state was not hostile to the practice of Kurdish language, dress and ways of life in public and private spheres (except for the use of the 'official' language and dress code in education and administration), Kurdish cultural forms continued to be represented by dress, Kurdish weddings and dance, and, crucially, music. (As discussed in the previous chapter, these aspects of life came increasingly under pressure as modernization led to categorization.) The continuation of Kurdish cultural ways of life was possible because numerous individuals endeavoured to preserve them through poetry, literature, folklore, historiography, and social and political actions. One artistic area, which represented Kurdish culture more freely, was undoubtedly the music. 'Local music', as it was referred to in contrast to 'Iranian music', featured in radio programmes, opening a new arena for Kurdish artists, musicians and singers to mature and commit themselves to Kurdish cultural practices. Like many other cultural areas, the interrelation of Kurdish and Persian music and the state's 'secular' attitude to music allowed Kurdish music to prosper. However, as oral history accounts confirm, the contribution of individuals was crucial to promoting Kurdish music. Radio and other technical means of communication made many signers household names within a short span of time. However, Kurdish music remained strictly 'local' because it never achieved the status of Persian music, which had Iran's television and radio stations at its disposal. The lack of state support and inadequate institutional resources hindered the artistic transformation of Kurdish music, while Persian music's enjoyment of infinite resources and new technology contributed to Persian cultural hegemony. Nevertheless, Kurdish music remained a formidable site of cultural resistance.

Kurdish cultural resistance was represented in various organizational and popular levels. In addition to music, other forms of cultural resistance included the establishment of libraries and bookshops, the distribution of books, poetry and musical cassettes. This occurred even though Kurdish literature was heavily suppressed by the state's oppressive apparatus, and the combination of linguistic policies and Persian linguistic hegemony prevented the popularization of Kurdish literacy skills. Due to resistance and formidable distinctive elements of Kurdish identity, homogenization failed in eradicating Kurdish identity, and for this matter other non-Persian identities, despite Persian cultural superiority. On the contrary, modernization and homogenization strengthened *Kurdayeti*, which endeavoured to emerge in new political and cultural forms.

Conclusion

Politically, the era of the White Revolution eventually came to be characterized by the concentration of political power and the state's oppressive measures against its opponents. As regards Kurdish opposition, it revived throughout the decades following the demise of the Kurdish Republic of 1946 while simultaneously encountering major intellectual transformations in the 1960s and 1970s, shaping new theories and political actions. Oral history, along with a closer analysis of the events, defies the myth of *the Rebellion of 1968-9* as merely a period of armed struggle. Instead, it presents it as a juncture when at least a decade-long activism was effectively suppressed by the Iranian army, partly in collaboration with the Barzani movement. The next decade marked the emergence of an educated generation of Kurdish political activists whose ideas and actions reflected a transforming age, subsequently forming the nuclei of modern political parties; a distinctive characteristic of this generation was its critique of guerrilla warfare. The reinvigoration of Kurdish opposition was directly linked to the socio-economic modernization of an exclusive state, a process which, while accelerated the incorporation of the Kurds into modern Iran, encountered resistance against homogenization.

Culturally, insofar as the Kurds were concerned, the main cultural consequence of modernization was the cultural hegemony of Persian. Until relatively recently, Iranian cultures had lived side by side and did not perceive each other as *alien*; they were communities with shared history and culture. Before modern cultural encounters, political and cultural domination by the ruling state was maintained mainly through coercive measures, while Persian culture and language relied on its literary prestige and administrative continuity and not on systematic marginalization of others – Ferdowsi's *Shahnameh* shaped the historical consciousness of the Kurds too while Sufism relied on Persian for its literary form of poetry. Although political centralization and institutional modernization, most importantly modern education, inaugurated a systematic promotion of Persian culture and language into 'mainstream' or 'Iranian' since the early decades of the twentieth century, Persian cultural hegemony was effectively achieved during the era of the White Revolution because it irretrievably transformed cultural dimensions through its proliferation of the audio and visual means of communication. Of course, by then literacy had also increased considerably, resulting in more effective impacts of written modes of communication in this respect. However, audiovisual means of communication revolutionized the nature of cultural encounters. Until its emergence, based on a national understanding of the past, modern education had continued to cultivate the idea of the cultural superiority of the Persian language over other languages, which were defined as its less significant branches. However, the new means of communication and their profound psychological impacts made Persian's 'normality' and 'superiority' common sense, thus giving Persian culture a hegemonic status. Simultaneously, the White Revolution institutionalized the concept of other cultures and languages, including Kurdish, as 'local'. This is best recognized in the state's prioritization of Persian as the official and state-preferred medium of communication regarding technological innovations and exemplified by the literary advances in Persian literature, supported by institutionalized education and innumerable publication houses. Nevertheless, Kurdish cultural and literary resistance continued with the effect that the Kurdish society of the end of the 1970s was culturally a product of the interactions of cultural homogenization and Kurdish cultural resistance since the Second World War.

Chapter 5

THE MODERNIZATION OF GENDER RELATIONS

Introduction

The new image of women in Kurdish-Iranian society at the end of the 1970s was inextricably related to and a product of the social change and transformation Iran had experienced, especially in the decades following the Second World War. However, although the gradual but profound changes in the position of women in society have been a hallmark of modern Iran, more interpretations of this process and analyses of the concepts involved are required to explain various aspects of that process. First and foremost, the idea of the 'new woman' formed part of the ideological package of modernity and was intimately linked to the idea of the 'nation'. Resulting in an intellectual foundation to deal with the women question in the process of modern nation-building, 'new women' accompanied the formation of the modern states, shaping conceptions, literature, movements, policies and laws. Furthermore, to present a more comprehensive analysis of this process, we need to transcend development and modernization theories and engage with a dynamic historical process that profoundly transformed the position of women in society.

Therefore, this chapter sets out to discuss the historical process in Iran, focusing on the era of the White Revolution and its impact on Kurdish society. Significantly, the era was characterized by important developments in both private and public spheres across Iran. For example, as the people's awareness of hygiene began to increase and medical care became available, the burden of childbearing lessened, and later, with the decrease in the size of families, women's presence in the public sphere increased, which, in turn, led to their growing independence. Legal, educational, medical and economic changes, which affected the social status of women, were taking place in the background. In a process that combined such factors to transform the place of women, women's agency was integral. That said, related to Kurdish society, this chapter starts with a brief discussion of modernity and the redefinition of the role of women, followed by an overview of women as subaltern within the gender order of society. Next, this chapter underlines the scientific, educational, legal and economic changes of the era which transformed the social status of women in Kurdish society and across Iran. The last sections of this chapter include assessments of the two important phenomena of collective agency and resistance, which impacted the course of social change.

Finally, an attempt to review the literature on women in the modernizing Kurdistan of the second half of the twentieth century quickly reveals, despite some exceptions, the scarcity, almost the absence, of gender studies approaches to the historical period.[1] Other exceptions are found in the recent, though inadequate, inclusion of women in Kurdish historiography. For source materials, this chapter relies on oral history, memoirs and official statistics. However valuable, these sources also expose the scarcity of the studies of social change and gender on the period; these studies have only begun to appear since the early 2000s, authored by researchers in the fields of social science.[2] To a great extent, however, this deficiency is compensated by the more established field of Iranian gender studies on the Pahlavi era, because the changes in Iran affected all women, regardless of cultural differences.[3] This is a crucial point to bear in mind because it is precisely for such a reason that any categorization of women based on ethnicity will blur the study of the process of change and transformation insofar as gender is concerned. Of course, in multi-ethnic Iran, this does not obviate the need for considering distinct cultural or political behaviours, which should be explained by referring to contexts that highlight them.

Modernity and the idea of the 'new woman'

The new discourses around the question of women and gender reforms in the modern Middle Eastern states were intellectually originated in the intellectual works, debates and critiques since the Enlightenment. This section concisely analyses the idea of the new woman as a crucial component of the ideological package of modernity alongside the ideas of the nation, progress and education. Throughout the nineteenth century and in tandem with Enlightenment ideas, classical liberalism's legalist and utilitarian approach to the question, and colonialism's justification of its presence in the Middle East also through the idea of the education of (Muslim) women, influenced the intellectual domains in Eurasian societies, as well as the Ottoman and Iranian-Qajar Empires.[4] As Elizabeth Frierson has shown in the case of the Ottoman Empire, the education of women for social and economic reasons became the rallying cry for a domestic movement.[5] The idea was embraced by reformists, intellectuals and literary figures, who were not passive receivers of new ideas but contributed to the debates, increased tension in the cultural sphere and shaped the new nation states' gender and educational reforms.

The idea of the new woman was inextricably linked to the concepts of progress and modern education, which, as discussed in the previous chapters, was perceived as the wheel of progress and an essential ingredient behind any nation's scientific and historical advance. Cultivating such ideas especially since the early twentieth century, intellectuals in Asian societies began a radical redefinition of the social place and role of women in modern times. Previous social movements throughout the nineteenth century such as Babism and Bahaism in Iran had addressed the oppression of women and encouraged their education.⁶ Furthermore, critiques of the unfavourable social status of women can be detected in literary and intellectual works since the early decades of the nineteenth century. A case in point is the female poet and historian Mastura Ardalan Kurdistani (1804-44), from the ruling family of the Kurdish Ardalan Emirate in Iran, who expresses discontent with a situation in which 'under the veil, there is a head worthy of a diadem'.⁷ Reflecting ongoing change and transformation, debates on the role of women in family and society intensified towards the end of the century. This was exemplified by criticizing patriarchal views propagated by an essay entitled *Ta'dib al-Nesvan* (The education of women), published in Tehran in 1887, which advised women to maintain self-isolation and social distancing amid the spread of new ways of life. The critic, Bibi khanom (lady Bibi) Astarabadi, whose mother Khadijeh khanom was the teacher of one of Naser al-Din Shah's (r. 1848-96) daughters, asserts in her aptly entitled book *Ma 'ayeb al-Rajjal* (Vices of men, written in 1894, published a century later) that reason is not the prerogative of men.⁸ As critiques of gender relations increased and masculinity and femininity redefined, education for women was explained as the first step towards changing the social status of women.⁹

However, the new era of nations and nationalism demanded more radical changes in perceptions and practice. In addition to the femininity given to *vatan* or *patrie* as Motherland, this was because the perceived progress of the 'nation' stipulated well-educated generations (of men). Therefore, 'new woman' was considered as both educated and the educator of the (masculine) nation. This notion began to be supported by both secular and religious nationalism, the latter represented by Islamic reformism, which was advocated, for example, by the Egyptian lawyer Qasim Amin in his *The Liberation of Women* (1899) and *The New Woman* (1900) – Amin also criticizes Western feminism.¹⁰ Furthermore, throughout the nineteenth century, intellectual groups or salons, as was the case in the Ottoman Empire, were crucial for disseminating such ideas.¹¹ The prominent Ottoman intellectual Namek Kemal linked the future development of the empire to educational efforts, and in his article, *Terbiye-i Nesvan* (The education of women, 1867), he explained the education of women as an effort to mobilize women as a resource to serve the future well-being of the empire.¹² Therefore, by the end of the century, an intellectual domain had been formed, shaping the debates on the question of women.

The idea of the new woman, intimately connected to the ideas of the nation, progress and education, was embraced by Kurdish intellectuals since the early twentieth century. This is reflected in Kurdish literature, mainly represented by poetry. For example, after returning from Istanbul to Ottoman Kurdistan in the early twentieth century to convey the message of modernity, Piramerd (1867-1950) was one of the early advocates of the idea of the new woman among Kurdish modernists, connecting *taraqi vatan* (the progress of the Motherland) along with *awladi chak* (good generation) to educated women.¹³ He insisted

> Only the educated girls
> Make the nation succeed

Raise [the kind of] children [needed]
For the nation to proceed.[14]

Therefore, the need to educate women was justified by emphasizing their roles as educated mothers in the progress of the new nation because, as Piramerd argued, progress stipulated a 'good [well-educated] generation'. Later literary figures such as Fayaq Bekas (1905–48), Qaneʿ, Goran (1904–62) and Hemin continued the promulgation of 'new woman' throughout the twentieth century amid social and political transformations.[15] However, there were others such as Aladdin Sajjadi (1907–84), whose national refashioning of the Kurds and their history rejected 'new woman' because, according to him, women remained men's intellectual inferiors despite education.[16]

Kurdish poetry also revealed the influence of other radical ideas. For example, seemingly influenced by the Iraqi poet Jamil Sidqqi al-Zahawi (1863–1936), Fayaq Bekas's poems explicitly demanded unveiling as an essential step towards the emancipation of women. This aspect later influenced the poetry of Hemin who in *Memory of Shirin*, which was both a break with nineteenth-century poetry and a redefinition of the social role of women against Nali's (1800–56) *Yarn knitting Shirin*, warned that 'Veiling is shameful in the twentieth century'. Such ideas were received and popularized in intimate connection with the modernization of 'the nation' in general and the institution of education in particular. Observing women's social inferiority, the idea of the new woman inspired educated and powerful women too who exerted a profound impact on social change. Meanwhile, this modern redefinition of gender roles intimately involved a redefinition of man aspiring to become a 'modern man' who had to play an active role in the making of the new woman; this indicated the modernization of both femininity and masculinity, new ways by which gender roles were socially and culturally reconstructed in a changing world, in connection with each other. The above-mentioned literary figures were mostly men, committed to that very goal. Alongside nation-building, the twentieth century can also be considered a century of making new women, while modernization transformed the social organization of sexual difference. From this perspective, one can argue that modern Iran had produced a modern image of women by the end of the 1970s fundamentally different from the earlier generations. This process involved challenging enormous social and discursive obstacles that worked to maintain the social inferiority of women. Nevertheless, any comparative study of the early decades with later decades of the twentieth century will quickly reveal the remarkable scope of change.

Women as subaltern

Historically, women of various communities had always played active roles in the family and the workplace. These two spheres of life became more distinct with the expansion of a capitalist economy. Women in Kurdish communities of village, towns and tribes contributed to economic production, and maintained the family, by undertaking more tasks and bearing more responsibilities than men. Prior to significant changes in the role of women in the family, women were mostly prepared for marriage; married women had to devote most of their time to childbearing or caring for children, with the effect that before they reached thirty-five many had already given birth to a high number of children. As a result, their chances of a better life were restricted. Several interrelated factors (as discussed later in the chapter) transformed the place of women in society in general, although for many, especially those in rural areas or the urban poor, conditions had not profoundly changed even by the end of the 1970s.

Despite social change, the hegemony of man and the subordination of woman were (re)produced by a constitutive discourse that banked on cultural symbols and social norms and was supported by the existing institutions such as religion. The interaction of these elements contributed to the definition of the woman who was represented by man, who 'sets the standards of propriety for women's behaviour, their role in society, and the kind of punishment meted out to women who did not abide by the social norms set for them'.[17] The woman's life, behaviour and dress code were shaped under both the visible and the invisible gazes of the patriarchal man. The continuation of the authority of the man through such norms and codes maintained a patriarchal system which was reinforced by a patriarchal language, biased religious practices and the politics of the ruling classes.[18] A good Kurdish woman was idealized as *pak* (Ku. pure) or *ma'sum* (Ku. pitiful and innocent), while one seen as immoral was addressed as *behaya* or *besharm* (shameless) to suggest that she lacked modesty and honour respectively.[19] In this definition, the woman was but a sex object, a childbearing person and a housekeeper. In a mostly rural society, the culture of the Kurdish *agha* (landowner) shaped important aspects of the existing gender relations. It was these relations that began to transform with the expansion of a capitalist market economy, urbanization and modern education. However, the conditions of the past, that is, religious norms, customs and cultural symbols, were also fundamental ingredients for (re)shaping gender relations. The transformation of the mode of production did not automatically transform social or cultural norms: as discussed further in Collective agency, agency was crucial for social change.

The linguistic reproduction of powerful masculinity and subordinated femininity was another crucial aspect of gender relations in Kurdish societies. As Hassanpour has shown, deviance from mainstream social norms was associated with negative, but firmly institutionalized, traits such as *hiz* (literally, always ready for sexual intercourse) and *makkar* (cunning), which were framed as feminine qualities. On the other hand, bravery, stamina and wisdom were qualities associated with men, who were naturally capable of ruling, judging and leading. Women of different social classes might have been distinguished materially or to some extent culturally, based on their degree of access to cultural capital. However, the definition of woman as the property of man, based on the norms of masculinity and femininity, applied more or less to any woman.

According to Hassanpour, who has conducted extensive and excellent research on the subject, 'the unequal distribution of gender power is recorded in the Kurdish language, which is one of the ignored yet powerful sites in the exercise of patriarchal rule' in Kurdish society.[20] For example, *zhn* (Ku. woman) and *piyaw* (Ku. man) represent diametrically opposed qualities. Man connotes 'human being', while *piyaw kushtn* and *piyaw khirap* are used to refer to 'to kill [a man]' and '[becoming] a bad man', respectively. Words for positive qualities are formed with a masculine suffix, for example, *piyawati* (manliness, manhood), *aza-yi* (bravery) and *netirs-i* (fearlessness). By contrast, the words most associated with woman are traditionally feminine qualities such as *namus* (honour), *abrru* (honour), *sharaf* (honour), *sharm* (shame, shyness) and *haya* (modesty, sense of shame). *Piyaw-ati*, manliness, is a positive virtue, while *wek-zhn* and *zhnana*, derived from the word for woman, connote being a coward and cowardly act respectively.

Moreover, language is not merely employed to maintain gender inequality and reinforce prejudice against women. At times, similar clichés are used to refer to women and minorities as a means of degradation. For instance, in Kurdish oral culture 'women and the Jews share the stereotype as timid [while] men signify bravery'.[21] To add to Hassanpour's study, such designations are closely linked to social practices and femininity, with the effect that the practices of marriage and divorce, genital mutilation and social exclusions, what are held to be 'acceptable' and 'unacceptable', etc., are shaped and supported by such discursive designations. Moreover, lexical, semantic and ideological constructions of patriarchy extend into every layer of Kurdish oral and written culture. This is clearly seen in the many Kurdish dictionaries which later emerged. For example, as Hassanpour explains, Hazhar's *Hambana Borina* reflects misogyny and functions to reproduce the existing power relations in Kurdistan.[22] Nevertheless, resistance to the linguistic foundations of gender order in Kurdish societies constituted a crucial aspect of life, recorded in the Kurdish language; examples of folklore and song which promoted the place of woman also reflected linguistic resistance.

Societal change and resistance to patriarchy, and obstacles to them, formed other aspects of women's lives. Into the 1970s, women remained deprived of medical assistance and knowledge, which were also scarcely available for the wider urban and rural populations. Pregnancy marked the most difficult time in women's lives, with childbirth proving the major challenge. As a teacher recalls,

> Farasat, a woman from Digin village, continued to work on the carpet-weaving machine despite being pregnant. She spent long hours behind the machine while seated, which threatened her health seriously. I warned her about the consequences, but she wanted to finish the carpet as quickly as possible because she would not be able to work for a while after giving birth to her child. I could not do more [because there were no medical centre or doctors nearby]. The night she gave birth to her child, there was only the midwife with her unhygienic equipment.[23]

Women in Iranian societies constantly encountered cultural and religious barriers set by the patriarchal system, determining what was 'allowed' or 'disallowed' for them. Women in conservative households were not supposed to share their problems with doctors and were frequently reminded of the unsuitability of women's education. Moreover, they were made to believe that 'women's diseases' were a natural part of life, which either went away or stayed, depending on the will of the Supreme Being.[24] Violence against women was widespread, and it was considered the duty of the man to ensure his woman's subordination. Women exercised no rights in marriage and had to succumb to norms and customs such as *zhn ba zhn* (exchange marriage) and early marriage engagement, even from birth. Writing about his childhood, the translator Muhammad Qazi (1913–98) recalls how violence extended to the disruption of the life of women who, becoming widows following the death of their husbands, had to succumb to decisions made by others in order to survive; in many cases, they were also separated from their children.[25] Woman's subordinated status was protected by the absence of rights to divorce husbands and choose partners.

These all took place in a culture in which masculine norms shaped common sense, which ruled social and cultural behaviours. Underneath were hidden forms of violence. One area was female genital mutilation (FGM), carried out in extremely unhygienic circumstances, inflicting enduring physical and psychological damage to young girls, some still in infancy. Another ugly side to this practice was its secrecy. The same teacher quoted earlier remembers that despite her close contact with the women of the village where she was teaching, she only found out about the practice of FGM by accident because women were forbidden to talk about their experiences in public.[26] It is impossible to provide precise data, but based on various reports, one can reasonably speculate that the practice was carried out as a social norm in some areas or communities.[27] In this way, control over both the woman's body and her sexuality was ensured, while the imposed silence confirmed the normality of the practice.

As noted in the previous chapters, in addition to household tasks and helping husbands or fathers on the land, women were exploited in carpet workshops across the Kurdish region. This economic role was not concealed. However, a woman's productive role on the land and in the family was not acknowledged as such, while working as skilled or semi-skilled labourers was linked to the economic needs of the family. As modernization intensified, women began to achieve a better social status in many respects in the urban centres, while the growing demand for carpets increased the exploitation of women in such workshops mostly in the rural areas. Moreover, low wages and long hours characterized the working conditions in the workshops. For example, in Sanandaj and its vicinity, carpet workshops were set up for low-income or migrant women, while machines were installed inside family houses to exploit women and benefit from their work.[28] According to Gulrukh Qubadi, a teacher and women's activist in the 1970s,

> Farah [Pahlavi] Agribusiness (*sherkat-e sahami-zara'i-e Farah*) for the cultivation of opium and poppy seeds (*Kheshkhash*) also set up a carpet

workshop in the Marenj Muzhezh region around Sanandaj. It only employed young girls to work under male or female managers who were trained in the art of carpet-weaving. They had long working hours, which lasted from 6 am to 6 pm. Breaks were every four or five hours during which the girls were taken out to do body exercise. Wages were paid to the girls' fathers. When these young girls grew up, they continued to work as 'self-employed' on a machine purchased by their parents. Families benefited from their children who were either working in carpet-weaving workshops or on a machine set up in the household, whereas young girls endured hardship and received their wages in a dress or custom jewellery only once a year. There were other carpet workshops in other cities such as Kermanshah, Mariwan, Saqqez, Bukan and Minanduab [indicating the growth of the carpet industry]. Physical or other kinds of punishment undoubtedly existed; however, we do not know if there was sexual harassment.[29]

Migration and the expansion of the economy, as discussed in the previous chapters, increased women's share in the workforce. More Kurdish women became brick-oven factory workers, cleaners, housekeepers and vendors. All these jobs involved harsh conditions. Female vendors included elderly women who had to sell their products, usually hot food, sometimes in extreme climates in open spaces of city bazaars. The need for more income was a decisive factor for the increase in the number of working women in urban centres, while considerably more rural women brought their products to sell in city markets. The women of the migrated families became residents of impoverished districts in the cities and began to work as cleaners or babysitters to increase family income. This change had of course cultural implications for these women, who began to become accustomed to an urban way of life.

At the same time, modernization was characterized by the growing employment opportunities for women who graduated from schools. Since the early 1960s, the number of women in teaching and nursing increased because of the spread of modern education. In a change from the early decades of the century, these women no longer exclusively came from aristocratic families, because more primary and secondary schools for girls, as well as teaching and nursing training colleges, had popularized literacy and created employment opportunities for women in certain jobs (see Table 6). A crucial aspect of this process was the increase in gender awareness of society, reflected in a generation of men in urban centres who were more open to the new ideas which aimed to enhance the social status of women. Furthermore, there were social customs and ways of life which prevented the seclusion of women and provided more space for their interaction with men, particularly in Kurdish communities. This was exemplified by the peculiarity of Kurdish wedding with mixed group dances and women's intermingling with men, and the absence of strict religious ceremonies that characterized the Shiʻa religion (e.g. the commemoration of Imam Hussein in Muharram), which effectively decreased the segregation of men and women.

Woman's subservience to man continued to be ensured and reinforced by religion in myriad ways. 'Appropriate' behaviour and dress code were required when a woman encountered religious authorities or entered sacred places. A woman's access to powerful positions was effectively restricted by assigning her to seemingly sacred roles whose fulfilments ensured her purity and God's satisfaction. The mosque too remained a masculine space; however, there were other spaces such as *Takya*, where they could perform religious ceremonies. Although such religious institutions for women increased in urban centres in the 1960s and 1970s, participation mainly came from an older generation of women, in search of spiritual help.

Women and the White Revolution

The era of the White Revolution was characterized by important interrelated factors which profoundly affected the social status of women in Kurdish society. The following section concentrates on the scientific, educational, legal and economic changes, as well as women's collective agency. The approach in identifying and explaining these factors is informed by a non-developmental view and the perception of the 'White Revolution' as primarily a phenomenon that modernized the existing gender relations.

The new science and modern education

The topic of the new science was discussed in relation to the expansion of modern healthcare in Chapter 3. However, a brief discussion of the topic is also required here. The introduction of women to new medical science in Kurdistan entailed their gradual emancipation from the previous conditions of childbirth and lack of hygiene, thus creating more opportunities in life. According to oral accounts, the introduction of contraceptives and their free distributions especially since the 1960s was a significant step in that direction.[30] This was not an isolated incident but was accompanied by the expansion of medical means and knowledge, hygienization and the increase in the number of women working as medical staff, who 'enthusiastically worked to ameliorate the existing conditions'.[31]

However, the urban and rural centres' share in the new scientific technologies and medicine was not equal. While cities continued to benefit from new healthcare, rural areas developed at a slow pace in that direction because of poor infrastructural and geographical conditions, as well as the absence of the state, as discussed in previous chapters. This asymmetrical relationship with technology had enduring effects and outlasted the era of the White Revolution. For example, a doctor recalled how he carried out an operation in the Kurdish city of Sardashat in 1979 to extract a stillborn child that had remained in the mother's abdomen for three days. This had caused the mother unbearable pains, without having access to any medical advice to identify what caused the pain.[32] Himself a doctor, the memoirs and writings of the renowned Iranian writer Gholamhossein Sa'edi (1936–85) also reflect the horrible conditions in Iran's rural areas or among the poor and the absence of medical services. Despite improvements in social or medical conditions, the urban–rural disparity remained a formidable obstacle to the improvement of conditions for many women.

Modern education in Iran was undoubtedly another significant institution the impact of which on women and society cannot be overestimated. The idea of modern education for girls in Iran had become more acceptable by 1918, when the first public school for girls was opened following a limited number of private or missionary schools, which had started operating since 1907. The first such schools in Sanandaj in Iranian Kurdistan were opened in the early years of the 1920s. Although more primary and secondary schools for girls were established in the bigger cities of Kurdistan by the end of the 1930s, schools for girls only proliferated in the second half of the century (see Chapter 3). Until there were more female teacher training institutions, the shortage of teachers was a significant factor that, combined with other educational deficiencies, hindered women's education.[33]

For women, modern education continued to distinguish the present from the past. Among the upper classes, as noted earlier, literacy and greater social and political roles for women were not alien concepts. Modern education, too, became more accessible to the women of the better-off families. For example, in Sanandaj during the early decades of the modern state women from aristocratic families, such as Mo'tamed Vaziri, went to primary schools for seven- to twelve-year-old girls. Based on the old six-class system, and due to the lack of secondary school, students could become teachers after accomplishing the six-year education. Some women founded other schools for girls in Sanandaj upon their graduation elsewhere and their return to the city.[34] By the end of the 1930s, across Kurdish cities, the number of girls and young women from prominent families in education increased, as did the number of schools. This process gradually impacted social attitudes towards women in education, and with the impact of political events, more women from the wider population were encouraged to seek education. For example, a women's society, *Yakiati Afratani Kurdistan* (Kurdistan's Women Union), was founded in Mahabad under the Kurdish Republic in 1946, possible because of a new intellectual atmosphere in the region since the early 1940s in which the Organization of Kurdish Revival stood out for its progressive publications and activities. The society aimed to educate women, while a modern image of woman was even advocated by prominent Kurdish men such as Qazi Muhammad, the head of the Republic.[35] Nevertheless, dominant patriarchal views continued to exclude women, including the members of the society, from political participation in the Republic. For example, as Mina Qazi, Qazi Muhammad's wife and a founder of the society, recalled later, 'when the Republic was announced in [Mahabad's] city square, we watched from afar in our home.'[36] No specific role was assigned to women in the Republic, other than a limited friendly attitude towards literacy for women. Nevertheless, the new idea of women's emancipation was incorporated into the political and social agendas of Kurdish activists, and the interruption of the experience of the Kurdish Republic was a serious setback for attempts to enhance the social status of women in society. The political situation of the early 1940s in general and the Republic in particular facilitated intellectual transformations, exemplified by *Nishtiman*, and enabled the formation of such societies. According to Mina Qazi, the society aimed to eradicate illiteracy and create opportunities for Kurdish women to prosper and 'serve their society'.[37]

The efforts of women of urban upper classes became the guidelines for modern education, encouraging the establishment of more schools for girls in Kurdish urban centres. Primary and secondary schools for women in Kurdistan proliferated during the 1970s, for which the determination of the previous generation of women who helped popularize modern education for women was essential. The introduction of the Literacy Corps in rural areas, according to a teacher from the time, was a turning point that presented women with an opportunity to teach. Simultaneously, the new perceptions of gender roles mobilized many men, too, while the intellectual atmosphere of the 1960s and 1970s encouraged political and cultural activists to advocate teaching in the most deprived regions.[38] In these circumstances, and encouraged by other activists, more educated Kurdish women chose to teach to expand literacy, which involved engaging with women in need.[39] The Literacy Corps was a crucial means to that end.[40] Although the presence of any member of the Literacy and Medical Corps in deprived regions was a new development per se, for those who had incorporated the era's ideological transformations and were receptive to progressive and left-wing ideas, this meant more active involvement in social change. For example, as Qubadi recalls,

> We [teachers] worked longer hours in the village school, organised after-school clubs, eschewed corporal punishment, and paid attention to the pupils' family circumstances. We were friendly, mixed with women and their families, and listened to their problems. Teachers taught large classes. For example, when I was a teacher in Zarrin Chia village around Kermanshah [in the middle of the 1970s], I had 30 to 40 (Year 1 to Year 5) pupils. All stayed in the same class. Ten were girls. People began to send their girls to school more than before. We established strong relationships with people to be able to convey progressive and emancipatory ideas [to them]. We organised meetings with women to discuss domestic violence, which was common, and find solutions when they sought advice on marriage and family problems. Despite unfavourable conditions, teaching was a thrilling experience that hugely impacted a community's life.[41]

The availability of female teachers also created a help point for women to seek advice, in most cases for the first time, on social or cultural issues. In the absence of relevant state institutions in the rural areas, the presence of female teachers and their community work had become very significant. While they had the authority of the state behind them, their constructive approach to work stemmed from their intellectual dispositions and their willingness to go to rural areas in need and spontaneously engage in extra social work merits recognition.

Legal and economic changes

The modern state was in favour of a new image for women, allowing legal changes in favour of women. In addition to new civil laws, the most significant event was the forced unveiling of 1936, which intended to 'emancipate' women but had the impact on shutting women back in the sphere of home. Although young schoolgirls had started to go to school in school uniforms even before this law, once the law passed their mothers in many cases preferred to stay home for fear of forced unveiling and abuse from the police.[42] The banning of the veil entailed (passive) resistance from women by staying home. Nevertheless, it gradually institutionalized a new women's dress code in schools and a less veiled type of dress in public. Its later implication was that legal and state support for women could be effective, eventually institutionalizing a new dress code for women.[43] Kurdish women, specifically those living in the village, were not accustomed to strict veiling. However, they had been veiled enough according to the Islamic dress code. The *chashew/chador* (Ku./Pe. open cloak) was customary, as was other forms of headgear for women. Initially, the proposed dress code (1936) seemed too foreign to the culture, and impractical (see Figure 8), to be implemented by force.

The new family laws were other crucial actions for which the pressure of women had been indispensable. However, without the power of the state, such laws could not have been materialized. Combined with other educational or medical developments, these laws increased the age of marriage for both sexes and bestowed upon women more rights in marriage, family and child custody.[44] Because of religious opposition and the Shah's conservatism, these laws had their own limits. Nevertheless, they represented major advances in the legal status of women.

While the increase in the number of women in new jobs also owed itself to the expansion of modern education, employment provided economic independence and empowered women both in the home and in public. The socio-economic transformation created or increased new opportunities in teaching, nursing and the private sector. The Kurdish society of the 1960s had significantly become accustomed to women working as teachers, secretaries or nurses and to their growing independent presence in public. Women had also been a part of the production, as noted before, and the expansion of the economy also expanded their economic involvement. However, the achieved degree of independence in new jobs, which required prior education, created a new dimension in the existing gender relations in favour of women. Indeed, this accentuated the resistance of men to women's empowerment, even in middle-class families.[45]

However, empowerment did not necessarily bring about an equal share because the positive legal and economic changes regarding women were not going to eradicate or reduce inequality in the income gap or the economic well-being of families across different classes and regions. Economically, the majority of women joined the new, growing Kurdish working class. Babysitters, cleaners, market vendors and housekeepers increased many-fold. The internal migrant women resided in the new poor city districts on the outskirts of the cities. Most of them had lost their previous productive role in agricultural production without being provided with better economic opportunities. As noted in the previous chapters, many women ended up in brick-oven factories, enduring harsh living and working conditions. There were no protective labour laws for anyone.

5. The Modernization of Gender Relations 157

Figure 8 Women: Past and present. Above: the women of landowners' households around Saqqez, Qajar Kurdistan, circa 1910. *Source*: courtesy of Kurdistan Photolibrary. Despite modification through time, women's dress, seen in this image, were preserved throughout the Pahlavi era and outlived it, effectively challenging the homogenization of culture. Below: Hapsa Khan Naqib among new Kurdish-speaking women, modern Iraq, circa 1950. *source*: author's collection.

Therefore, the relationship between the economy and gender followed an undulating pattern, while economic well-being and educational background affected the degree of economic empowerment of women. Nevertheless, socio-economic changes introduced women to new possibilities in life that could not have been imagined a few decades earlier. For example, despite the hardship involved, working outside the home or residing in cities entangled women with others who endeavoured to enhance women's social status.[46] Actively pursued by Iranian women's organizations, new laws to improve working conditions for women followed the expansion of the women workforce.[47] This involved a discursive battle on behalf of the Woman's Organization to create a fertile ground for the public supporting laws protecting women workers. The organization proclaimed that 'Today, working is an honour for a woman',[48] and advised women that 'Evening times are the time for doing household tasks and helping the children with their homework'.[49] Nevertheless, this conservatism was compensated by ardent cultivation of the notion of 'the equality between men and women', and providing previously non-existent advice for working women and mothers.[50] These created the ground for a possible labour law, which promised the support of the state. The following message of the organization reflected the realities of the time, including cultural resistance to improving the place of women, the ambivalent position of the White Revolution – that is, both its modernizing impact and its conservatism – and the significance of women's agency:

> The White Revolution placed our country at the crossroads of progress and development. The share of women, especially that of working women, has been more than others. [This is] because, on the one hand, their right to vote was recognized and, on the other, in the same way as their brothers, they became shareholders in factories [...] [unlike before] the wages for men and women are equal [...] working is an honour for woman and a woman is worth more if she can work because her wages will enhance the economic well-being of the family and bring prosperity.[51]

Finally, the appearance of women in the domains of sports and the arts, as further significant aspects of socio-economic and cultural modernizations, should alert us to other significant, thus far neglected, aspects of modernization. In Iran, physical education constituted an aspect of modern education and grew with the latter's expansion. Like modern education, it gained a special place in the modern, nationalizing state; however, new sports required pioneers who, influenced by progressive and national ideas of the time, actively advocated a *healthy* education at least since the 1930s.[52] Although by the mid-1970s the expansion of sports had considerably included school girls and created a firm foundation for women in sport, descriptive histories of *men* in sport in Kurdistan have completely ignored women.[53] According to official statistics, quantitatively, in 1973–4 in table tennis, basketball, fencing, volleyball and handball, there were respectively 474, 248, 57, 366 and 76 female participants in the Kurdistan Province, compared to 1,124, 336, 84, 1,123 and 82 male participants.[54] Combined with oral accounts and photographic evidence, a rising proportion of women in sport can be seen, which signalled the profound transformation of conventional sports which had been dominated by men. The growing presence of women in sport could not have been possible without the firm foundation which was laid during the modernization of education.

Music and cinema became other spheres in which the traditional conception of women was challenged, with the creation of new roles for women and the modernization of the existing perceptions. The cinematic arts perpetuated the image of women, now literate and working, as sexual beings facing the constant threat of offensive attitudes, or as sexually vulnerable to prostitution because of poverty; for these reasons, the protection of men as their saviours was constantly required. At the same time, the increasing number of women employed in education and healthcare or as singers, writers and poets with literary and artistic influence helped create and transform the perceptions of the new generation of educated, urban men. The growing presence of women in such fields coincided with the proliferation of audio and, especially, visual means of communication such as radio and television, which maximized their impact on society, forcing the reconfiguration of the boundaries of masculinity and femininity. Qualitatively, the women of the early twentieth century and women of the 1970s could not be compared in their social position and attitudes, which also applied to men.

In 1978,

> The women's share in Iran's work force was approximately two million, including 190,000 with university education and expert training. 144,000 women worked as civil servants, including 1,666 women with various managerial posts. The number of [female] university lecturers exceeded 1,800 [while] there were women working in the army and police force or as lawyers, judges and engineers. The theology faculties [in the universities] were the only institutions which did not have any place for women. In 1978, as a result of the endeavours of organised women's groups for encouraging the political and electoral participation of women, 333 women were elected the members of local councils. In the same year, there were 22 [female] members of the Majlis [Parliament] and another two members of the Senate.[55]

Collective agency

Interrelated with other factors discussed earlier, women's agency was an indispensable factor in the transformation of the place of women in Iran in general. To include this factor in an analysis of the cultural transformation of the period is to emphasize the actions undertaken by a generation of educated women, who were intellectually shaped by progressive ideas of the time. These actions included the establishment of schools, women's organizations, help points, social work in difficult conditions in villages or among the poor, and political agitation towards forcing new elections and the legislation of family laws. These actions were not meagre. It was women's collective agency that primarily explains the distinction between Iran, which experienced a notable transformation of gender relations, with some other neighbouring countries, which went through much more limited, institutional changes. Precisely because of the profound institutional changes, the higher status of women was still preserved through resistance in Iran when a woman-friendly state had been eventually replaced by a regime of gender apartheid following the 1979 Revolution. Furthermore, incessant intellectual transformations in Iran since the Constitutional Revolution, and later the emergence of political parties in the 1940s (the Tudeh) and 1960s, for example, Fedayyan, which became a platform for women's activism, cannot be overemphasized.

The connection with the outside world, the expansion of the new means of communication, and revolutions and movements, including the advance of feminism, were all reflected in a generation of Iranians' writers, poets, and social and cultural critics among which women stood out and provided role models. Confirmed by the oral accounts of women workers, teachers and local activists, this occurred in a situation of extreme hardship, within a hostile culture and under a politically oppressive state during the era of the White Revolution. The collective agency proved to be a crucial factor for bringing about the institutional transformations regarding women in Iran. Presenting a challenge to visible and invisible practices involving women, directly or indirectly, was possible because of 'new women', whose emergence owed itself to many interrelated factors, discussed earlier.

That said, as Kurdish society's socio-economic integration into modern Iran continued, the place of women became increasingly linked with the way gender relations in Iran were being transformed. By the 1940s, feminism in Iran had entered public discourse as a consequence of Iranian women's activism, reforms and new laws in the preceding years.[56] Two world wars, which brought women of many countries into factories on a massive scale, the Russian Revolution and other social movements, were as crucial in spreading the ideas of women's emancipation and gender equality. As a result, by the 1960s a widespread *nehzat-e zanan* or women's movement in Iran had gradually taken form, represented by various women's organizations.[57] Without the pressure from this movement, the right of women to vote would not have materialized in 1963. Indeed, family laws, ratified by the Parliament in the following years, which radically altered the gender relations in Iran, were owed to the actions of the women's organizations. However, the movement still needed to become more powerful and self-aware if women were to achieve more rights and enhancement of their social status.[58] This led to more liaisons with the state, the support of which the movement hoped to attract by appealing to Princess Ashraf, the reigning Shah's twin sister. As a result of several months of research by a group of women's leaders, *Tashkilat-e Zanan-e Iran* or Iran Women Organization was formed with the princess as its honorary president. The organization's first congress in 1966 consisted of 5,000 members who had come from different parts of Iran to ratify the Organization's Constitution.[59]

The Women Organization was an amalgamation of many smaller organizations, which had been launched by women's activists and had been proliferating across Iran. As a result of its liaison with the state and, positively, with male ministers in power, the organization became more powerful. Its efforts affected, for example, school textbooks, a more favourable labour law for working women, family law and penal codes.[60] Its branches spread across Iran – there were ten branches in the Kurdistan Province – encouraging women's more active participation in society.[61] According to the director of the organization, Mahnaz Afkhami, the Shah was supportive but remained conservative for fear of the reaction of the religious hierarchy.[62] The biggest hurdle was an ingrained patriarchal ideology, supported by culturally deep-rooted religious institutions. The Shah's support emanated from a secular nationalism, which needed women for state-led modernization but remained characteristically conservative towards mainstream religion.

Although the women's societies continued their existence independently, Iran's Women Organization gradually became more centralized as the result of its liaison with the state. Seeking to accumulate political influence through powerful individuals and ministers initially yielded the desired results. However, in the long run, according to Mahnaz Afkhami, the organization became too aligned with the state, especially when making a mistake of supporting the new one-party system, which only recognized the Rastakhiz Party:[63] 'This made many dissidents of the [Shah's] regime suspicious of the Organisation.'[64] Nevertheless, the women's movement and the organization left an indelible mark on Iran with their major contributions to the enhancement of the social status of women in Iran.

Resistance

A significant aspect of the existing gender relations was undoubtedly women's resistance to different forms of male dominance, manifest in the various ways in which they interacted with their environment. Examining the conditions of women from this perspective allows for a change of perception from women as a category in development theories or an en masse force, to women as human beings with names and faces. In this regard, it is very productive to use Ilan Pappe's notion of 'autonomous space', which women created to cope with a male-dominated society or to organize and manage their lives.[65] While Pappe concisely stresses the importance of legal and social 'reforms from above [. . .] initiated by the state, and by the well publicized feminism of "women worthies"',[66] the roles of educated women and organized feminism in Iran which made 'reform from above' and changes in the legal system possible need to be underlined. Therefore, it was not simply the 'secularisation of the legal system' by the state but pressure from below along with the ongoing tension between (organized) women, the state and the religious establishments, on the one hand, and between the state and the religious institutions, on the other, which determined the scope of change of the social status of women. Admittedly, as Pappe argues, the secularization of the Middle Eastern states after the Second World War created 'better opportunities for effecting a significant transformation in the position of women through legal reforms'. However, he maintains, 'it was left to state officials in high positions to formulate and execute new policies in women's favour if they were inclined to do so.'[67]

In the case of Iran, women's activism, exemplified by publications and organizations, had preceded the modern state of Iran;[68] 'same-tireless dedication was responsible for bringing about the passage of Family Protection Law in 1967 and its amendment in 1973.'[69] State officials' dispositions were decisively affected by the existence of such pressure and, insofar as the state was concerned, it relied on political acts to have an impact on women's social or legal status. The infamous *kashf-e hejab*, or unveiling, was a case in point. It aimed to create a superficial modern image of Iranian women while women organizations such as the Women's

League were being eliminated and disbanded.[70] As another illustration of this, the right of women to vote in Iran, which was incorporated into the principles of the White Revolution, only came after the symbolic participation of women in the previous election, which forced the state to change the election laws in favour of women in 1963. As Pappe rightly argues, the state's reforms related to women resulted from economic or political considerations.[71] Although the support of the state, especially in the face of the mounting opposition of religious forces, was crucial, a study of women's activism since the Constitutional Revolution of 1906 shows that 'above all, it was the tireless effort of hundreds of committed women for more than fifty years that finally brought about the passage of this [election] law'.[72] This point is further illuminated by comparative studies of the status of women in Iran and other regional countries. As a case in point, as Pappe noted, Jordan failed to keep pace with others in introducing reforms related to the status of women.[73] There may be many reasons for the different chronologies and paces of change related to women; however, the tradition of organized feminism and the impact of pressure from below are significant factors that explain the differences of processes related to women in different countries, from Tunisia to Iran to Afghanistan.[74] Indeed, the histories of women are intertwined with women's efforts to reform their societies' gender order.

As their incorporation into modern Iran continued to accelerate, Kurdish-speaking women in Iran were increasingly affected by the gradual modernization of gender relations. In different ways, changing historical and social contexts presented new opportunities for them to challenge social norms. In Kurdish society, microhistories can be uncovered through the seemingly trivial stories of excluded women, or of major histories relating to the educated, urban generation which redefined women's role in both private and public spheres. These stories include cases in which women, encountering a female teacher for the first time in the 1970s, express opinions on customs such as forced marriage and FGM and against domestic violence. Another interesting tale is the cooperation of the wives of the same landowner to maintain a role in the management of the community, even though polygamous marriage created unfavourable conditions for the women involved. Represented by prominent women, women's societies, and educated and working women, the microhistories record social and political activism throughout the twentieth century.

The presence of prominent women throughout Kurdish history undoubtedly exerted a great impact on their communities' perceptions of gender. The existence of such 'women worthies' was not, however, exclusive to the Kurds, and more importantly the acceptance of their powerful role, according to studies on women in the early modern times, probably stemmed from the fact that the hierarchies of social class or genealogy outweighed gender as a determinant of social role.[75] The upper class in pre-modern Kurdish principalities, for example, Soran, Ardalan and Baban, contained 'women worthies' throughout successive centuries. They emerged as poets (Mastura Ardalan), or as activists (Hapsa Khan Naqib, 1891–1953), who is believed to have founded the first women's society in 1930 in Sulaimaniya in modern Iraq, or as community leaders (the provincial governor of Halabja, 'Adila

Khanim, 1848–1924). Many such individuals functioned as points of support for women of the lower strata, too. The women of the landowner's household did not always belong to the upper class. According to published memoirs, in the first decade of the twentieth century, the three wives of the *agha* of Delawan village worked as a team, under the supervision of the older wife, to manage the myriad tasks of the landowner's household and also the community around it.[76] In this way, they created their own autonomous space, including a help point for other women to rely on.

In some Kurdish regions, *radu khstn* (Ku. elopement) challenged forced marriage in favour of mutual love. In a region like that of Sardasht in the west of Iranian Kurdistan, a woman could succeed in choosing her partner for life by conducting marriage through elopement. The eloped couple took refuge in a powerful household, usually that of a landowner or a tribal chief, after which attempts were made to achieve the consent of the woman's family to the marriage. Pejoratively, a woman could be mocked by other women for not being fit for elopement. However, not all cases of elopements ended peacefully. In some regions such as Mangorayeti, located between Sardasht and Mahabad, elopement continued to be practised until the 1980s.

As noted in Chapter 1, women formed the most vulnerable section of society throughout the vicissitudes of the twentieth century. Rafiq Hilmi reported how women, who had to leave their homes in Iranian Kurdistan during the Second World War and enter Ottoman Kurdistan, were forced to engage in prostitution to survive, while Hemin recalled the trading of young girls for a sack of flour during the next war. Consistently missed by national historiography, Kurdish movements relied heavily on women; while the men were fighting, women endured hunger and the consequences of forced banishment. They were always the first to suffer from the governments' brutal oppressive machine. A typical example was Haybat whose husband was a peshmarga of Mullah Mustafa Barzani during the 1960s and 1970s. In *My Father's Rifle*, her son, Azad, recalls,

> Suddenly I heard very agitated voices. [. . .] When I reached the back of the house, I saw my mother come out, distraught, grasping the Koran wrapped in its green cloth. She held it out toward tense armed men. In a shaken voice, she screamed at them, 'For the love of the Koran, don't touch my house'. Right before my eyes, she was hit with the butt of a rifle and collapsed to the ground.[77]

Yet, in Kurdish history-writings women remained mostly nameless, without history and faceless.

Political movements, often rather indirectly, engaged women in politics. Later political upheavals and uprisings during or in the post–Second World War era, such as the Kurdish Republic, the crisis of the nationalization of oil in Iran and the peasant uprisings across Bukan region in Iranian Kurdistan, increased women's direct participation in politics. Village councils included female representatives in many cases.[78] Such historical events affected the social, political and gender awareness of all. An illustration of this is the story of Mina from Qoital village around Sardasht, told by a teacher she met at the end of the 1970s. Among the local people, Mina was known for being brave and free-minded. Her husband, Hussein, had regularly defied the landowners and later began to help the group around Sharifzada and Muʿeini (see the previous chapter) during the 1960s. After marrying Hussein, Mina became engaged in political activities. She would hide and escort other activists to pass checkpoints safely, deliver correspondence and undertake logistic tasks. At the end of the 1970s, 'Mina had three children whose characters resembled hers in many ways.'[79] Finally, the new educated, urban generation could count on unwavering support from their mothers, who encouraged their daughters to change the way women lived.

Conclusion

'Modernity' in Iran, including Kurdish society, entailed new institutions of education and civil and political bodies (women's societies, political parties and the 'secular' state), which challenged the inferior social status of women in both family and public. For statesmen and intellectuals alike, transforming Iran into a modern nation postulated the 'new woman', vital for a progressive image. Consequently, the state-led modernization restructured the existing gender relations, which came to be characterized by the growing presence of women in various social, cultural and economic fields. This process involved significant scientific, educational, social and legal achievements for women, for which, taking into account the pressure which women put on the state, women's activism was indispensable. The histories of women in Iran in general, and in Kurdistan in particular, demonstrate this activism that defied the existing gender order. Although the development discourse, which guided the Pahlavi state's modernization, discovered women as a category, reformism in Iran had preceded the new discourse by many decades. Later efforts both from above and from below to improve the place of women in society were a synthesis of that reformism and development discourse. The state's constructive approach to the question of women was crucial for realizing the above achievements. It comes as no surprise that the women of Iran of the 1970s, particularly urban women, generally considered themselves better-off in comparison with the women of the past. Furthermore, the new image of woman continued stubbornly to distinguish Iran in the region, despite the change in the nature of that state at the end of the 1970s, indicating women's agency as a significant factor to obtain, and preserve, such achievements.

Statistics show the inclusion of many women in ministerial and governmental posts or with responsibilities in executive and judicial power centres during the era of the White Revolution.[80] In Kurdish society, this was reflected in a higher number of educated women who became teachers, nurses, lawyers, secretaries, doctors, etc., accompanied by a new perspective on the role of women in society, effectively formed during the second half of the twentieth century. As argued in this chapter, this needs to be linked to social change across Iran as another significant aspect of the socio-economic incorporation of Kurdish society into modern Iran.

The televised 1979 Revolution presented women as a social force and revealed an *institutionalized* women's activism. This activism continued to characterize Kurdistan in the following years, despite the disappearance of the women-friendly Pahlavi state and its replacement with a state committed to gender discrimination and segregation. A case in point presents itself in the fact that the White Revolution socially changed and modernized the place of women in Kurdish society, yet the disparity between the urban and rural areas regarding the place of women stubbornly remained and continued to characterize the Kurdish region still in the 1980s. Women's activism continued to promote the expectations of rural women who waited to take their chances when the state-led modernization finally and more properly reached them in the next two decades following the 1979 Revolution, of course prioritizing its own needs as the Pahlavi state had done before.

CONCLUSION

KURDISH SOCIETY: PAST AND PRESENT

The central idea of this study posits that the modernization of Iran and the formation of Iran's modern nation state involved a dual process of socio-economic transformation and homogenization of identity and culture based on Persian as the perceived nation's core-ethnocultural community. This process, by the end of the 1970s, had resulted in profound social, economic, political and cultural transformations of Kurdish society in Iran. It also created new conditions for resistance to homogenization and the struggle for political and cultural rights of the Kurds to continue, according to various historical contexts.

Each chapter in this study sets out to demonstrate in different, but interwoven, ways how this dual process takes place, and what impact it has on the formation of modern Iranian Kurdish society. They shed light on two crucial aspects of that process. First, socio-economic modernization results in the (unequal) integration of Kurdish society in modern Iran. For example, urbanization, the expansion of the economy, the successive centralizing, urban-oriented development programmes, the new modernizing institutions of education and healthcare, and cultural modernization, all strengthened or created new bonds between Kurdish society and other societies in modern Iran in a single political and economic entity. Therefore, while it endeavoured to promote its political and social positions in the new nation state and preserve its commonality with other Kurdish societies located in adjacent nation states, Iranian Kurdish society followed the integrating tendency of social change and modernization.

Second, the dual process involves the Kurds' resistance to a homogenizing modernization while their struggle for cultural and political rights continues. This reflects a Kurdish society – the political and cultural structures of which were (re)shaped according to the policies of the state in the context of modern cultural encounters. The Kurdish struggle represents this aspect of the dual process. It continued to be reconfigured according to historical contexts, for example, the quasi-autonomous period of the early 1940s and the revolutionary activities of the 1960s and the 1970s, and to be affected by intellectual transformations, a case in point being the inspirational Thirdworldist ideologies of the 1960s. Meanwhile, discourses of power, based on the concept of the Kurds as *aqaliat-e qaumi* along with misrepresentation, justified the Kurds' marginalized position in the modern nation state of Iran, as well as political suppression and militarization; however, this was unceasingly defied by political, social and cultural activisms of a new educated generation of men and women especially in the second half of the twentieth century. From this perspective, this book concludes that to understand the consequences of modernity and modernization for the Kurds in Iran, we need to look at the dialectics of the dual process, because the Kurdish society of the second half of the century is effectively a synthesis of that multifaceted process.

As discussed in Chapter 2 and the following chapters, during this process the era of the White Revolution distinguishes itself for the intensification of modernization and unprecedented social transformations it entailed. It is important to avoid mythologizing or trivializing the era and acknowledge its significance for twentieth-century Iran, by a critical reading of the state-led modernization in that period. In fact, rather than being an invention of the ruling Shah, the 'White Revolution', as a reform programme in a specific historical context, was a synthesis of the existing ideas to reform Iran and the development discourses or theories which emerged in the aftermath of the Second World War. This becomes more evident if we underline two facts. First, explained by political scientists, the aim of the modernizing programmes of post–Second World War era, including the White Revolution, was to thwart revolution by neutralizing the threat posed by discontented social classes or groups. As the historians of Iran have also noted, the inception of the White Revolution to implement the existing reformist ideas of the time in Iran was an attempt to preserve the monarchy during a tumultuous period of regional revolutions and coups. The second fact pertains to the emergence of what it holds to be *generations for change*, who, ultimately failed by a personified dictatorship, left an enduring legacy through, for example, social, cultural and literary activism. Simultaneously, as discussed in Chapter 4, the proliferation of the audio and visual means of communication made the era a unique and challenging episode in the formation of modern Iran.

The consequences of the state-led modernization during the White Revolution for Iranian Kurdish society were significant; however, they simultaneously revealed the project's centralizing orientation. Analysed in Chapters 3 and 4, since the mid-twentieth century, development programmes became increasingly centralized and continued to be characterized by the absence of any provincial (or more precisely regional) planning. Until then, the lack of revenue was one of the main problems which had paralysed the effective execution of economic plans in Iran. As a mainly rural and agricultural society, the Kurdish region under Reza Shah, but also in later periods, suffered from both the orientation and deficiencies of the economic policies. In this respect, the Plan Organization of the 1950s under Ebtehaj symbolized centralization and set a precedent for the economic plans that followed during the White Revolution. Indeed, the Second Development Plan (1956–62) effectively marked the triumph of centralization in its tension with decentralization or more regional-oriented, plans.

This remained the case even when more comprehensive and sophisticated plans emerged, owing to the spiralling oil revenues of the early 1970s. Consequently, the development plans retained their focus on the expansion of modernization from the centre, with the effect that their emphasis on industrialization or privatization excluded regions that lacked capital and the potential of which was ignored. The notion of 'provincial development' died with the White Revolution. Moreover, insofar as the Kurdish region was concerned, political considerations also affected the state's economic policies, while economic changes reflected the economic expansion of the state, symbolized, for example, not by 'industrialisation' but by a thriving, labour-intensive, construction industry. Therefore, the general improvement of socio-economic conditions in Kurdistan depended on the effectiveness of the development plans to address, for instance, infrastructure, urbanization, transportations, communications, healthcare and education. Nevertheless, and in this respect, the urban-oriented development plans of the 1960s and 1970s were socio-economically more effective than their predecessors.

Furthermore, the scope of change was significantly extended during the era of the White Revolution to include, for example, modern education and healthcare (with major results), while land reform as its centrepiece effectively replaced the political and social authority of the Kurdish landowner class with that of the state. Although debilitated, the Kurdish *agha* class did not disappear but maintained their economic and social power in different ways, or remained dormant to re-emerge opportunistically to claim the restitution of their lost lands; a unique opportunity presented itself when the central power lost its coercive forces and subsequently its grip on society in 1979. Moreover, the land reform led to unprecedented migration and social movements of Kurdish peasantry, with their social consequences. For example, as a unit of the workforce, migrating peasant families endured harsh working conditions in brick-oven factories, while an army of seasonal workers was also created. This attests to the shortcomings of the reform as an uneven and prolonged process with serious social consequences. However, as confirmed by contemporaries, the reform inaugurated massive social movements also with further dynamic ramifications: it linked the village to constantly changing economic and social spheres and marked the effective start of the end of its social isolation. As noted, this had not yet been realized by the end of the 1970s, though significant changes in many respects could be detected. Finally, the long-term demise of both the foundations of tribalism and the social and political cohesiveness of the Kurdish *agha* class, a reality of twenty-first-century Iranian Kurdistan, could not have happened without the White Revolution's land reform; this is a distinguishing characteristic of Iranian Kurdish society compared with other Kurdish societies of the region.

Moreover, modernization entailed a profound transformation of social formations. Most notably, the expansion of a market economy, along with a conventional mercantile economy, modern education and healthcare, and civil administration, yielded a Kurdish middle class, whereas the land reform, unplanned urbanization which produced impoverished city neighbourhoods, and the growth of the economy, contributed immensely to the formation of modern Kurdish working class, a significant proportion of which, in addition to farmworkers, consisted of seasonal workers and unskilled urban labourers.

Regionally, insofar as the disparity between urban and rural areas in Kurdistan was concerned, it was sustained – in many cases the gap even widened – during the era of the White Revolution; no economic plan concerned with urbanization, industrialization, modern healthcare and education addressed that issue effectively. Culturally, this disparity applies to the unequal distribution of cultural capital too. While the urban centres continued to benefit from cultural innovations in an increasingly mediatized society, a significant part of the rural areas remained isolated from a rapidly changing world.

Furthermore, two other major areas of change pertained to political and cultural spheres. Above all, the (re)formation of both political and cultural structures of Kurdish society corresponded to the process of homogenization. A crucial element in this respect was political and cultural resistance to the homogenizing policies of an authoritarian state which continued to be a prominent characteristic of Iranian Kurdistan. Between 1946 and 1979, except for short intervals, dictatorship and militarization characterized the political situation of Kurdistan and continued to undermine civil and democratic means of political participation. By the 1970s, the absolute power of the monarch over Iranians had been established. These factors kept the idea of armed struggle both relevant and attractive, especially in an era during which the Thirdworldist ideologies became inescapably influential. Insofar as Iranian Kurdish political activists were concerned, this was specifically the case with the movement of the 1960s, the end of which marked a critique of guerrilla warfare in favour of social revolution theories. Moreover, administratively, in the same period the motives behind modern administrative divisions differed from pre-modern, largely geographical and administrative considerations and began to serve a nationalist, homogenizing modern state. This resulted in further re-divisions of the region and led to the marginalization of communities such as the Failis in the south, and less-privileged cities and regions in the northwest of Iran's Kurdish region such as Somabradost. Finally, modern education, social change, urbanization and the intellectual transformations of the post–Second World War era yielded modern Kurdish political parties, which, in the long run, proceeded to completely replace tribal politics in Iranian Kurdistan.

As explicated in Chapter 4, this book illuminates the most significant aspect of the era's cultural transformation, that is, modern cultural encounters within a multicultural nation state, in contrast to a colonial or imperial context, which resulted in the establishment of Persian cultural hegemony. The state and its modern education had effectively paved the way in that direction; however, the proliferation of audio, but crucially also visual means of communication such as television and cinema, was crucial to this end.

Although resistance to a hegemonic culture persisted, the cultural structure of Kurdish society continued to (re)form according to the way cultural encounters between intimate, and not alien, cultures were taking place. It was in this context that the hegemonic notions of 'mainstream' or 'official' and 'local', to describe Persian language and culture and that of other non-Persian-speaking peoples in Iran respectively, became deeply ingrained in society in the era of the White Revolution. Admittedly, since the early years of the formation of the modern Iranian state, the literary prestige of Persian had begun to enjoy a state-sponsored political authority. However, the cultural superiority of Persian became hegemonic when the cultural inferiority of others was further institutionalized also as a consequence of the visualization of the means of communication, which proliferated alongside the expansion of modern education in Iran, transcending any literacy skills required for using the written modes of communication. Finally, the modernization's unequal distribution of cultural capital hindered the cultural potential of Kurdish society, especially in its rural regions. Therefore, championed by cultural and political activism, Kurdish society came to be characterized by Kurdish cultural resistance to the advance of hegemonic culture. Such a tension between a homogenizing culture and a resisting culture meant that Kurdish cultural production continued to be either hindered or promoted according to variable social conditions.

Methodologically, insofar as the concepts of 'Kurd' and 'Kurdistan' are concerned, this book's heterogeneous approach renders insufficient a well-established homogenous approach, which has been historically advocated by an intellectual tradition since the end of the nineteenth century and sustained vigorously throughout the next century. In this respect, a unique contribution of this study is a methodological break with the intellectual tradition to be able to approach the Kurds not as a monolithic entity but as members of *various* Kurdish societies, each affected by almost a century-old social change and transformation in *various* nation states. This approach does not undermine the Kurds' cultural commonalities, which exist regardless of their geographic locations, nor attempts to erode their distinct histories. It simply asks for their assessments in their own terms, based on both their own and common histories with others around them. It is only this heterogeneous, theoretically informed approach that can help the scholarship to leap forward in its analysing the social and historical formations of modern Kurdish societies.

Furthermore, a study of the formation of modern Kurdish society needs to underline the role of non-state agents of change and their interaction with the state as the central player. This study's examination of the expansion of modern education and healthcare reveals the significance of including non-state agents of change. Although urban-oriented, these institutions were two leading areas of change in Kurdistan, also because their expansions involved the endeavours of non-state agents of change such, symbolized by the educator ʿAziz Al-Muluk and the poet Qaneʿ, who made the promotion of the social and cultural awareness of people a major part of their mission; the role of non-state agents of change is often overlooked by theories of modernization. The crucial interaction of the state and non-state agents of change is also revealed in the process involving the modernization of gender relations. Women's agency was crucial in the institutionalization of a promoted social status of women in Iranian societies.

Iran's Kurdish society in the present

This book's analysis of twentieth-century Kurdish-Iranian society reveals the roots of many prominent trends in the present. The Islamic Republic of Iran's state-led modernization has been all but the continuation of the Pahlavi modernization, albeit with paying close attention to agriculture too. While quantitatively everything points to the staggering scope of change in the context of globalization, the question of (centralized) *touse'e* or socio-economic development regarding a periphery region such as Kurdistan has remained the main question. Politically, militarization and the heavy presence of the central government in the Kurdish region since the revolution has worked to the detriment of civil society movements, encouraging violent forms of resistance. This was embodied by the intense armed struggle of the entire decade of the 1980s, on which memoirs are proliferating. However, civil society movements along with the spread of non-governmental organizations have proliferated in the last two decades. This is also the case with the academic, intellectual, literary and journalistic efforts, which fundamentally distinguish contemporary Kurdish society from the one under the Pahlavis. Overshadowed by the recent wars and political developments in the wider region, such movements are not at least sufficiently acknowledged in the scholarship. This is due to the apparent absence of an active, armed Kurdish movement in Iran, often explained by Iranian Kurds' 'acquiescence' or owing to their more Iranian 'racial' roots. The 1990s and the 2000s are marked by a revolution in communication, exemplified by satellite television stations and, of course, the internet. This significant historical moment seems to comprise *terra* nearly incognito, to borrow from Frierson, a frontier, of history for historians, seeming to have made the preceding decades along with historical actors lost to amnesia.[1] There is a danger that whenever the heroic or horrific events across the wider region are captured, magnified and then circulated by the astonishing speed of the internet, everything that happened before, if not completely forgotten, pales into insignificance. The reason that the post-1979 Kurdish society remains, at least until quite recently, largely understudied, is partly because the usually shallow analyses of the pre-1979 period or the dominance of political history – significant works are the exception – have not been surpassed by more in-depth, comprehensive studies of the formation of modern Kurdish society.

Yet this book shows that resistance has been a permanent, indeed an exciting, aspect of the modern history of Iran's Kurdish society, which simultaneously continues both its intimate interaction with social change and transformation across Iran and resistance to political, cultural, gender and religious oppression. Various literary, women's rights, labour, students and environmental societies or groups characterize present-day Kurdish society. Furthermore, the establishment of the institutions of higher education, for example, the University of Kurdistan, the increase in the number of bilingual journals despite financial difficulties – under the Iranian press law, Kurdish journals have to include articles in Persian too – producing Kurdish textbooks for secondary schools, organizing conferences and seminars, the presence of more Kurdish-speaking individuals in the management of the local and provincial authorities, the expansion of the academia, the considerable increase in the number of women, for example, also from the rural regions, in higher education, etc., could not have been achieved in the absence of persistent activism or by being acquiescent. These are taking place despite the fact that Kurdish activists continue to face a constant threat of imprisonment with its dire consequences. On the other hand, non-violent, intermittent general strikes along with maintaining pressure on the state through various means of communication, demonstrate other aspects of the political situation in Kurdistan. Civil society, social or grassroots movements are also reflected in large and far-ranging literary records produced mainly in Kurdish-Sorani. Interestingly, not only the boundaries of the state and society have constantly continued to be redrawn, but another aspect of life has also been engagement with dominant culture as a communicative medium in order to change it as a cultural producing system. This is exemplified by the translations of literary works, for example, the poetry of Sherko Bekas, from Kurdish into Persian and the increasing inclusion of Kurdish cultural traits in award-winning Persian literary works such as *Joghd-E Barfi* (The snowy owl, 2018).[2] This has been the case with symbolic acts of defiance, too. For example, in the wake of the 2017 deadly earthquake, which devastated the Kermanshah Province and other parts of the Kurdish region, many Persian daily newspapers expressed solidarity in Kurdish on their front pages. It was breathtaking and unprecedented at the same time, giving a new meaning to the Iranian people's humanitarian aid pouring into the Kurdish region. Indeed, Persian cultural hegemony in modern times has never been impervious to resistance, while engagement with dominant culture is seen as an alternative, to borrow from Ashcroft, to isolation and remaining as the *other* forever, and, to borrow from Bazafkan and Rezaei, to antagonism.[3] Indeed, the Kurds of Iran have been, and continue to be, the leading actors in changing their society, shaping the course of the history of Iran at the same time.

That said, this raises two new sets of questions for future research around (1) Kurdish identity and (2) social change studies. As regards the former, how do the dialectics of modernization and homogenization continue to (re)shape Iranian Kurdish society in the periods that follow the era of the White Revolution? How do cultural encounters manifest themselves? To identify any advances of Kurdish cultural practices in Iran, what course, to borrow from Williams, has the tension between emergent and hegemonic cultures taken since the 1970s? How prominent has Kurdish culture and literature become in recent decades? These and many more questions reveal that the dual process incorporates infinite sources which affect the formations of Kurdish identity and modern Kurdish society. The other set of questions bears on a decisive turn to social change studies, whose themes need to be examined in the light of constant methodological and theoretical endeavours in relevant fields. This means engaging, among scholarly fields, with studies of economy and society; gender order and reproduction of masculinity and femininity; the class structure; education and healthcare; the disparity between city and village; and historiography, political science, literature and cultural studies. This is also necessary to defy national narratives which continue to claim these fields to the detriment of social history and social change studies.

The result of the expansion of the scholarship will be the demarginalization of Iranian Kurdish studies in the face of homogenous, national narratives, on the one hand, and making such studies central to Iranian Studies, on the other. The achievement of this is presupposed by an approach which, founded on common social, economic, cultural, political and historical concerns between Kurdish society and other societies in Iran, regards Kurdish and Iranian Studies as complementary. Such concerns are as significant as any society's peculiarity in all those aspects because they reflect a common experience of change and transformation in the last century.

NOTES

Introduction

1 On the ascendancy of Europe since the early modern times, see John Darwin, *After Tamerlane: The Global History of Empire since 1405* (London: Allen Lane, 2007), 162–98; and Nikki R. Keddie (ed.), *The French Revolution and the Middle East*. Iran and the Muslim World: Resistance and Revolution (London: Macmillan Press, 1995).
2 Andrew Linklater, 'The Problem of Community in International Relations', *Alternatives: Global, Local, Political* 15, no. 2 (Spring 1990): 149.
3 Hegemony, in Gramscian terms, is maintaining authority through consent rather than coercion. An intellectual hegemony is achieved when a set of ideas becomes a point of departure, making a conception 'instinct', 'spontaneously' conceived, as 'common sense'. See Quintin Hoare and Geoffrey Nowell Smith (eds), *Selections from the Prison Notebooks of Antonio Gramsci* (London: Lawrence and Wishart, 1971), 198–9.
4 For more on Heidegger and his influence on important thinkers such as Ahmad Fardid, Ali Shari'ati and Jalal Al-e Ahmad, see Ali Mirsepassi, *Political Islam, Iran, and the Enlightenment* (Cambridge: Cambridge University Press, 2011), 85–128.
5 On gender see Joan Wallach Scott, 'Gender: A Useful Category of Historical Analysis', in Sue Morgan (ed.), *The Feminist History Reader* (New York: Routledge, 2006); Merry E. Wiesner-Hanks, 'Gender', in Garthine Walker (ed.), *Writing Early Modern History* (London: Hodder Arnold, 2005); Dorothy Ko, 'Gender', in Ulnika Rublack (ed.), *A Concise Companion to History* (Oxford: Oxford University Press, 2012); Stefan Dudink et al. (eds), *Masculinities in Politics and War: Gendering Modern History* (Manchester Manchester University Press, 2004); Raewyn Connell, *Gender*, 2nd edn (Cambridge: Polity, 2009); James W. Messerschmidt, *Hegemonic Masculinity: Formulation, Reformulation, and Amplification* (London: Rowman & Littlefield, 2018).
6 See Lokman I. Meho and Kelly L. Maglaughlin, *Kurdish Culture and Society: An Annotated Bibliograph* (Westport: Greenwood Press, 2001).
7 One notable exception is the works of Amir Hassanpour.
8 See Ahmad Mohammadpur and Taqi Iman, 'Taqhirate Ejtemai Dar Sardasht' (Social Chang in Sardasht), *Nameye Ensanshenasi* 1, no. 5 (1383 (2004)): 11–39; Mehdi Rezayi et al., 'Sonnat, Nosazi Wa Khanewade' [Tradition, Modernization and Family], *Pazhoheshe Zanan* 7, no. 4 (2010): 71–93; Omid Qaderzade et al., 'Tejarate Marzi Wa Tafsire Mardom Az Taghirate Jahane Ziste Khanevade' [Border Trade and People's Perception of Family], *Rahbord Farhang* 6, no. 22 (Summer 1392 [2013]): 61–84.
9 Illan Pappe, *A History of Modern Palestine*, 2nd edn (Cambridge: Cambridge Univeisity Press, 2004), 1–13.
10 Ibid., 7.

11 Michel Foucault, *The Archaeology of Knowledge* (London: Routledge, 1972), 24–5 and Ch. 2; Edward Said, *Orientalism* (New York: Vintage Books, 1978), 3.
12 According to Bourdieu, economic theory has reduced 'the universe of exchanges to mercantile exchange, which is objectively and subjectively oriented toward the maximization of profit, i.e., (economically) self-interested', and 'has implicitly defined the other forms of exchange as non-economic, and therefore, disinterested'. See Pierre Bourdieu, 'The Forms of Capital', in John G. Richardson (ed.), *Handbook of Theory and Research for the Sociology of Education* (London: Greenwood Press, 1986), 242.
13 Ibid.
14 On development theory, see Arturo Escobar, *Encountering Development: The Making and Unmaking of the Third World* (Princeton: Princeton University Press, 1995). For critiques of modernization, tradition and modernity, and modernization theories, see Reinhard Bendix, 'Tradition and Modernity Reconsidered', in Reinhard Bendix (ed.), *Embattled Reason* (New Jersey: Transaction, Inc., 1988); Ilan Pappe, *The Modern Middle East* (New York: Routledge, 2005), 1–13; Zachary Lockman, *The Contending Visions of the Middle East: The History and Politics of Orientalism*, 2nd edn (New York: Cambridge University Press, 2010), 134–48.
15 Cf. Max Weber, *Economy and Society: An Outline of Interpretive Sociology* (Berkeley: University of California Press, 1978).
16 John Stevenson, *British Society 1914-1945* (London: Penguin, 1984), 17.
17 Ibid.
18 Reinhard Bendix, 'Tradition and Modernity Reconsidered', *Comparative Studies in Society and History* 9, no. 3 (April 1967): 331.
19 Ibid., 293.
20 Lawrence Cahoone (ed.), *From Modernism to Postmodernism: An Anthology* (Australia: Blackwell Publishing Ltd, 2003), 9.
21 Lockman, *The Contending Visions*, 137–8.
22 Ibid., 134.
23 Ibid.
24 Ibid., 88.
25 Ibid., 134–41.
26 Ibid., 280.
27 Ibid.
28 On political developments, cf. W. W. Rostow, *The Stages of Economic Growth: A Non-Communist Manifesto* (Cambridge: Cambridge University Press, 1990); and Samuel Huntington, *Political Order in Changing Societies* (New Haven and London: Yale University Press, 1968).
29 Huntington, *Political Order in Changing Societies*, 155.
30 TNA, FO371 157605 EP 1015/123 24 May 1961, quoted in Ali M. Ansari, 'The Myth of the White Revolution', in Ali M. Ansari (ed.), *Politics of Modern Iran* (London: Routledge, 2001), 262.
31 Ervand Abrahamian, *Iran between Two Revolutions* (Princeton: Princeton University Press, 1982), Ch. 9.
32 Bendix, 'Tradition and Modernity Reconsidered', 315–16.
33 Ibid., 316.
34 Daniel Lerner, *The Passing of the Traditional Society: Modernizing the Middle East* (Glencoe: Free Press, 1958), 44.
35 Nation as an imagined community and a product of print capitalism is represented in Benedict Anderson, *Imagined Communities* (London and New York: Verso,

2006), 37–47; nation as a product of industrialization is discussed in Ernest Gellner, *Nationalism* (New York: New York University Press, 1997); while for Anthony Smith nationalism is not only an ideology but also a cultural phenomenon which is closely related to national identity: Anthony Smith, *National Identity* (London Penguin Books, 1991), 19–42; nation and nationalism as inventions of the nineteenth-century Europe are represented in Eric Hobsbawm and Terrence Ranger (eds), *The Invention of Tradition* (Cambridge: Cambridge University Press, 1983), 1–15 and in Eli Kedouri, *Nationalism in Asia and Africa* (London: Weidenfield and Nicolson, 1971), 1–188; and for nation as narration, see Homi K. Bhabha (ed.), *Nation and Narration* (New York: Routledge, 1990).

36 See Stefan Berger and Chris Lorenz (eds), *The Contested Nation: Ethnicity, Class, Religion and Gender in National Histories* (Basingstoke: Palgrave McMillan, 2008).
37 Anthony Smith, *Nationalism and Modernism* (New York: Routledge, 1998), 3 and 1–24.
38 See Roger Brubaker, *Nationalism Reframed: Nationhood and the National Question in the New Europe* (Cambridge: Cambridge University Press, 1996); on Iran see Touraj Atabaki (ed.), *Iran in the 20th Century: Historiography and Political Culture* (London: I. B. Tauris, 2009); Ali M. Ansari, *Politics of Nationalism in Modern Iran* (Cambridge: Cambridge University Press, 2012); Afshin Marashi, *Nationalizing Iran: Culture, Power and the State* (Seattle and London: University of Washington Press, 2008).
39 Andreas Wimmer, *Nationalist Exclusion and Ethnic Conflict: Shadows of Modernity* (Cambridge: Cambridge University Press, 2002), 1.
40 Denis Natali has attempted to explain *Kurdayeti* or 'Kurdish national identity' and 'its similarities and variations in its manifestation [. . .] based on the nature of political space' in the nation states of Turkey, Iraq and Iran. While a useful approach, it is limited because it is only concerned with political aspects of the formation of national or ethnic identities. In contrast, the current study stresses a dynamic, multifaceted dual process of modernization and homogenization which also contains social and cultural aspects. See Denise Natali, *The Kurds and the Stat: Evolving National Identity in Iraq, Turkey, and Iran* (New York: Syracuse University Press, 2005), Introduction.
41 Cf. Husein Huzni, 'Ghunchai Baharistan: Tarikhi Kurdan' [Blossoms of Spring: The History of the Kurds] in Badran Ahmad Habib (ed.), *Collected Works* (Aras: Hawler, 2011), 67; and Muhammad Mardukh, *Mezhui Kurd Wa Kurdistan* [The History of Kurd and Kurdistan] (Hawler: Rozhhalat Press, 2011), 25.
42 On state formation see Heather Rae, *State Identities and the Homogenisation of Peoples* (Cambridge: Cambridge University Press, 2002), 1–54; and on the politicization of ethnicity see Wimmer, *Shadows of Modernity*, Chs. 3 and 6.
43 Rae, *State Identities*, 2.
44 On periodization and spatialization, see Fred M. Donner, 'Periodization as a Tool of the Historian with Special Reference to Islamic History', *Der Islam* 91, no. 1 (2014): 20–36.
45 Ideology as meaning in the service of power is discussed in John B. Thompson, *Ideology and Modern Culture: Critical Social Theory in the Era of Mass Communication* (Cambridge: Polity Press, 1990), 6–7. Terry Eagleton points out that this definition is 'the single most widely accepted definition of ideology', rightly asserting that not all 'ideologies are oppressive and spuriously legitimating' and that ideology 'is any kind of intersection between belief systems and political power'. See Terry Eagleton, *Ideology: An Introduction* (London and New York: Verso, 1991), 5–7.

46 The records and catalogues held by the National Archives are cited in this order: 'Title, (other references), date, TNA, Reference.
47 Lynn Abrams, *Oral History Theory* (London: Routledge, 2010), 1.
48 For more on oral history, cf. Donal A. Ritchie (ed.), *The Oxford Handbook of Oral History* (Oxford: Oxford University Press, 2011).

Chapter 1

1 Cf. Evliya Chelebi, *An Ottoman Traveller: Selections from the Book of Travels of Evliya Çelebi*, trans. Robert Dankoff and Sooyong Kim (London: Eland, 2010).
2 Masoud Karshenas, *Oil, State Ad Industrialisation in Iran* (Cambridge: Cambridge University Press, 1990), Ch. 2. For example, 'while in 1844 more than 70 per cent of Iranian exports were composed of handicraft manufactures, by 1910 the share of manufactures, with the exception of carpet, was reduced to virtually nil.' Ibid., 48.
3 Ibid., 47-8.
4 Eric Hobsbawm, *The Age of Revolution: Europe, 1789-1848* (London: Weidenfeld & Nicolson, 1962), 181.
5 Isabella Bishop, *Journeys in Persia and Kurdistan*, Vol. 2 (London John Murray, 1891), 207. According to Bishop, the city had 'twenty small mosques, three *hammams* [public bath], some very inferior caravansaries and a few coffee houses' and its *bazaar* well supplied. Ibid., 206.
6 Ibid., 207.
7 Ibid., 208.
8 *Sur Esrafil* 18 (November 1907): 1-2.
9 Cf. C. Rich, *A Narrative of Residence in Koordistan*, 2 vols (London: W. Clowes and Sons, 1836); James B. Fraser, *Narratives of a Journey into Khurasan in the Years 1821 and 1822* (London: n.p., 1825); Bishop, *Journeys in Persia and Kurdistan*, Vol. 2; and, first published in 1915, Sir Mark Sykes, *The Chalifs' Last Heritage* (Reading: Garnet Publishing, 2002).
10 See Sykes's observation of Kurdish and Armenian markets in Sykes, *The Chalifs' Last Heritage*, 403 and Ch. V.
11 A case in point is the famous Barzani tribal community. For a brief account, see William Eagleton, *The Kurdish Republic of 1946* (London: Oxford University Press, 1963), 47-54. Referring to the Young Turks government, Sir Mark Sykes argued that the aim of the policy of the settlement of tribes was 'the pacification of so-called turbulent [Kurdish] tribes, who, as history has shown, never gave the least trouble to a just or even moderately strong government, and, who, if treated with ordinary kindness, are a bulwark of strength in time of war'. For this see Sykes, *The Chalifs' Last Heritage*, 404.
12 Fraser, *Narratives of a Journey into Khurasan*, 160.
13 Ibid., 173.
14 For more discussions on such terms, see Ira M. Lapidus, *A History of Islamic Societies*, 3rd edn (Cambridge: Cambridge University Press, 2014), 220-3 and 81.
15 See, respectively, Sharaf Khan Bitlisi, *Sharafnameh: Tarikhe Mofassale Kurdistan* [The Sharafnameh: The Complete History of Kurdistan] (in Persian) (Iran: Asatir, 1377 [1998]), 9; and Haji Qadir Koyi, *Diwan* (Kurdish) (Stockholm: Nefel, 2004), 106-7.

16 'Abd-Allāh Mardūk, 'The Madrasa in Sunni Kurdistan', in *Encyclopaedia Iranica*, http://www.iranicaonline.org/articles/education-vi-the-madrasa-in-sunni-kurdistan, accessed 15 March 2017.
17 Ibid.
18 C. J. Wills, *In the Land of the Lion and Sun or Modern Persia* (London: Ward, Lock and Co., 1891), 336.
19 See ibid., 37–9.
20 Ibid., 338–9.
21 See ibid., 339.
22 Mardūk, 'The Madrasa in Sunni Kurdistan'.
23 Maref Khaznadar, *Mezhui Adabi Kurdi: Sadai 19 W Saratai Sadai 20* [The History of Kurdish literature: The 19th Century and the Early 20th Century], ed. Dr Kurdustan Mukriani, Vol. 4 (Kurdistan, Hawler: The Education Ministry Publication, 2004).
24 Vasili Nikitin, *Kord Wa Kordestan* [Kurd and Kurdistan], trans. M. Qazi (Iran: Nilufar, 1363 [1984–5]), 230–31.
25 Abrahamian, *Iran between Two Revolutions*, 13.
26 See Khaznadar, *The History of Kurdish Literature*, Vol. 4.
27 Maref Khaznadar, *Mezhui Adabi Kurdi: Sadei Nozda W Bistam* [The History of Kurdish Literature: the Nineteenth and Twentieth Centuries] (Kurdish), Vol. 4 (Kurdistan, Hawler: The Education Ministry, 2004), 21. Another example is Sayyid Abdulrahim known as Mavlavi (1806–83) who frequently travelled to Iran.
28 Bishop, *Journeys in Persia and Kurdistan*, Vol. 2, 207. Unveiled Kurdish women attracted all Europeans like Sykes who contrasted them to (Turkish) women in 'Turkified' Anatolia. Sykes, *The Chalifs' Last Heritage*, 405.
29 Cf. Nikitin, *Kord Wa Kordestan*, 223–8.
30 The French ambassador, Eugene Aubin, recalls in his travelogue (1907–8) 'beautiful carpets which had been weaved for the *agha* by women in their free time in winter'. Eugene Aubin, *Iran Emrouz 1907-1908* [Iran Today] (Iran: Zawarm 1985), 110.
31 Maref Khaznadar, *Mezhui Adabi Kurdi La Saratawa Ta Sadai Chwarda* [The History of Kurdish Literature: From the Beginning until the Fourteenth Century], Vol. 1 (Kurdistan, Hawler: Education Ministry, 2001), 17–18.
32 Abrahamian, *Iran between Two Revolutions*, 12.
33 Ibid.
34 Mehdi Rezayi, 'A Study of Low-Birth Rate in Iranian Kurdistan' (PhD Thesis, University of Tehran, 2011).
35 Bishop, *Journeys in Persia and Kurdistan*, Vol. 2, 207.
36 Cf. document 31 and 32, correspondence of spring 1911, in Reza Azari Sharzayi (ed.), *Asnade Baharestan (1): Gozideye Asnadi Az Waqaye' Mashroote Dar Kordestan Wa Kermanshahan* [Bahrestan Documents (1): A Selection of Documents Pertaining to the Constitutional Events in the Kurdistan and Kermanshahan [Provinces]] (Tehran: Library of Islamic Consultative Assembly, 1385 [2007]), 68–73.
37 Eagleton, *Kurdish Republic*, 7.
38 According to the 1960 census in Iran, there were 4,400 Shikak families (in Iran). For this see Muhammadrasul Hawar, *Simko W Bzutnawey Natawayeti Kurd* [Simko and The Kurdish National Movement] (Sweden: APEC, 1995), 210. Lord Curzon's estimation in 1892 was 1,500 families.
39 Sanar Mamedi, *Khaterat Wa Dardha* [Memorandom and Pains], Vol. 1 (Sweden: Alfabet Maxima, 2000), 14 and 14–16.

40 Cf. document 54, which contains a correspondence as of 1911, in Sharzayi, *Asnade Baharestan*, 98–101.
41 As Eagleton noted, 'the Republic overcame the most disrupting factors in large-scale tribal movements, i.e. the foraging which often led to looting'. Eagleton, *Kurdish Republic*, 94.
42 'The Kurds of Persia', dated 28 March 1946, TNA, FO371/52702 E2782/104/34 confirms a previous statement that 'The Kurds of Persia are hopelessly divided among themselves'.
43 For more on Kurdish tribes, see Eagleton, *Kurdish Republic*, 16–23.
44 Muhammad Mardukh claimed that in June 1907 'along with several respected and intelligent men from the first class of Kurdistan, we decided to form an anjoman [called Sadaqat] in Sanandaj without including any *mushir*s or *asafs*', that is, the government's representatives or city rulers. He also mentions the formation of a 'workers union' by 'a group of bazaar vendors and merchants (Bazargan). See Mardukh, *Mezhui Kurd*, 483.
45 For the representatives from the Kurdish region see *Kaveh*, Year 1, ns. 29 and 30, 8–9.
46 A correspondence as of May 1911 addressed to the *Majlis* complains about 'bad intentions' on behalf of some [powerful people] and demands the reopening of *Ma'refat* school which had been functioning for the previous three years. For this see document 49 in Sharzayi, *Asnade Baharestan*, 91–3.
47 Eagleton, *Kurdish Republic*, 33. For their names see ibid., 133.
48 For a list of the Republic's ministries see ibid., 134.
49 See Touraj Atabaki, *Azerbaijan: Ethnicity and Struggle for Power in Iran* (London: I. B. Tauris, 2000), 54–9. For example, since the start of the Constitutional Revolution, Iranian Azerbaijan had become a testing ground for such ideas exemplified famously in the short-lived government of Khyiabani (1918–20), for which see ibid., 46–51.
50 Sir Arnold Wilson, *Sw. Persia: A Political Officer's Diary 1907-1914* (London: Oxford University Press, 1941), 267–98.
51 The 1913 commission's work was based on previous attempts by Britain and Russia since 1847, ibid., 269. The new commission 'procured the consent of the Sublime Court Porte and the Imperial Persian Government to a definite frontier line from Fao on the Persian Gulf to Ararat in the north', ibid., 270.
52 Ibid.
53 Ibid., 284.
54 *Kaveh*, 127–9.
55 *Ayandeh* (1925) 1:82 and (1926) 13:7.
56 Rafiq Hilmi, *Yaddasht* [Notes] (Iraq: Roshinbiri Lawan Press, 1988), 32–3.
57 David McDowall, *A Modern History of the Kurds* (London: I. B. Tauris, 2004), 108.
58 Quoted in ibid., 109.
59 Cf. documents 32 Sharzayi, *Asnade Baharestan*, 69–73.
60 E. M. H. Lloyd, *Food and Inflation in the Middle East, 1940-45* (California: Stanford University Press, 1956), 240–1.
61 Ibid., 241.
62 Ibid., 242.
63 Eagleton, *Kurdish Republic*, 87–8.
64 Mohammad Amin Sheikholeslami-Hemin, *Tarik W Roon* [Dark and Light] (n.p: n.p), 34–5.
65 Ibid.

66 Sami Zubaida defines political field as 'a whole complex of political models, vocabularies, organisations and techniques which have established and animated [. . .] a political field of organisation, mobilisation, agitation and struggle', Sami Zubaida, *Islam, the People and the State: Political Ideas and Movements in the Middle East* (New York: I. B. Tauris, 2009), 145–6.
67 Politico-cultural stance is a term borrowed from Brubaker, *Nationalism Reframed*, 60.
68 See Smith's discussion on the role of organized religion in ethnic persistence among 'vertical' communities. Smith, *National Identity*, 62.
69 For a good discussion of the priority of national identity over religious identity, see ibid., 6–8.
70 Mola Qadir Modarresi, 'Komalay Zhekaf', in ʿAli Karimi, *Zhiyan W Basarhati Abdulraham Zabihi* [The Life and Fortune of Abdulrahman Zabihi] (Sweden: Zagros Media, 1999), 68.
71 For a history of theological transformations in the Shiʿa thought, see Said Amir Arjomand, *The Shadow of God and the Hidden Imam* (Chicago: University of Chicago Press, 1984). On the ideologue of the Islamic Revolution, see Hamid Dabashi, *Theology of Discontent: The Ideological Foundation of the Islamic Revolution in Iran* (New Brunswick: Transaction Publishers, 2006).
72 Saeed Talajooy, 'Rostam and Esfandiyar: From a Heroic Age to Page, Stage and Screen', unpublished article, 2011.
73 See R. John Perry, 'Language Reform in Turkey and Iran', *International Journal of Middle East Studies* 17, no. 3 (August 1985): 295–311; Mehrdad Kia, 'Persian Nationalism and the Campaign for Language Purification', *Middle Eastern Studies* 34, no. 2 (1998): 9–36; and Mohsen Rustayi, *Tarikhe Nokhostin Farhangestane Iran* [The History of Iran's First Academy] (Iran: Nei Publications 1385 [2006–7]).
74 For more on this, see Stephanie Cronin, *Soldiers, Shahs and Subalterns in Iran: Opposition, Protest and Revolt, 1921-1941* (New York: Palgrave, 2010), Ch. 1.
75 See *Sur Esrafil*, *Hab al-Matin*, *Akhtar*.
76 *Sur Esrafil* 17 (November 1907): 1.
77 *Kaveh*, Year 1, no. 27 (15 April 1918): 2–5.
78 *Kaveh*, Year 2, no. 1 (22 January 1921).
79 On material and spiritual domains, see Kia, 'Persian Nationalism', 9–10; and Darwin, *After Tamerlane*, 339–49, for a general discussion on 'culture wars' in relation to non-European societies.
80 *Kaveh*, Year 2, no. 1, 2.
81 Mardukh, *Mezhui Kurd*, 628–9.
82 For more on Foroughi, see Ali M. Ansari, 'Mohammad Ali Foroughi and the Construction of Civic Nationalism in Early Twentieth-Century Iran', in H. E. Chehabi, et al. (eds), *Iran in the Middle East: Transnational Encounters and Social History* (London: I. B. Tauris, 2015). On Taqizadeh see Homa Katouzian, *State and Society in Iran: The Eclips of the Qajars and the Emergence of the Pahlavis* (London: I. B. Tauris, 2000), 307.
83 Mohammad Ali Foroughi, 'The History of the Modernization of Law', *Journal of Persianate Studies* 3, no. 1 (2010): 44.
84 Katouzian, *State and Society in Iran*, 308.
85 Touraj Atabaki, 'The First World War, Great Power Rivalries and the Emergence of a Political Community in Iran', in Touraj Atabaki (ed.), *Iran and the First World War: Battleground of the Great Powers* (London: I. B. Tauris and Co., 2006), 6.

86 *Kaveh*, no. 8 (16 August 1921): 3.
87 see Fakhreddin Azimi, *Iran: The Crisis of Democracy, 1941-1953* (London: I. B. Tauris, 1989); and Gholam Reza Afkhami, *The Life and Times of the Shah* (California: University of California Press, 2006), 61–207.
88 Mohammad Reza Shah Pahlavi, *Mission for My Country* (London: Hutchinson, 1991), 220–1.
89 Another example is Ghani Blouryan (1924–2011) who was a young activist in the time of the Republic and later spent almost three decades in prison. For this see Ghani Blouryan, *Alakok* (Tehran: Farhange Rasa, 1384 [2005]); for the peasant uprising see Amir Hassanpour, 'Raparini Verzerani Mukriyan, 1331-1332', [The Peasant uprising of Mukriyan, 1952-1953], *Derwaze*, no. 1 (April–May 2017).
90 Muhammad Ali Jamalzadeh's *Yeki Bud Yeki Nabud* (1921), a collection of short stories, was primarily a fierce criticism of using French and Arabic words not necessarily for their 'nationality' but for being incomprehensible.
91 Rustayi, *Tarikhe Nokhostin Farhangestane Iran*.
92 Ibid., 345–478.
93 Husein Makki, *Tarikhe Bist Saleye Iran* [Twenty Years History of Iran], Vol. 6 (Tehran: Entesharat Elmi, 1374 [1995]), 235 cited in Ansari, *Politics of Nationalism*, 99.
94 See chapters on the role of gendarmerie and these rebellions in Cronin, *Soldiers, Shahs and Subalterns in Iran*.
95 S. Bakhash, 'Administration in Iran Vi. Safavid, Zand, and Qajar Periods', in *Encyclopaedia Iranica*, Online edition, http://www.iranicaonline.org/articles/administration-vi-safavid, accessed 23 April 2018.
96 Ibid.
97 Rahim Rezazade Malek (ed.), *Enqelabe Mashruteye Iran Be Rawayate Asnade Wazarate Kharejeye Englis* [Parliamentary Papers, Correspondence Respecting the Affairs of Persia] (Iran: Mazyar, 1377 [1998–9]), 270.
98 'Intelligent report amended provincial administrative division', FO 371 21895 E672/167/34, dated 15 January 1938, quoted in Ali M. Ansari, *Modern Iran: The Pahlavi and After*, 2nd edn (England: Pearson Education Limited, 2007), 56. Ali Akbar Davar (1885–1937), minister of justice in 1927, was the founder of modern Persian judicial system.
99 See Bahador 'Alami, *Naqd Wa Arziyabie Qanoon Taqsimate Keshwarie Iran* [A Study of Iran's Administrative Divisons Law] (Tehran: Iran Parliament's Research Centre, 2013).
100 Mahmud Afshar, *Ayandeh*, 1925, no. 1.
101 Hamed Nohekhan, 'Me'yarhaye Taqsimate Keshwari Dar Doreye Pahlavi' [Criteria of Administrative Divisions under the Pahlavi], *Kheradnameh* 4, no. 9 (1391 [2012]): 113–36.
102 The Faili Shi'a Kurds have suffered in both Iran and Iraq. They faced constant banishment and forced settlements by the Ba'th regime in Iraq in the 1970s. The administrative divisions of Iran complicated life for the Failis by ignoring their religious and ethnic identities. Studies on the Failis are rare. However, for a background reading of the Faili Kurds in modern Iraq, see *State and Society in Iran*; and on the Faili Kurds in Iran, see Jamil Rahmani, Said Hossein Sarrajzadeh and Omid Qaderzadeh, 'Motale'eye Kaifie Mazhab Wa Qomgaraiy Dar Mian Kordhaye Shi'e' [A Qualitative Study of Religion and Ethnicity Among Shia Kurds], [in Persian], *Jame'eshenasi [Sociology]* 15, no. 4 (2015): 3–29. On imposing national

identities on Faili Kurds, 'allowing them to become inadvertent victims of nationalist regimes' see Sabri Ateş, *The Ottoman-Iranian Borderlands: Making a Boundary, 1843-1914* (Cambridge: Cambridge University Press, 2013), 165-71.

103 'The Kurds of Persia', dated 28 March 1946, TNA, FO371 52702 E2782/104/34; see also the first proclamation of the Republic in Muhammad Ezzat, *Hukkamati Komari Kurdistan: Namekan W Balgekan* [Kurdish Republic: Correspondece and Documents] (n.p: n.p, 1995), Document 1, 18.

104 Jahangir Amuzegar, 'Capital Formation and Development Finance', in Ehasan Yarshater (ed.), *Iran Faces the Seventies* (England: Praeger Publishers, 1971), 67.

105 On famine and poverty in Kurdistan in this period, see Karim Hesami, *Le Bireweriekanim* [From My Memoirs], Vol. 1 (Uppsala: Jina Nu Forlaget, 1986); and Abdulrahman Sharafkandi-Hazhar, *Cheshti Mijawir* [A Mosque Servant's Stew] (Iraq: Kitebi Mehregan, 2007).

106 For more on economic objectives of Reza Shah, see Kamran Mofid, *Development Planning in Iran: From Monarchy to Islamic Republic* (England: MENS Press, 1987), 7-33; and for a brief account of economic development under Reza Shah, see M. E. Yapp, *The near East since the First World War: A History to 1995* (London: Longman, 1996), 177-8.

107 Yapp, Yapp, *The Near East*, 177. For more on economic policies of Reza Shah and the neglect of agriculture, see Mofid, *Development Planning in Iran*, 19.

108 Julian Bharier, *Economic Development in Iran 1900-1970* (Oxford: Oxford University Press, 1971), 84. For more on the role of the Iranian state in economy, see ibid., 87.

109 Mallispaugh in ibid.

110 Hesami, *Le Bireweriekanim*, Vol. 1, 83.

111 Ibid.

112 Mofid, *Development Planning in Iran*, 8.

113 Bharier, *Economic Development in Iran*, 65-6.

114 Mofid, *Development Planning in Iran*, 8.

115 Quoted in ibid.

116 For pre-modernization cities and modern urbanization in Iran, see Eckart Ehlers, 'Modern Urbanization and Modernization in Persia', in *Encyclopaedia Iranica*. Available online at http://www.iranicaonline.org/articles/cities-iv, accessed 16 July 2016.

117 Byron J. Good, 'The Transformation of Health Care in Modern Iranian History', in Michael E. Bonine and Nikki R. Keddie (eds), *Modern Iran: The Dialectics of Continuity and Change* (Albany: State University of New York Press, 1981).

118 Ibid., 69.

119 Kakshar Oremar, *Dimana Lagal Mina Qazi* [Interviw with Mina Qazi] (Sulaimaniya: Karo, 2013), 35.

120 Quoted in Good, 'The Transformation of Health Care', 70.

121 Cf. Bishop, *Journeys in Persia and Kurdistan*, Vol. 2.

122 Hoare and Smith, *The Prison Notebooks of Antonio Gramsci*, 137-8.

123 Good, 'The Transformation of Health Care', 63.

124 Ibid., 70.

125 Quoted in ibid.

126 Borhan Ayazi, *Ayyine-Ye Sanandaj* [The Mirror of Sanandaj] (Iran: Payam, 1991), 24.

127 Ibid.

128 in 'Ali Karimi, *Zhiyan W Basarhati Abdulraham Zabihi* [The Life and Fortune of Abdulrahman Zabihi] (Sweden: Zagros Media, 1999), 633.
129 Plan and Budget Organisation, *Statistical Yearbook of Iran 1352 [March 1973 - March 1974]* (Iran: Statistical Centre of Iran, 1975), 108.
130 L. P. Elwell-Sutton, 'Alam-E Nesvan', in *Encyclopaedia Iranica*, Vol. I, 8, 795–6. Available online at http://www.iranicaonline.org/articles/alam-e-nesvan-a-magazine-founded-in-mizan-1299-s, accessed 23 August 2016.
131 Jasamin Rostam-Kolayi, 'Expanding Agendas for the "New" Iranian Woman', in Stephanie Cronin (ed.), *The Making of Modern Iran: State and Society under Reza Shah, 1921-1941* (London: Routledge, 2003), 158.
132 Hassan Taqizadeh, 'Nokat Wa Molahezat' [Points and Observations], *Kaveh* 5, no. 11 (1920): 1.
133 Sheikholeslami-Hemin, *Tarik W Run*. For more on religious education in Kurdistan, see Mardūk, 'The Madrasa in Sunni Kurdistan'.
134 Sharafkandi-Hazhar, *Cheshti Mijawir*, 28.
135 Ibid.
136 See Burhan Qane' (ed.), *Divani Qane'* [Qane's Poetry Collection] (Iran: Dalaho Publications, 2014).
137 Ibid.
138 As 'the son of a refugee who had rebelled against the landowner class', Qane' was lucky to have a relative who became his guardian after his father died and enrolled him in a *Hojra* around Mariwan. See ibid., 3.; Hazhar's acquisition of education was also accidental. See Sharafkandi-Hazhar, *Cheshti Mijawir*, 13.
139 Hesami, *Le Bireweriekanim*, Vol. 1, 18–23.
140 For a history of education in Iran, see Marashi, *Nationalizing Iran*, Ch. 3; Ahmad Ashraf, 'General Survey of Modern Education', in *Encyclopaedia Iranica*, http://www.iranicaonline.org/articles/education-vii-general-survey-of-modern-education, accessed 02 August 2016; David Menashri, *Education and the Making of Modern Iran* (Ithaca and London: Cornell University Press, 1992). On the Ottoman Empire, see Şerif Mardin, *The Genesis of Young Ottoman Thought: A Study in the Modernisation of Turkish Political Ideas* (Syracuse: Syracuse University Press, 2000), 283–4; and M. Sukru Hanioglu, *The Young Turks in Opposition* (Oxford: Oxford University Press, 1995).
141 Michael Bentley, *Modernizing England's Past: English Historiography in the Age of Modernism, 1870-1970* (Cambridge: Cambridge University Press, 2005), 5–6.
142 Cf. Koyi's poetry in Koyi, *Diwan*, 61; and Piramerd's memoir in Omed Ashna (ed.), *Piramerd*, Vol. 1 (Hawler: Aras, 2001).
143 Cf. Mola Qadir Modarresi, 'Komalay Zhekaf', in Karimi, *Zabihi*, 67.
144 Karimi, *Zabihi*, 82–3.
145 Modarresi, 'Komalay Zhekaf', 67. A useful comparison is the opposition of the clergy to the establishment of a modern judicial system in Iran in the aftermath of the Constitutional Revolution. See Foroughi, 'Modernisation of Law'. Foroughi recounts that wearing hats, neckties and glasses were 'considered as ostentatious and westernised tendency'.
146 Rezayi, 'A Study of Low-Birth Rate'. Other representatives from the Kurdish region to the Third *Majlis* included Asadula Haji Mirza Khan, Sardar Mu'azam (Farajola Khan), Qasem (Mirza Khan Tabrizi) from Sauj Belagh, and A'zaz al-Saltaneh. For this see *Kaveh*, Year 1, nos 29 and 30, 8–9.
147 Ibid.

148 Cf. *Ta'lim va Tarbiyat* (*Amuzesh va Parvaresh* since 1938) between 1925 and 1938. Published by the Ministry of Education, the earlier issues of this journal contained more educational statistics and articles on provinces. Later issues, however, gradually became embroidered with the pictures of Reza Shah and his son, accompanied by eulogizing articles; Modarresi, 'Komalay Zhekaf'.
149 Qane', *Divani Qane'*, 3–17.
150 Ashraf, 'General Survey of Modern Education'.
151 Ibid.
152 Ibid.
153 Mohammadpur and Iman, 'Taqhirate Ejtemai Dar Sardasht', 25.
154 Rezayi, 'A Study of Low-Birth Rate'.
155 A number of factors enabled the practice of Kurdish language in education and administration in modern Iraq. This included political considerations to create a balance of Kurd-Sunni against the Shi'a majority in Iraq and cultural measures to satisfy the Kurds in the modern nation state of Iraq. However, as the League of Nations reported in 1932, 'Up to the present day, measures designed to meet Kurdish desires have been fairly successfully sabotaged. This may have been due in part to lack of energy in tackling natural difficulties but, on the whole, it must be regarded as the result of deliberate reluctance to take steps believed to tend towards the separation rather than the unity of the community of Iraq.' For this see 'League of Nations' (E2640/140/34), dated 23 March 1946, TNA, FO371 52702; and Shahram Chubin and Charles Tripp, *Iran and Iraq at War* (London: I. B. Tauris and Co Ltd, 1988). For politicization of ethnicity in modern Iraq, see Wimmer, *Shadows of Modernity*, Ch. 6.
156 Mahmud Afshar, 'Shureshe Kordhaye Osmani Wa Masaleye Kordestan' [The Revolt of the Ottoman Kurds and the Kurdistan Question], *Ayandeh*, no. 1 (Tir 1304 [1925]), 62.
157 Ibid.
158 Sharafkandi-Hazhar, *Cheshti Mijawir*, 47.
159 Ibid., 49.
160 Mardukh, *Mezhui Kurd*, 628–9.
161 Sharafkandi-Hazhar, *Cheshti Mijawir*, 12–13. Hazhar explains that although 'ajam 'means a powerful Iranian, the Kurds of the Mokrian region [the region between Saqqez and Mahabad] use 'ajam to refer to their Turkish-speaking neighbours because they have been ruled by and suffered under Turkish-speaking administrators'. See ibid., 47.
162 Mujtaba Berzuyi, *Vaz'iyate Siasie Kurdistan* [Political Situation in Kurdistan] (Tehran: Fekre Nou, 2000), 240–52.
163 See Said Borhan Tafsiri and Mansour Ahmadi, 'Ile Galbakhi', *Pazhoheshname Tarikhe Mahalie Iran* [Journal of Iran's Local History] 8, no. 1 (1398 [2019]): 259–70.
164 Richard Tapper, *Frontier Nomads of Iran: A Political and Social History of the Shahsevan* (Cambridge: Cambridge University Press, 1997), 289.
165 See Sharafkandi-Hazhar, *Cheshti Mijawir*, 52–3.
166 Cf. Mahmood Afshar, *Ayandeh*, no. 1 (1925).
167 Ibid.
168 Mahmud Afshar, *Ayandeh* 4. nos 1–2 (Mehr-Aban 1338 [October–November 1959].
169 Ibid.
170 Abbas Vali, *Kurds and the State in Iran* (London: I. B. Tauris, 2011), 19.

171　For the link between the idea of 'core nation' and a nationalizing and modernizing state, see Brubaker, *Nationalism Reframed*, 83.
172　Ibid., 26 and Ch. 2.

Chapter 2

1　Quoted in Afkhami, *The Shah*, 768.
2　Reza Barahani, *Tarikhe Mozakkar* [Masculine History] (Tehran: Nashre Awwal, 1984), 79.
3　Mahmud Afshar, 'Enqelabe Sefid' [The White Revolution], *Ayandeh* 3, nos 14–16 (1946): 767–8.
4　Ibid., 768.
5　Cf. Manucher Farmanfarmaian and Roxane Farmanfarmaian, *Blood and Oil: A Prince's Memoir of Iran, from the Shah to the Ayatollah* (New York: Random House, 1997); and Jami, *Gozashte Cheraghe Rahe Ayande Ast* [Past Is the Torch of Future's Path] (Tehran: Qaqnus, 1998).
6　William Roger Louis, *The British Empire in the Middle East 1945-1951* (Oxford: Clarendon Press, 1984), 632.
7　Afkhami, *The Shah*, 231.
8　As Afkhami has noted, the idea of the Literacy Corps came from the Education Minister Parviz Khanlari. See also Khanlari's speech at Tehran College Training on 'the situation and the future of education', entitled by the journal of Education as 'To Accomplish the Shah's Command [to form the Literacy Corps]'. For this see Khanlari, 'The Situation and the Future of Education', [in Persian], *Amuzesh wa Parvaresh* New Era, Year 33 [Esfand], no. 1 (1963): 9–22.
9　Dariush Homayun, 'Eslahate Arzi Dar Iran' [Land Reform in Iran], *Tahqiqate Eqtesadi [Economic Research]*, nos 5 and 6 (Khordad 1342 [June 1963]): 38.
10　*'Alam-e Naswan* (the World of Women) was one of the earliest journals advocating women's rights and advising women on social issues. For more see Elwell-Sutton, 'Alam-E Nesvan'.
11　Afkhami, *The Shah*, 227–9.
12　Mahnaz Afkhami, *Dowlat, Jame'e va Jonbeshe Zanan Dar Iran: 1342-1357* [State, Society, and the Women Movements in Iran: 1963-1979] (Bethesda: Foundation for Iranian Studies, 2003), 124–35.
13　Afkhami, *The Shah*, 227.
14　For the political crisis of this period cf. Azimi, *Iran: The Crisis of Democracy*.
15　Afkhami, *The Shah*, 219.
16　See *bayaniye-ye Jebhey-e Melli dr barey-e Enqelab-e Sefid va Referandom-e 6 Bahman 1341* (The National Front's announcement on the White Revolution and the Referendum of 19 February 1963).
17　Quoted in Afkhami, *The Shah*, 220–1.
18　Yadola Biglari, 'Kurdistan and the White Revolution', interview with author, 6 July 2017.
19　Ibid.
20　Yadola Biglari who worked as a judge between 1354 and 1357 [1975–9] in Kermanshah recalls a meeting of the Union with the National Front, represented by Siyawash Mokri (Kermanshahi) and Kayumars Baghbani, a follower of Foruhar,

in which the Union rejected any cooperation for fear of losing its organizational independence, ibid.
21 Ibid.
22 Mahmud Kaiwan, 'Kurdistan and the White Revolution', interview with author, 4 July 2017.
23 Ibid.
24 Biglari, Interview.
25 Ibid.
26 Ibid.
27 Rahim Amini, 'Kurdistan and the White Revolution', interview with author, 10 July 2017. A teacher in the mid-1970s and an activist since the early 1960s, Amini grew up in a village near Saqqez and witnessed the inception of land reform in the area.
28 Ibid.
29 Ibid.
30 Ibid.
31 Ibid.
32 Reshad Mustafasultani, 'Kurdistan and the White Revolution', interview with author, 3 July 2017.
33 Ibid.
34 Amuzegar, 'Capital Formation', 67.
35 Ibid., 68; Plan Organization, *Report on the Operation of the Second Seven-Year Plan* (Tehran, 1964), appendix 5.
36 Abrahamian, *Iran between Two Revolutions*, 427.
37 See ibid., 426–35. Ibid.
38 See ibid., 427–8.
39 On Centre for Economic Research see Afkhami, *The Shah*, 334; and the journal of *Tahqiqat-e Eqtesadi* (Pe. Economic Research) published by the Faculty of Law, Political and Economic Sciences, University of Tehran, which contained high quality scholarly articles.
40 Afkhami, *The Shah*, 322–33.
41 Amuzegar, 'Capital Formation', 69.
42 Ibid.
43 Ibid.
44 Abulhasan Ebtehaj, *Khaterate Abulhasane Ebtehaj* [Ebtehaj's Memoirs], Vol. 1 (London: Paka Print, 1991), 336–8.
45 'Provincial Development Work', (EP1102/4), dated 31 December 1958, TNA, FO 371/140822.
46 Ibid.
47 Ebtehaj, *Khaterat*, Vol. 1, 409.
48 'Provincial Development Work', (EP 1103/2), dated 8 June 1959, TNA, FO 371/140822.
49 Cf. 'Provincial Development Work', (EP 1103/1), dated 31 December 1958, TNA, FO 371/140822.
50 Ibid. (EP1103/5), dated 10 June 1959.
51 'Development of Provinces of Iran', (EP1103/7), dated 27 January 1959, TNA, FO 371/140822.
52 Afkhami, *The Shah*, 208.
53 Ebtehaj, *Khaterat*, Vol. 1, 375.
54 Ibid., 376.

55 'Development of Provinces in Iran', (EP1103/14), dated 25 February 1959, TNA, FO 371/140822.
56 Ibid.
57 Ebtehaj, *Khaterat*, Vol. 1, 406–7.
58 'Development of Provinces in Iran', (EP1103/14), dated 25 February 1959, TNA, FO 371/140822.
59 ibid.
60 'Development of Provinces in Iran', (EP1103/18), dated 13 April 1959 TNA, FO 371/140822.
61 Afkhami, *The Shah*, 70.
62 Ibid.
63 Farhad Daftary, 'Development Planning in Iran: A Historical Survey', *Iranian Studies* 6, no. 4 (1973): 181–2.
64 See Said Amir Arjomand, *The Turban for the Crown: The Islamic Revolution in Iran* (Oxford: Oxford University Press, 1988), Ch. 5; and on the background and formation of religious political organization, see Izzat-Allah Sahabi, *Nim Qarn Khaterah Va Tajrubeh* [Half a Century Memoirs and Experiences], Vol. 1 (Tehran Farhange Saba Publication, 2009), 107–222 and 229–326.
65 For more on the Fourth Plan cf. Amuzegar, 'Capital Formation', 74–83; and on both plans, see Afkhami, *The Shah*, 326–8 Abrahamian, *Iran between Two Revolutions*, 428.
66 Afkhami, *The Shah*, 326–7.
67 This was in 'the fields of basic metals (e.g., steel, aluminium, copper, lead, and zinc) and minerals (e.g., petro-chemicals) scientific water preservation and water resources development, rapid expansion of power generation both for industry and agriculture and the construction of a national grid system, and utilization of natural gas for domestic consumption as well as exports'. For this see Amuzegar, 'Capital Formation', 76–8.
68 Ibid., 79.
69 Afkhami, *The Shah*, 324.
70 Abrahamian, *Iran between Two Revolutions*, 448.
71 Afkhami, *The Shah*, 329.
72 Farmanfarmaian and Farmanfarmaian, *Blood and Oil*, 69.
73 Afkhami, *The Shah*, 333.
74 For more on the National Spatial Strategy Plan see ibid., 330–3.
75 Ibid., 233.
76 Ibid.
77 Cf. Ann K. S. Lambton, *Landlord and Peasant in Persia* (London: I. B. Tauris, 1991); and James A. Bill, 'Modernization and Reform from Above: The Case of Iran', *The Journal of Politics* 32, no. 1 (February, 1970): 19–40.
78 Baqer Momeni, *Masalaye Arzi Wa Jange Tabaqati Dar Iran* [The Land Question and Class Struggle in Iran] (Tehran: Payvand, 1979), 81–109.
79 Abol Hassan Danesh, 'Land Reform, State Policy, and Social Change in Iran', *Urban Anthropology and Studies of Cultural Systems and World Economic Development* 21, no. 2 (1992): 164. See also Abbas Amanat, *Iran: A Modern History* (New Haven and London: Yale University Press, 2017), 577–84.
80 For more cf. Nikkie R. Keddie, *Modern Iran: Roots and Results of Revolution* (New Haven: Yale University Press, 2003); Momeni, *The Land Question*.

81 In addition to the articles on social change in Kurdistan, cited in the literature review, see Shahin Ra'naiy, 'Barresiye Ejraiye Eslahate Arzi Wa Payamadhaye an Dar Ostane Kordestan' [Land Reform in the Kurdistan Province and Its Consequences], PhD Thesis Thesis, University of Shahid Beheshti, 2017.
82 Cf. Fiaz Zahed, 'Gozari Bar Qanune Eslahate Arzi Dar Iran' [A Review of Land Reform in Iran], *Pazhohesnameye Tarikh [Historical Research]* 3, no. 11 (Winter 1394 [2016]): 91–122; Ra'naiy, 'Land Reform in Kurdistan'.
83 Homayun, 'Land Reform in Iran', 38.
84 Biglari, Interview.
85 Ibid.
86 Homayun, 'Land Reform in Iran'.
87 Ibid., 39.
88 For more on this uprising, see Hassanpour, 'The Peasant Uprising'.
89 Plan and Budget Organisation, *Statistical Yearbook of Iran 1352 [March 1973 - March 1974]*, 199.
90 Ibid.
91 Zahed, 'Land Reform'.
92 Ibid., 107.
93 Ibid., 98. Momeni highlights the problem of official statistics during the land reform. According to him, both the number of villages 'claimed to be around 72,000', and the number of landowners varied according to official sources. For this see Momeni, *The Land Question*, 259–69.
94 Bahram Davari, 'Tarhi Baraye Ehiyaye Keshawarzi Wa Bazsaziye Roosta' [A Plan for the Revival of Agriculture and Reconstruction of the Village], *Keyhan* 1351 [1972–3], 6.
95 Biglari, Interview.
96 Mustafasultani, Interview.
97 *Keyhan*, 19 Ordibehesht 1358 [9 May 1979], 7.
98 Fuad Mustafasultani, 'Dar Bareye Chegunegiye Ijade Etehadyeye Dehqanan' [On the Foramtion of the Peasant Union] in Malaka Mustafasultani et al. (eds), *Kak Fuad Mustafasultani* (Stettin: Print Group, 2017), 317.
99 Cf. document number 44/1 of *Edareye Rah* [Road Office] dated 25 August 1331 [16 September 1952] in Presidential Office Document Centre, *Documents on Truman's Point Four in Iran (1946-1947)* (Tehran: Vizārat-i Farhang va Irshād-i Islamī, 1382 [2003]).
100 Kaiwan, Interview.
101 Mustafasultani, Interview.
102 Daftary, 'Development Planning', 204.
103 Farmanfarmaian and Farmanfarmaian, *Blood and Oil*, 149.
104 Biglari, Interview.
105 Ibid.
106 See Document 161 in Sharzayi, *Asnade Baharestan*, 35–6.
107 Biglari, Interview.
108 Dr Ahmad 'Azizpur, 'Kurdistan and the White Revolution', interview with author, 8 July 2017.
109 See Zahed, 'Land Reform'.
110 For a theoretical analysis of the institutional dimensions of modernity, cf. Anthony Giddens, *The Consequences of Modernity* (Cambridge: Polity, 1990), 55–78.

Chapter 3

1. Farhad Kazemi, *Poverty and Revolution in Iran: The Migrant Poor, Urban Marginality and Politics* (New York: New York University Press, 1980), 42.
2. Jahangir Amuzegar, *Iran: An Economic Profile* (Washington, DC: Middle East Instiue, 1977), 15.
3. Theorists of sociology such as Spencer and Durkheim specify differentiation as the modernizing, evolutionary pattern of social change in the direction of improved material well-being of all. See Malcolm Waters, *Modern Sociological Theory* (London: Sage Publications, 1994), 320.
4. Ibid., 302–5. For more on these theorists and a discussion of stratification and differentiation, see ibid., Ch. 9.
5. Quoted in ibid., 302.
6. Ibid., 302–3.
7. Ibid., 303.
8. Wills, *The Land of the Lion and Sun*, 5.
9. Although the workers of the Abadan oil refinery had set a precedent in the 1940s, minimum wage probably remained a concept among industrial workers and was certainly not developed by any government. There were two pieces of minimum wage legislation. The 1959 Labour Law ruled minimum wage to be set every two years through a high labour council while in 1973 companies with more than 100 employees were required 'with the concurrence of labor representatives or syndicates, to prepare detailed job classifications to be used for determining employee's wages'. For this see Amuzegar, *Iran*, 233–4; and for the first imposition of a minimum wage in Iran, see Farmanfarmaian and Farmanfarmaian, *Blood and Oil*, 186–7.
10. Biglari, Interview.
11. It seems that some forms of social insurance for employees to benefit from healthcare or a retirement salary in the Kurdish region were introduced by the end of the 1950s. Although with civil servant or teaching jobs came such schemes, these jobs only increased with the expansion of bureaucracy, governmental offices and modern education since the 1950s.
12. Kaiwan, Interview.
13. Amini, Interview.
14. Biglari, Interview.
15. Cross-border trade continued to defy the national economy and remained a crucial part of economic life for communities living in coterminous regions divided by national borders.
16. See Hesami, *Le Bireweriekanim*, Vol. 1; Sharafkandi-Hazhar, *Cheshti Mijawir*; Sheikholeslami-Hemin, *Tarik W Run*.
17. Amini, Interview.
18. Kaiwan, Interview.
19. Mustafasultani, Interview.
20. Amuzegar, *Iran*, 260.
21. See Gholamhossein Sa'edi, *Azadarane Bayal* [The mourners of Bayal] (1964).
22. Ḥosayn Farhūdī, 'City Councils', in *Encyclopaedia Iranica*, http://www.iranicaonline.org/articles/city-councils-anjoman-e-sahr-in-persia, accessed 27 August 2017.
23. Ibid.

24 Kaiwan, Interview.
25 See Menashri, *Education and the Making of Modern Iran*; Ashraf, 'General Survey of Modern Education'; Marashi, *Nationalizing Iran*, Ch. 3.
26 Abdulhamid Heyrat Sajjadi, *Pishineye Amuzesh Wa Parvaresh Dar Kurdistan (1320-1357)* [The History of Education in Kurdistan (1941-1957)], Vols 2 and 3 (Sanandaj: Kurdistan Publications, 2004), 330.
27 Ibid., 343-6.
28 See *Amuzesh wa Parvaresh*, no. 5 (Mordad 1321 [July-August 1939]) 70.
29 See *Amuzesh wa Parvaresh* 28, no. 1 (Farvardin 1335 [March-April 1956]).
30 Cf. *Amuzesh wa Parvaresh* 28, no. 4 (Dey 1335 [December 1957-January 1958]).
31 Cf. *Amuzesh wa Parvaresh* 28, no. 3 (Khordad 1336 [May-June 1957]).
32 Sajjadi, *Pishineye Amuzesh Wa Parvaresh*, Vols 2 and 3, 209. By 1960, Baneh city had acquired 12 primary schools and 1 secondary school, albeit with very limited classes for their 945 students.
33 Azizpur, Interview. According to Azizpur, with a population of around 15,000, Baneh city's secondary school for boys in 1968 did not have any teacher to teach experimental sciences. Moreover, by the end of the 1950s, only the provincial centres – there were twelve provinces in Iran in this year – and not all the growing cities, acquired *Daneshsara* or training colleges for teachers and nurses. See *Amuzesh wa Parvaresh* 28, no. 3 (Khordad 1336 [May-June 1957]): 71.
34 For a brief background of the journal, see *Amuzesh was Parvaresh* 23, no. 1 (Mehr 1327 [September-October 1948]).
35 *Amuzesh wa Parvaresh* 12, nos 8-11 (Aban-Azar 1321 [October 1942-February 1943]): b.
36 *Amuzesh wa Parvaresh* 27, no. 3 (Mehr 1335 [September-October 1956]).
37 See *Amuzesh va Parvaresh* 29, no. 10 (Tir 1337 [June-July 1958]): 27.
38 Ibid.
39 *Amuzesh va Parvaresh*, no. 9 (Azar 1323 [August-December 1950]): 469.
40 Cf. *Amuzesh va Parvaresh*, ibid., no. 5 (Mordad 1323 [July-August 1944]): 271; ibid., no. 6 (Shahrivar 1323 [August-.September 1944]): 324-9; no. 9 (Azar 1323 [November-December 1944]): 469.
41 Cf. a translation of a work on education in rural areas which draws lessons from 'new and democratic education in the U.S.A'. For this see *Amuzesh va Parvaresh* 15 (1324 [1945-6]).
42 Cf. *Amuzesh wa Parvaresh* 12, nos 1 and 2, Farvardin-Ordibehesh 1321 [April-June 1942]).
43 *Amuzesh va Parvaresh* 30, no. 4 (Bahman 1337 [January-February 1959]): 61-3.
44 Gonabadi Mohammad Parvin, 'Amuzeshe Zabane Farsi Va Hadafe Tarbiyatie An' [Teaching Persian Language and Its Educational Aim], *Amuzesh wa Parvaresh* 35, nos 9 and 10 (1344 [1965]).
45 *Amuzesh va Parvaresh* 30, no. 8 (Khordad 1338 [May-June 1959]); and ibid., no. 9 (Tir 1338 [June-July 1959]).
46 *Amuzesh wa Parvaresh*, nos 11 and 12 (Bahman and Esfand 1323 [January-February 1945]).
47 Plan and Budget Organisation, *Statistical Yearbook of Iran 1352 [March 1973 - March 1974]*, 62.
48 Ibid.
49 Ibid.

50 *Amuzesh va Parvaresh* 33, no. 1 (Esfand 1341 [February–March 1963]): 10. For this law see *Amuzesh va Parvaresh* 12, nos 8–11 (Aban-Bahman 1321 [January 1943]), Alef [A]. UNESCO estimated the number of illiterates in Iran to be more than twenty million or 75 per cent of the population.
51 See the Shah's message in *Amuzesh va Parvaresh* 33, no. 1 (Esfand 1341 [February–March 1963]).
52 Ibid., 12. This plan was divided into four parts the first of which had been included in the five-year economic plan. See *Amuzesh va Parvaresh* 33, no. 1, 11.
53 *Amuzesh va Parvaresh*, 'Payame Shahaneh' [A Kingly Message] 33, no. 1 (Esfand 1341 [February–March 1963]).
54 *Amuzesh va Parvaresh* 33, no. 1, 60.
55 Kaiwan, Interview.
56 Ibid.
57 Biglari, Interview.
58 Ibid.
59 Ibid.
60 Kaiwan, Interview.
61 Ibid. Biglari, Interview.
62 ʿAzizpur, Interview.
63 Weber, *Economy and Society*, 24–5.
64 Ibid., 25.
65 ʿAzizpur, Interview.
66 *Amuzesh va Parvaresh*, no. 3 (Ordibehesht 1342 [April–May 1963]), 60.
67 Ibid.
68 *Amuzesh va Parvaresh*, 'Amare Farhangi' [Educational Statistics], 34, no. 1, 53.
69 *Amuzesh va Parvaresh* 34, no. 1 (Farvardin 1343 [1964]): 52–3.
70 With an area of 25,000 square kilometres, the Kurdistan Province in 1972 consisted of six counties (shahrestan), sixteen districts (bakhsh), eight *shahredari*s (city councils), and forty-nine *dehestan* (rural centres), thus excluding a considerable part of the Kurdish region in the west of Iran. For this see Plan and Budget Organisation, *Statistical Yearbook of Iran 1352 [March 1973 - March 1974]*, 2.
71 Ibid.
72 *Amuzesh va Parvaresh*, no. 2 (Ordibehesht 1343 [April–May 1964]): 61–2.
73 See *Amuzesh va Parvaresh* 37, nos 7 and 8 (1346 [1967]): 116.
74 Ibid., 117.
75 Plan and Budget Organisation, *Statistical Yearbook of Iran 1352 [March 1973 - March 1974]*, 66.
76 Ibid., 68.
77 Ibid., 69.
78 Ibid., 65.
79 *Amuzesh va Parvaresh* 35, no. 6 (Azar 1344 [December–January 1965]), 14–16.
80 Akbar Moarefi, 'Behdāštbarā-Ye Hama', [Health for All] in *Encyclopaedia Iranica*, http://www.iranicaonline.org/articles/behdast-bara-ye-hama, accessed 02 August 2017.
81 Ibid.
82 B. Alen, 'Behdashte Rustayi', [Rural Healthcare], *Amuzesh va Parvaresh* 14, no. 5 (Mordad 1332 [July 1953]): 274.
83 Mustafasultani, Interview.
84 Biglari, Interview.

85 ʿAzizpur, Interview. According to Azizpour, local experts used conventional methods to 'immunise' against smallpox by having the patient make early contact with the virus.
86 Ibid.
87 Ibid.
88 Ibid.
89 Ibid.
90 Ibid.
91 Moarefi, 'Behdāštbarā-Ye Hamaʾ.
92 Mohammad Ali Faghih, 'Behdārī', [Health Centre] in *Encyclopaedia Iranica*, IV/1, 100–4. Available online at http://www.iranicaonline.org/articles/behdari, accessed 30 December 2012.
93 Moarefi, 'Behdāštbarā-Ye Hamaʾ.
94 See Hamid Dabashi, *Iran: A People Interrupted* (New York: New Press, 2007), Ch. 4. Devoid of any reference to Kurdish cultural modernity or the contributions of Kurdish literary individuals to the literary movement of the era, Dabashi's book nevertheless provides valuable insight into the literary, intellectual and social movements of the era.
95 Plan and Budget Organisation, *Statistical Yearbook of Iran 1352 [March 1973 - March 1974]*, 102–4.
96 Ibid.
97 Ibid., 159.
98 Ibid., 90; and Faghih, 'Behdārī'.
99 ʿAzizpur, Interview; Amini, Interview.
100 ʿAzizpur, Interview.
101 Ibid.
102 Faghih, 'Behdārī'.
103 ʿAzizpur, Interview.
104 Ibid.
105 'Request for technical assistant', (MID 242/86/02), dated 10 July 1969, TNA, OD 34/272.
106 'Request for social welfare experts', (MID 242/86/02), dated 2 July 1969, TNA, OD 34/272.
107 'Request for social welfare experts', (MID 242/86/02), dated 8 July 1969 TNA, OD 34/272.
108 Ibid.
109 'Request for social welfare experts', (MID 242/86/02), dated 20 June 1969, TNA, OD 34/272.
110 'Request for social welfare experts', (MID 242/86/02), dated 27 September 1968, TNA, OD 34/272.
111 'Request for social welfare experts', (ES 332/213/03), dated 24 September 1968, TNA, OD 34/272.
112 Amuzegar, *Iran*, ix. Otherwise a very informative source with valuable data on the economic performance of Iran, its optimistic and uncritical approach to economic or social policies of the state is accompanied by avoiding any discussion of social consequences of modernization.
113 According to Yadola Biglari, a family judge, giving custody of a child to a person married to a citizen of a foreign country was not desirable; however, in one case he gave custody of a child to an Iranian man and his Swedish wife. See Biglari, Interview.

114 ʿAzizpur, Interview.
115 Zubaida, *Islam, the People and the State*, 64–82.
116 Amuzegar, *Iran*, 260.
117 Quoted in ibid., 259.
118 William H. Sullivan, *Mission to Iran* (New York: W.W. Norton and Company, 1981), 57.

Chapter 4

1 Masud Ahmadzadeh, *Mobareze Mosalahane: Ham Estrategy Va Ham Taktik* [Armed Struggle as Both Strategy And Tactic] (1970). For more on Fedayyan, see Peyman Vahabzadeh, 'A Generation Myth: Armed Struggle and the Creation of Social Epic in 1970s Iran', in H. E. Chehabi, et al. (eds), *Iran in the Middle East: Transnational Encounters and Social History* (London: I. B. Tauris, 2015).
2 Thompson, *Ideology*, 11.
3 See Sharafkandi-Hazhar, *Cheshti Mijawir*.
4 See Karim Hesami, *Khaterate Karim Hesami* [Karim Hesami's Memoirs] (Sweden: Arzan, 2011), 102–31.
5 Muhammad Khezri, *Laparayek La Tekoshan W Julanaway Salakani 42-47 Hezbi Dimukrati Kurdistan* [A Page from the Struggle and Movement of the Democratic Party of Kurdistan (1963–8)] (Sweden: n.p., 2003), 13.
6 Ibid., 13 and 26.
7 On the impact of the movement in Iraq, see Saʿid Kawa Kwestani, *Awerrek La Basarhati Khom* [Looking Back on My Life] (1996), 54–5. Available at http://said.kurdland.com in PDF format, accessed on 23 May 2018.
8 Ibid.
9 Khezri, *Laparayek*, 13.
10 Ibid., 129.
11 On such assumptions cf. Farideh Koohi-Kamali, *The Political Development of Kurds in Iran* (New York: Palgrave, 2003), 168–71.
12 Hesami, *Khaterat*, 121.
13 Khezri, *Laparayek*, 155.
14 See Kwestani, *Awerrek*, 72–115.
15 Biglari, Interview.
16 Khezri, *Laparayek*, 83.
17 On the uprising see Hassanpour, 'The Peasant Uprising'.
18 See Khezri, *Laparayek*, 186–7. According to contemporary and eyewitness accounts, in another incident in Iraqi Kurdistan in spring 1968, five members were arrested in a house in Alane village in a common operation by forces of the Barzani movement and the Iranian gendarmerie. Four were taken to Jeldiyan military base where they were tortured and then executed there or in the Kurdish city of Piranshar's military base; the body of the fifth person called Ebrahim Dalawaiy (sur), who had been wounded in this raid and died later, was displayed in public in Piranshar. For this see ibid., 164–5.
19 Ibid., 162–6.
20 Ibid., 156.
21 Biglari, Interview.
22 Ibid.

23 Ibid.
24 Ibid.
25 Ibid.
26 Ibid.
27 The Third Party Conference of DPIK in June 1971 ratified the party's programme. For this see Hesami, *Khaterat*, 129.
28 Biglari, Interview; Bahman Saʿidi, *Penj Sal Lagal Abdulla Muhtadi* [Five Years with Abdulla Mohtadi] (Sulaymaniya: n.p., 2010); Bahman Saʿidi, *Khabat Baraw Sarkawtin: Didarek Lagal Ebrahim Alizada* [Struggle Towards Victory: A Meeting with Ebrahim Alizadeh] (Kurdistan: Komala Central Committee Publication, 2012); Shoʿeib Zakaryayi, *Tharikhe Bazandeh: Naqdi Bar Husein Moradbegi's Tarikhe Bazandeh* [The Lost History: A Critical Review of Hossain Moradbegi's 'Living History'] (Sulaymaniya: Rawand, 2010).
29 See Farmanfarmaian and Farmanfarmaian, *Blood and Oil*, 54 and 382.
30 Ibid., 370.
31 Ibid., 395–401.
32 Henry Tudor, *Political Myth* (London: Pall Mall Press, 1972), 138.
33 Stephen Howe, *Ireland and Empire: Colonial Legacies in Irish History and Culture* (Oxfor: Oxford University Press, 2002), 139.
34 Ibid., 230.
35 Cf. Ibid., Ch. 7; Stephen Howe, 'Historiography', in Kevin Kenny (ed.), *Ireland and the British Empire* (Oxford: Oxford Unviersity Press, 2004).
36 For more on Ireland in this regard, see Howe, *Ireland and Empire*, Ch. 7.
37 Bill Ashcroft, *Post-Colonial Transformation* (New York: Routledge, 2001), 46 and see Ch. 2.
38 Cf. Peter Burke, *History and Social Theory* (New York: Cornell University Press, 2005), 162–5.
39 Raymond Williams, *Problems in Materialism and Culture* (London: Verso, 1980), 38.
40 Ibid.
41 Ibid., 40–1.
42 Ibid., 41.
43 Ibid., 39.
44 Raymond Williams, 'From Base and Superstructure in Marxist Cultural Theory', in Kiernan Ryan (ed.), *New Historicism and Cultural Materialism: A Reader* (London: Arnold, 1996), 23.
45 Ibid.
46 Ibid., 24.
47 Ibid., 28.
48 Pierre Bourdieu, *Language and Symbolic Power* (Cambridge: Polity Press, 1991), 166, and Ch. 7; see also David Swartz, *Culture and Power: The Sociology of Pierre Bourdieu* [Culture and Power] (Chicago: University of Chicago, 1997), Ch. 1.
49 Bourdieu, *Language and Symbolic Power*, 167.
50 On symbolic system as a classification system, see Swartz, *Culture and Power: The Sociology of Pierre Bourdieu*, 84.
51 On various forms of cultural capital (embodied, objectified and institutionalized), see Bourdieu, 'The Forms of Capital'.
52 Barahani, *Tarikhe Mozakkar*, 105–6.
53 Ibid., 106.
54 Ibid., 110.

55 Ibid.
56 Ibid., 13.
57 Rasmus Christian Elling, *Minorities in Iran: Nationalism and Ethnicity after Khomeini* (Basingstoke: Palgrave Macmillan, 2013), 167.
58 Cf. Asad Behrangi (ed.), *Namehaye Samad Behrangi* [Samad Behrangi's Letters] (Tehran: Amir Kabir, 1357 [1979]); Samad Behrangi, *Qessehaye Behrang* [Behrang's Stories] (Tehran: Donya, 1359 [1980]).
59 Asad Behrangi (ed.), *Majmuʻe Assare Samad Behrangi* [An Anthology] (Tabriz: Behrangi, 1382 [2005]), 67.
60 Ziyaedin Sajjadi, 'Saʻid Nafisi and Shenasandane Farhange Iran' [Saʻid Nafisi and Introducing the Culture of Iran], *Nashriyeye Adabiyat wa Olume Ensanie Daneshkadeye Tehran* 14, no. 3 (1967): 363.
61 Cf. Dr Bahram Frewshi, 'Zabanhaye Irani Dar Kharej Az Iran' [Iranian Languages Outside of Iran], *Nashriye Adabiyate Daneshkade Tehran* 12, nos 3–4 (1344 [1965]): 320–38; Dr Mansur Ekhtiyar, 'Shiweye Barresiye Guyeshha' [The way to Analyse Dielects], *Nashriyeye Adabiyate Daneshkadeye Tehran* 12, no. 2 (1343 [1964]): 170–215.
62 Frewshi, 'Zabanhaye Irani Dar Kharej Az Iran', 326.
63 Cf. ʻUbeidulla Ayyubiyan, 'Barresiye Tahqiqie Chrikai Mam U Zin' [An Analysis of Mam and Zin Epic Story], *Nashriyeye Adabiyate Daneshkadeye Tabriz* 13, no. 2 (1340 [1961]): 164–240.
64 See Stefan Berger and Christoph Conard, *The Past as History: National Identity and Historical Consciousness in Modern Europe* (Basingstoke: Palgrave, 2015), 28–79.
65 ʻUbeidulla Ayyubiyan, 'Taqwime Mahalliye Kurdi' [The Kurdish Local Calendar], *Nashriyeye Adabiyate Daneshkadeye Tabriz* 16, no. 2 (1343 [1964]): 179–280.
66 Qader Fattahi Qazi, 'Chand Baite Kurdi' [Some Kurdish Couplets], *Nashriyeye Adabiyate Daneshkadeye Tabriz* [the Journal of the University of Tabriz Faculty of Literature] 16, no. 3 (1343 [1964]): 307–20.
67 Sajjadi, 'Saʻid Nafisi', 361.
68 Saʻid Nafisi's literary works included (national) historiography. Cf. Saʻid Nafisi, *Tarikhe Ejtemaʻi Wa Siyasiye Iran Dar Doreye Moʻaser* [The Social and Political History of Modern Iran] (Tehran: Ahoura, 1383 [2004]), first published in the summer of 1956; Saʻid Nafisi, *Babak Khorramdin* (Tehran: Asatir, 1384 [2005]), first published in 1954.
69 Williams, *Problems in Materialism and Culture*, 40–1.
70 Homi K. Bhabha, *The Location of Culture* (London: Routledge, 1994), 1–18.
71 Thompson, *Ideology*, 225.
72 Ibid., 265.
73 Ibid.
74 Bhabha, *The Location of Culture*, 66.
75 Edward Said, *Culture and Imperialism* (London: Vintage Books, 1994), 276.
76 Cf. Bhabha, *Nation and Narration*.
77 A recent article develops a concept of 'internal cultural imperialism' in relation to Turkey from a juridico-political point of view. See Mohammed A Salih, 'Internal Cultural Imperialism: The Case of the Kurds in Turkey', *The International Communication Gazette* (June 2020), doi.org/10.1177/1748048520928666.
78 For more on these themes see Ashcroft, *Post-Colonial Transformation*; and on post-colonial studies, see Bill Ashcroft et al. (eds), *The Post-Colonial Studies Reader* (New York: Routledge, 1995).

79 Raymond Williams, *Television* (New York: Routledge, 1974), 17. Interestingly for this study focusing on the same period, in the early 1970s Williams conducted research in the United States 'to describe the relationship between television as a technology and television as a cultural form'. Ibid., xiv. As a result, *Television* discussed how TV as a cultural product had become a vital part of American culture.
80 Plan and Budget Organisation, *Statistical Yearbook of Iran 1352 [March 1973 - March 1974]*, 143.
81 Amanat, *Iran*, 684.
82 Ibid.
83 Amuzegar, *Iran*, 125.
84 Ibid.
85 Mustafasultani, Interview.
86 Biglari, Interview.
87 Ayazi, *Sanandaj*, 727. Radio Sanandaj was set up by army personnel and broadcast for one hour per week. Wireless was used to 'broadcast army news and local music using loudspeakers. People gathered in front of the army base to listen. More advance broadcasting began a few years later, increasing the length of broadcasting from three to four hours per week to 24 hour a day when many individuals began to contribute to the programme. At least until the early 1970s, its most notable aspect was Kurdish music'. Ibid., 724–6.
88 Mustafasultani, Interview.
89 Biglari, Interview. Radio Kurdish Tehran was founded as a result of efforts by prominent Kurdish individuals such as Shokrolla Baban and Mr Situdeh, a teacher of literature. Ibid.
90 Such literary figures or social and political activists of later decades remained influential especially where written, audio and visual means of communication were not available. Another figure is undoubtedly Mala Awara (Mala Ahmad Shalmashi, 1934–68), mentioned earlier.
91 Biglari, Interview; Amini, Interview, Kaiwan, Interview.
92 Biglari, Interview.
93 Cf. *Kurdistan* 4, no. 25, 2 Galarezan 1341 [24 October 1962].
94 Biglari, Interview. The editor of *Kurdistan* was Muhammad Sediq Muftizada and its owner was ʿAbdulhamid Baʿidulzamani, a professor of Arabic. It is believed that Pezhman, a SAVAK employee in Tehran, was responsible for the Kurdish section of Radio Tehran. Ibid. Swara Ilkhanizada (1937–76) was a gifted poet whose life was cut short in a tragic car accident. He graduated from Tehran University in 1968 with a degree in law and worked at the Kurdish service of Radio Tehran since 1968.
95 Amini, Interview.
96 Ibid.
97 On this see Amuzegar, *Iran*, 125; Hamid Nafisi, 'Cinema as a Political Instrument', in Ali M. Ansari (ed.), *Politics of Modern Iran* (New York: Routledge, 2011), 192.
98 Amuzegar, *Iran*, 125–6.
99 Ibid., 126.
100 Cf. Ayazi, *Sanandaj*, 727.
101 Amuzegar, *Iran*, 126.
102 Ibid.
103 Ibid., 127.
104 Ibid., 126.

105 Amir Hassanpour, 'Farhangi Zaraki Le Khuli Teknolozhiy Zamanda' [Oral Culture in the Age of Technology], http://en.calameo.com/read/0011170694fd3b13133a7, accessed 6 November 2017.
106 Nafisi, 'Cinema as a Political Instrument', 205.
107 Ibid.
108 Barahani, *Tarikhe Mozakkar*, 88.
109 Ibid.; Nafisi, 'Cinema as a Political Instrument'.
110 Edward Said explains this link between culture and imperialism. See Said, *Culture and Imperialism*, xiii.
111 Hassan Mir ʿAbedini, *Sad Sal Dastan Newisi Dar Iran* [One Hundred Years of Story-Writing in Iran] (Tehran: Nashre Cheshme, 1998), 408–9.
112 Ibid., 418.
113 Ibid., 408.
114 For more on this period, see ibid., 405–21.
115 Cf. Barahani, *Tarikhe Mozakkar*, Ch. 10.
116 Mehrzad Boroujerdi, *Iranian Intellectuals and the West: The Tormented Triumph of Nativism* (Syracuse: Syracuse University Press, 1996), 54–63.
117 Dariush Ashuri, *Ma Wa Moderniyat* [We and Modernity] (Tehran: Tolouʾ Azadi, 1998), seven.
118 See Masʿud Noqrekar, *Bakhsi Az Tarikhe Jonbeshe Rowshanfekrie Iran* [A Phase of the Enlightenment History of Iran], Vol. 1 (Sweden: Baran, 1382 [2002–3]), 24.
119 ʿAbedini, *Sad Sal Dastan Newisi Dar Iran*, 420.
120 Gulrokh Qubadi, 'Women and the White Revolution', interview with author, 20 September 2017.
121 Biglari, Interview.
122 ʾOmar Faruqi, *Nazari Be Tarikh Wa Farhange Saqqez* [A Glance at Saqqez's Culture and History] (Muhammadi Publication: Saqqez, 1369 [1991]), 163.
123 ʿUbaidulla Ayyubiyan, 'Mire Nowruzi' [The Nowruz Prince], *Nashriyeye Adabiyate Daneshkadeye Tabriz* 14, no. 1 (Bahar 1341 [Spring 1962]): 102.
124 Ibid., 101.
125 Ibid., 111–12.
126 Faruqi, *Saqqez*, 163.
127 Ibid.; secondary schools were encouraged by books on theatre. According to a contemporary observer, a case in point was a play entitled *dozd-e nashiy be Kahdan Mizanad* performed by Saqqez's Saʿdi Secondary School students in Persian. Amini, Interview.
128 Faruqi, *Saqqez*, 164.
129 ʾOmar Faruqi, who composed and performed plays in the 1970s, names a number of these artists: Muhammad Muhammadpanah, Fayeq Adami, Naser Ardalan, Majed Hamzaiy, Muhammad Zarendy, Muhsen Khursand, Abdulrahman Andishe, Ali Esfand, Jʿafar Jaʿfardust, Ebrahim Vaisiyn, Khalid Khaki and Amjad Alimuradi. Many became well-known artists towards the end of the 1970s. Ibid., 163–5.
130 Nikki R. Keddie, 'Secularism and State: Towards Clarity and Global Comparison', *New Left Review*, no. 226 (1997): 21–40.
131 David Forgacs (ed.), *The Gramsci Reader: Selected Writings 1916-1935* (New York: New York University Press, 2000), 53.
132 Arjomand, *The Turban for the Crown*, 96–7.
133 Ibid., 96.
134 Yapp, *The near East*, 337.

135 Ibid., 343.
136 Ali Ezzatyar, *The Last Mufti of Iranian Kurdistan: Ethnic and Religious Implications in the Greater Middle East* (New York: Palgrave, 2016), 55–6. The book claims that to address a religious question, the Qajar Shah demanded opinions also 'from a scholar who could provide a Sunni interpretation on the matter' (ibid., 55) and that against odds a certain Abdulla Dishi, Ahmad Muftizada's grandfather, was found in Qajar Kurdistan. Dishi participated in a meeting with Shiʿa scholars in the presence of the Shah and made such an impact by his 'knowledge on diverse Islamic matters' that he was given the 'nickname of Al-Farabi'. As a result 'he was named the "Mofti" of Iran's Sunnis by Nasser al-Deen Shah'. Ibid., 56. Although it is unlikely that there had been no other well-informed Sunni scholars at the time, this indicates to the family's religious prestige which lasted, first, institutionally and, later, spiritually.
137 Ibid., 82; Biglari, Interview.
138 Ezzatyar, *The Last Mufti*, 69.
139 Biglari, Interview.
140 Ibid.
141 Ezzatyar, *The Last Mufti*, 108.
142 Biglari, Interview.
143 Ezzatyar, *The Last Mufti*, 107. Ezzatyar's main aim is to show that Ahmad Muftizada, who became a prominent *religious* figure in revolutionary Kurdistan in 1979, is a historical example to prove the Kurds' aversion to both political Islam and religious extremism, making the Kurds ideal allies of the West. The book does not concern itself with the intellectual or cultural transformations of the era, in which the rise of Muftizada can be explained.
144 Ibid., 101; on his idea of the Islamic government, cf. Ahmad Muftizadeh, *Hokumat-E Eslami* [Islamic Government] (Sanandaj: Shuray-e Modiryat-e Maktab-e Qoran, 1979).
145 Ezzatyar, *The Last Mufti*, 101.
146 Biglari, Interview.
147 Ibid.
148 Amini, Interview; Biglari, Interview.
149 Biglari, Interview; Kaiwan, Interview; Amini, Interview.
150 Amini, Interview.

Chapter 5

1 See Shahrzad Mojab (ed.), *Women of Non-State Nation: The Kurds* (Costa Mesa: Mazda Publishers, 2001).
2 See Rezayi et al., 'Sonnat, Nosazi Wa Khanewade'; Mohammadpur and Iman, 'Taqhirate Ejtemai Dar Sardasht'.
3 See Guity Nashat (ed.), *Women and Revolution in Iran* (Colorado: West View Press, 1983); Afkhami, *Zanan*; Women's Organization of Iran, *Hoquqe Zan Dar Iran (1357-1346)* [Women and Law in Iran (1967-1978)] (n. p.: Foundation for Iranian Studies, 1994).
4 For classical liberalism's approach cf. John Stuart Mill, *The Subjection of Women* (London: Longman, 1870); and for colonialsim cf. Evelyn Baring Cromer, *Modern Egypt*, Vol. 1 (New York: Macmillan, 1916).

5   Elizabeth B. Frierson, 'Unimagined Communities: Women and Education in the Late Ottoman Empire 1876-1909', *Critical Matrix: The Prinston Journal of Women, Gender, and Culture* 9, no. 2 (1995): 74.
6   See Peter Smith, *The Babi and Baha'i Religions: From Messianic Shiism to a World Religion* (Cambridge: Cambridge University Press, 1987).
7   'Be zir-e maqna'e ma ra sarist layeq-e afsar'. Quoted in Mastoura Kurdistani, *Tarikhe Ardalan* [The History of the Ardalans] (Kermanshahan: Bahrami, 1946), ت [T].
8   See Bibi Khanom Astarabadi, *Ma'ayebe Rajjal: Dar Pasokh Be Ta'dibe Zanan* [Vices of Men: A Response to *the Education of Women*] (Chicago: Midland Press, 1992); and the translation of both texts in Hasan Javadi and Willem Floor, *The Education of Women and the Vices of Men: Two Qajar Tracts* (New York: Syracuse University Press, 2010).
9   Cf. Taj al-Saltanah, *Khaterate Taj Al-Saltanah* [The Memoirs of Taj al-Saltanah] (Tehran: Tarikhe Iran, 1992).
10 Cf. Qasim Amin, *The Liberation of Women [and] the New Woman* (Cairo: American University in Cairo Press, 2000).
11 On the intellectual debates in the Ottoman Empire regarding education and education for women, see Mardin, *The Genesis of Young Ottoman Thought*.
12 Ibid., p. 323: footnote 135.
13 Omed Ashna (ed.), *Piramerd*, Vol. 1, 2nd edn (Hawler: Aras, 2009), 27.
14 Piramerd, *Diwani Piramerdi Namir* [The Eternal Piramerd's Collection of Poetry], ed. Muhammad Rasul Hawar (Hawler: Shivan, 2007), 30–1.
15 See Qane's and Goran's *diwan*s or collections of poetry.
16 'Aladdin Sajjadi, *Mezhui Adabi Kurdi* [The History of Kurdish Literature] (Sanandaj: Kurdistan, 2013), 139.
17 Nashat, *Women and Revolution in Iran*, 5.
18 For the role of Kurdish language, see Amir Hassanpour, 'The (Re)Production of Patriarchy in the Kurdish Language', in Shahrzad Mojab (ed.), *Women of Non-State Nation: The Kurds* (Costa Mesa: Mazda Publishers, 2001).
19 See ibid.
20 Ibid., 227.
21 Hassanpour, 'Farhangi Zaraki Le Khuli Teknolozhiy Zamanda'.
22 Hazhar's misogynist stance towards women can be seen in his celebrated book, *Cheshti Mijawir*. The fact that he was a prominent poet with an interesting, somewhat nebulous, background, gave him a linguistic authority; hence, his dictionary instantly became very popular.
23 Gulrukh Qubadi, *Shaqayeqha Bar Sanglakh: Zendegi Wa Zamaneye Yek Zane Kord Az Kordestane Iran* [Poppies on Rocks: The Life and Times of a Kurdish Woman from Iran] (2015), 84.
24 Mustafasultani, Interview.
25 Muhammad Qazi, *Khaterate Yek Motarjem* [A Translator's Memoir] (Tehran: Zenderud, 1992), 19.
26 Qubadi, *Shaqayeqha*.
27 For a recent published work on the subject, cf. Fatema Karimi, *Tragediye Tan: Khosunat 'Aleyhe Zanan* [The Tragedy of the Body: Violence Against Women] (Tehran: Roushangaran, 1389 [2010]). The author explains in a video clip that she found out through her research, conducted in the 2000s in the Pava region, how FGM was considered by affected women as both normal and a religious duty, while

the idea involved widespread stress and fear endured by girls who expected the same fate. See https://vimeo.com/51060946, accessed 13 December 2017.
28 Qubadi, Interview.
29 Ibid.
30 'Azizpur, Interview.
31 Ibid.
32 Ibid.
33 Qubadi, *Shaqayeqha*.
34 Qubadi, Interview. A teacher in the 1970s, Qubadi can recollect stories told by her mother about women education in the early decades of the twentieth century.
35 Oremar, *Dimana Lagal Mina Qazi*, 16–18.
36 Ibid.
37 Ibid., 17–18.
38 Kaiwan, Interview.
39 Qubadi, Interview.
40 Ibid.
41 Ibid.
42 Qubadi, *Shaqayeqha*, 21–2.
43 Camron Michael Amin, *The Making of the Modern Iranian Women* (Gainesville: California University Press, 2002).
44 See these laws in *Hoquqe Zan Dar Iran (1357-1346)*, 351–62.
45 Qubadi, Interview.
46 Ibid.
47 *Hoquqe Zan Dar Iran (1357-1346)*, 362–74.
48 Cf. Ibid., 314.
49 Cf. Ibid., 322.
50 Cf. Ibid., 312, 15, 19 and 23–48.
51 Ibid., 310–11.
52 Cf. *Amuzesh wa Parvaresh* 9, no. 5 (Mordad 1318 [1939]): 7.
53 Cf. Bahram Mehrpaima, *Pishineye Warzesh Dar Saqqez-Kordestan* [The Genesis of Sport in Saqqez-Kurdistan] (Tehran: Tavakoli, 1390 [2011]).
54 Plan and Budgent Organisation, *Daftarcheye Amare Iran* [Statistical Notebook of Iran] (Iran: Statistics Centre, 1976), 133–6.
55 *Hoquqe Zan Dar Iran (1357-1346)*, 18–19.
56 Amin, *The Making of the Modern Iranian Women*, 7–8.
57 Afkhami, *Zanan*, 39.
58 Ibid.
59 Ibid., 39–40.
60 In textbooks working women were represented as *better mothers* in order to appease the patriarchal system. They did also advocate eight-hour work days and the establishment of nurseries within factories. *Hoquqe Zan Dar Iran (1357-1346)*, 316.
61 Ibid., 387.
62 Afkhami, *Zanan*, 101.
63 Ibid., 217.
64 Ibid.
65 Pappe, *Modern Middle East*, 224.
66 Ibid., 232.
67 Ibid., 234.

68 For example, as Nashat shows, early publications included *Shukufeh* (Blossom), *Zaban-e Zanan* (The Women's Voice) and *Alam-e Naswan* (The World of Women), 'undertaken by the women activists to enlighten women'. Two early societies formed in the aftermath of the Constitutional Revolution of 1906 were *Anjoman-e Azadi-ye Zanan* (the Women's Freedom Movement) and *Anjoman-e Mukhadarat-e Vatan* (National Ladies' Society). For this see Guity Nashat, 'Women in Pre-Revolutionary Iran: A Historical Overview', in Guity Nashat (ed.), *Women and Revolution in Iran* (Colorado: West View Press, 1983), 22 and 24.
69 Ibid., 30.
70 Ibid., 28.
71 This chapter's observations on Pappe's argument, which is in favour of writing women histories with a new methodology, complements his valuable study and his deconstructive approach to concepts popularized by modernization and development theories.
72 Nashat, 'Women in Pre-Revolutionary Iran', 30.
73 Pappe, *Modern Middle East*, 235.
74 The absence of this factor becomes more conspicuous when Pappe seems to attribute the process of change mainly to the state changes related to the status of women in Iran under the Pahlavis, without making the pressure from below central to these changes. This leads to an incorrect conclusion about women not defending the Pahlavi state during the 1979 Revolution. For this ibid., 237–8.
75 Wiesner-Hanks, 'Gender', 107.
76 Hesami, *Le Bireweriekanim*, Vol. 1, 22. The author (1926–2001) was a Kurdish political activist and a teacher. His memoirs contain valuable observation on such women's life, however, without providing any analysis.
77 Hiner Saleem, *My Father's Rifle: A Childhood in Kurdistan* (New York: Picador, 2006), 4–5.
78 Amini, Interview.
79 Qubadi, *Shaqayeqha*, 95.
80 *Hoquqe Zan Dar Iran (1357-1346)*, 19.

Conclusion

1 Frierson, 'Unimagined Communities'.
2 See Fatemeh Mehr Khansalar, *Joghd-E Barfi* [The Snowy Owl] (Tehran: Markaz, 2018).
3 Ashcroft, *Post-Colonial Transformation*, 45; Mohammad Bazafkan and Mohammad Rezaei, 'Othering the Ethnic Groups: A Meta-Analysis of Iranian Identity Studies', *The International Journal of Divers Identities* 20, no. 2 (2020): 1–17.

BIBLIOGRAPHY

Journals, newspapers, reference tools

Amuzesh wa Parwaresh (1938–77)
Asnad-e Baharestan (1): Documents Pertaining to Kurdistan and Kermanshahan in the Constitutional era, 1910–14
Ayandeh (1925–70)
Barresiha-ye Tarikhi (1966–70)
Daneshkade-ye Adabiat-e Tehran (1960–79)
Daneshkade-ye Adabiat-e Tabriz (1960–79)
Encyclopaedia Iranica
Encyclopaedia of Islam
Gowhar (issues published in the 1970s)
Kaveh (1916–22)
Keyhan (issues published in the 1970s)
Kurdistan (Tehran, 1959–63)
Nishtiman (1939–46)
Rahnema-ye Ketab (issues published in the 1960s and 1970s)
Rega (1949)
Sokhan (issues published in the 1960s and 1970s)
Sur Earafil (1907–8)
Tahqiqat-e Eqtesadi (Issues: 5–14, June 1963–December 1966)
Ta'lim wa Tarbiyat (1925–38)

The National Archives (London)

FO 371 – Foreign Office: Political Departments: General Correspondence from 1906–66. POLITICAL EASTERN (E): Persia.
Intelligent report amended provincial administrative division, (E672/167/34), dated 15 January 1938, FO 371 21895.
Internal political situation, (EP1015/123), dated 24 May 1961, FO371 157605.

Kurdish Situation, FO371/52702 Code 34 File 104. 1946

League of Nations, (E2640/140/34), dated 23 March 1946.
The Kurds of Persia, (E2782/104/34), dated 24 March 1946.
The Kurds of Persia, (E2782/104/34), dated 28 February 1946.
The Kurds of Persia, (E2782/104/34), dated 28 March 1946.
Manchester Guardian: 'On Situation in Iran' (E2268/104/34), dated 28 February 1946.

FO 371/140822 Development of provinces of Iran. Code EP file 1103. 1959.

Provincial Development Work, (EP1102/4), dated 31 December 1958.
(EP 1103/1), dated 31 December 1958.
(EP1103/7), dated 27 January 1959
(EP1103/14), dated 25 February 1959
(EP1103/18), dated 13 April 1959.
(EP 1103/2), dated 08 June 1959.
(EP1103/5), dated 10 June 1959.

OD 34/272 Technical assistance for social welfare, Iran. Ministry of Overseas Development (OD): Middle East Department (MID). 1968–9.

Request for social welfare experts, (MID 242/86/02), dated 02 July 1969.
(MID 242/86/02), dated 27 September 1968.
(ES 332/213/03), dated 24 September 1968.
(MID 242/86/02), dated 08 July 1969.
(MID 242/86/02), dated 10 July 1969.
(MID 242/86/02), dated 20 June 1969.

Interviews

Amini, Rahim. "Kurdistan and the White Revolution". Interview with author, 10 July, 2017.
Azizpur, Dr Ahmad, "Kurdistan and the White Revolution," interview with author, 8 July, 2017.
Biglari, Yadola. "Kurdistan and the White Revolution". Interview with author, 6 July, 2017.
Kaiwan, Mahmud, "Kurdistan and the White Revolution," interview with author, 4 July, 2017.
Mustafasultani, Reshad, "Kurdistan and the White Revolution," interview with author, 3 July, 2017.
Qubadi, Gulrokh, "Women and the White Revolution," interview with author, 20 September, 2017.

Documents by the government and other organizations

Plan and Budget Organisation. *Daftarcheye Amare Iran* [Statistical Notebook of Iran]. Iran: Statistics Centre, 1976.
Plan and Budget Organisation. *Statistical Yearbook of Iran 1352 [March 1973–March 1974]*. Iran: Statistical Centre of Iran, 1975.
Women's Organization of Iran. *Hoquqe Zan Dar Iran (1357–1346)* [Women and Law in Iran (1967–1978)]. n.p.: Foundation for Iranian Studies, 1994.

Other References

Abedini, Hassan Mir. *Sad Sal Dastan Newisi Dar Iran* [One Hundred Years of Story-Writing in Iran]. Tehran: Nashre Cheshme, 1998.

Abrahamian, Ervand. *Iran between Two Revolutions*. Princeton: Princeton University Press, 1982.
Abrams, Lynn. *Oral History Theory*. London: Routledge, 2010.
Afkhami, Gholam Reza. *The Life and Times of the Shah*. California: University of California Press, 2006.
Afkhami, Mahnaz. *Zanan, Dowlat Va Jame'e Dar Iran: 1941–1978* [Women, State, and Society in Iran]. Maryland: Foundation for Iranian Studies, 2003.
Afshar, Mahmud. "Enqelabe Sefid". [The White Revolution] *Ayandeh* 3 (1946): 14–16.
Afshar, Mahmud. "Shureshe Kordhaye Osmani Wa Masaleye Kordestan". [The Revolt of the Ottoman Kurds and the Kurdistan Question] *Ayandeh* 1 (Tir 1304 [1925]).
Ahmadzadeh, Masud. *Mobareze Mosalahane: Ham Estrategy Va Ham Taktik*. [Armed Struggle As Both Strategy And Tactic] n.p: n.p, 1970.
al-Saltanah, Taj. *Khaterate Taj Al-Saltanah* [The Memoirs of Taj al-Saltanah]. Tehran: Tarikhe Iran, 1992.
Al-Shaykh, Hanan. *I Sweep the Sun of Rooftops*. Trans. Catherine Cobham. New York: Anchor Books, 1998.
Alami, Bahador. *Naqd Wa Arziyabie Qanoon Taqsimate Keshwarie Iran* [A Study of Iran's Administrative Divisons Law]. Tehran: Iran Parliament's Research Centre, 2013.
Alen, B. "Behdashte Rustayi". [Rural Healthcare] *Amuzesh va Parvaresh* 14, no. 5 (Mordad 1332 [July 1953]): 273–5.
Amanat, Abbas. *Iran: A Modern History*. New Haven, London: Yale University Press, 2017.
Amin, Camron Michael. *The Making of the Modern Iranian Women*. Gainesville: California University Press, 2002.
Amin, Qasim. *The Liberation of Women [and] the New Woman*. Cairo: American University in Cairo Press, 2000.
Amuzegar, Jahangir. "Capital Formation and Development Finance". In *Iran Faces the Seventies*, edited by Ehasan Yarshater, 66–87. England: Praeger Publishers, 1971.
Amuzegar, Jahangir. *Iran: An Economic Profile*. Washington, DC: Middle East Institue, 1977.
Anderson, Benedict. *Imagined Communities*. London and New York: Verso, 2006.
Ansari, Ali M. *Modern Iran: The Pahlavi and After*. 2nd ed. England: Pearson Education Limited, 2007.
Ansari, Ali M. "Mohammad Ali Foroughi and the Construction of Civic Nationalism in Early Twentieth-Century Iran". In *Iran in the Middle East: Transnational Encounters and Social History*, edited by H. E. Chehabi, 11–26, Peyman Jafari and Maral Jefroudi. London: I. B. Tauris, 2015.
Ansari, Ali M. "The Myth of the White Revolution". In *Politics of Modern Iran*, edited by Ali M. Ansari, 261–82, Vol. 2. London: Routledge, 2001.
Ansari, Ali M. *Politics of Nationalism in Modern Iran*. Cambridge: Cambridge University Press, 2012.
Arjomand, Said Amir. *The Shadow of God and the Hidden Imam*. Chicago: University of Chicago Press, 1984.
Arjomand, Said Amir. *The Turban for the Crown: The Islamic Revolution in Iran*. Oxford: Oxford University Press, 1988.
Ashcroft, Bill. *Post-Colonial Transformation*. New York: Routledge, 2001.
Ashcroft, Bill, Gareth Griffiths, and Helen Tiffin (eds.). *The Post-Colonial Studies Reader*. New York: Routledge, 1995.
Ashna, Omed (ed.). *Piramerd*. Vol. 1. Hawler: Aras, 2001.
Ashna, Omed (ed.). *Piramerd*. Vol. 1. 2nd ed. Hawler: Aras, 2009.

Ashraf, Ahmad. "General Survey of Modern Education". In *Encyclopaedia Iranica*, http://www.iranicaonline.org/articles/education-vii-general-survey-of-modern-education, accessed 02 August 2016.
Ashuri, Dariush. *Ma Wa Moderniyat* [We and Modernity]. Tehran: Tolou' Azadi, 1998.
Astarabadi, Bibi Khanom. *Ma'ayebe Rajjal: Dar Pasokh Be Ta'dibe Zanan* [Vices of Men: A Response to the Education of Women]. Chicago: Midland Press, 1992.
Atabaki, Touraj. *Azerbaijan: Ethnicity and Struggle for Power in Iran*. London: I. B. Tauris, 2000.
Atabaki, Touraj. "The First World War, Great Power Rivalries and the Emergence of a Political Community in Iran". In *Iran and the First World War: Battleground of the Great Powers*, edited by Touraj Atabaki, 1–8. London: I. B. Tauris and Co., 2006.
Atabaki, Touraj (ed.). *Iran in the 20th Century: Historiography and Political Culture*. London: I. B. Tauris, 2009.
Aubin, Eugene. *Iran Emrouz 1907–1908* [Iran Today]. Iran: Zawarm, 1985.
Ayazi, Borhan. *Ayyine-Ye Sanandaj* [The Mirror of Sanandaj]. Iran: Payam, 1991.
Ayyubiyan, Ubaidulla. "Mire Nowruzi". [The Nowruz Prince] *Nashriyeye Adabiyate Daneshkadeye Tabriz* 14, no. 1 (Bahar 1341 [Spring 1962]): 99–112.
Ayyubiyan, Ubaidulla. "Barresiye Tahqiqie Chrikai Mam U Zin". [An Analysis of Mam and Zin Epic Story] *Nashriyeye Adabiyate Daneshkadeye Tabriz* 13, no. 2 (1340 [1961]): 164–240.
Ayyubiyan, Ubaidulla. "Taqwime Mahalliye Kurdi". [The Kurdish Local Calendar] *Nashriyeye Adabiyate Daneshkadeye Tabriz* 16, no. 2 (1343 [1964]): 179–208.
Azimi, Fakhreddin. *Iran: The Crisis of Democracy, 1941–1953*. London: I.B. Tauris, 1989.
Bakhash, S. "Administration in Iran Vi. Safavid, Zand, and Qajar Periods". In *Encyclopaedia Iranica*, Online edition, http://www.iranicaonline.org/articles/administration-vi-safavid, accessed on 23 April 2018.
Barahani, Reza. *Tarikhe Mozakkar* [Masculine History]. Tehran: Nashre Awwal, 1984.
Bazafkan, Mohammad, and Mohammad Rezaei. "Othering the Ethnic Groups: A Meta-Analysis of Iranian Identity Studies". *The International Journal of Divers Identities* 20, no. 2 (2020): 1–17.
Behrangi, Asad (ed.). *Majmu'e Assare Samad Behrangi* [An Anthology]. Tabriz: Behrangi, 1382 [2005].
Behrangi, Asad (ed.). *Namehaye Samad Behrangi* [Samad Behrangi's Letters]. Tehran: Amir Kabir, 1357 [1979].
Behrangi, Samad. *Qessehaye Behrang* [Behrang's Stories]. Tehran: Donya, 1359 [1980].
Bendix, Reinhard. "Tradition and Modernity Reconsidered". In *Embattled Reason*, edited by Reinhard Bendix, 279–320, Vol. 2. New Jersey: Transaction, Inc., 1988.
Bendix, Reinhard. "Tradition and Modernity Reconsidered". *Comparative Studies in Society and History* 9, no. 3 (April 1967): 292–346.
Bentley, Michael. *Modernizing England's Past: English Historiography in the Age of Modernism, 1870–1970*. Cambridge: Cambridge University Press, 2005.
Berger, Stefan, and Christoph Conard. *The Past as History: National Identity and Historical Consciousness in Modern Europe*. Basingstoke: Palgrave, 2015.
Berger, Stefan, and Chris Lorenz (eds.). *The Contested Nation: Ethnicity, Class, Religion and Gender in National Histories*. Basingstoke: Palgrave McMillan, 2008.
Berzuyi, Mujtaba. *Vaz'iyate Siasie Kurdistan* [Political Situation in Kurdistan]. Tehran: Fekre Nou, 2000.
Bhabha, Homi K. *The Location of Culture*. London: Routledge, 1994.
Bhabha, Homi K. (ed.). *Nation and Narration*. New York: Routledge, 1990.

Bharier, Julian. *Economic Development in Iran 1900–1970*. Oxford: Oxford University Press, 1971.
Bill, James A. "Modernization and Reform from Above: The Case of Iran". *The Journal of Politics* 32, no. 1 (Feb,1970): 19–40
Bishop, Isabella. *Journeys in Persia and Kurdistan*. Vol. 2. London: John Murray, 1891.
Bitlisi, Sharaf Khan. *Sharafnameh: Tarikhe Mofassale Kurdistan* [The Sharafnameh: The Complete History of Kurdistan]. Iran: Asatir, 1377 [1998].
Blouryan, Ghani. *Alakok*. Tehran: Farhange Rasa, 1384 [2005].
Boroujerdi, Mehrzad. *Iranian Intellectuals and the West: The Tormented Triumph of Nativism*. Syracuse: Syracuse University Press, 1996.
Bourdieu, Pierre. "The Forms of Capital". In *Handbook of Theory and Research for the Sociology of Education*, edited by John G. Richardson, 241–58. London: Greenwood Press, 1986.
Bourdieu, Pierre. *Language and Symbolic Power*. Cambridge: Polity Press, 1991.
Brubaker, Roger. *Nationalism Reframed: Nationhood and the National Question in the New Europe*. Cambridge: Cambridge University Press, 1996.
Burke, Peter. *History and Social Theory*. New York: Cornell University Press, 2005.
Cahoone, Lawrence (ed.). *From Modernism to Postmodernism: An Anthology*. Australia: Blackwell Publishing Ltd, 2003.
Chelebi, Evliya. *An Ottoman Traveller: Selections from the Book of Travels of Evliya Çelebi*. Trans. Robert Dankoff and Sooyong Kim. London: Eland, 2010.
Chubin, Shahram, and Charles Tripp. *Iran and Iraq at War*. London: I. B. Tauris and Co Ltd, 1988.
Connell, Raewyn. *Gender*. 2nd ed. Cambridge: Polity, 2009.
Cromer, Evelyn Baring. *Modern Egypt*. Vol. 1. New York: Macmillan, 1916.
Cronin, Stephanie. *Soldiers, Shahs and Subalterns in Iran: Opposition, Protest and Revolt, 1921–1941*. New York: Palgrave, 2010.
Dabashi, Hamid. *Iran: A People Interrupted*. New York: New Press, 2007.
Dabashi, Hamid. *Theology of Discontent: The Ideological Foundation of the Islamic Revolution in Iran*. New Brunswick: Transaction Publishers, 2006.
Daftary, Farhad. "Development Planning in Iran: A Historical Survey". *Iranian Studies* 6, no. 4 (1973): 176–228.
Danesh, Abol Hassan. "Land Reform, State Policy, and Social Change in Iran". *Urban Anthropology and Studies of Cultural Systems and World Economic Development* 21, no. 2 (1992): 153–79.
Darwin, John. *After Tamerlane: The Global History of Empire since 1405*. London: Allen Lane, 2007.
Davari, Bahram. "Tarhi Baraye Ehiyaye Keshawarzi Wa Bazsaziye Roosta". [A Plan for the Revival of Agriculture and Reconstruction of the Village] *Keyhan*, 1351 [1972–3].
Donner, Fred M. "Periodization as a Tool of the Historian with Special Reference to Islamic History". *Der Islam* 91, no. 1 (2014): 20–36.
Dudink, Stefan, Karen Hagemann, and John Tosh (eds.). *Masculinities in Politics and War: Gendering Modern History*. Manchester: Manchester University Press, 2004.
Eagleton, Terry. *Ideology: An Introduction*. London and New York: Verso, 1991.
Eagleton, William. *The Kurdish Republic of 1946*. London: Oxford University Press, 1963.
Ebtehaj, Abulhasan. *Khaterate Abulhasane Ebtehaj* [Ebtehaj's Memoirs]. Vol. 1. London: Paka Print, 1991.
Ehlers, Eckart. "Modern Urbanization and Modernization in Persia". In *Encyclopaedia Iranica*, http://www.iranicaonline.org/articles/cities-iv, accessed 16 July 2016.

Ekhtiyar, Dr Mansur. "Shiweye Barresiye Guyeshha". [The way to Analyse Dielects] *Nashriyeye Adabiyate Daneshkadeye Tehran* 12, no. 2 (1343 [1964]): 170–215.
Elling, Rasmus Christian. *Minorities in Iran: Nationalism and Ethnicity after Khomeini.* Basingstoke: Palgrave Macmillan, 2013.
Elwell-Sutton, L. P. "Alam-E Nesvan". In *Encyclopaedia Iranica* I, no. 8: 795–96, http://www.iranicaonline.org/articles/alam-e-nesvan-a-magazine-founded-in-mizan-1299-s, accessed on 23 August 2016.
Escobar, Arturo. *Encountering Development: The Making and Unmaking of the Third World.* Princeton: Princeton University Press, 1995.
Ezzat, Muhammad. *Hukkamati Komari Kurdistan: Namekan W Balgekan* [Kurdish Republic: Correspondece and Documents]. n.a: n.a, 1995.
Ezzatyar, Ali. *The Last Mufti of Iranian Kurdistan: Ethnic and Religious Implications in the Greater Middle East.* New York: Palgrave, 2016.
Faghih, Mohammad Ali. "Behdārī". [Health Centre] In *Encyclopaedia Iranica* IV, no. 1: 100–04, http://www.iranicaonline.org/articles/behdari, accessed on 30 December 2012.
Farhūdī, Ḥosayn. "City Councils". In *Encyclopaedia Iranica*, http://www.iranicaonline.org/articles/city-councils-anjoman-e-sahr-in-persia, accessed 27 August 2017.
Farmanfarmaian, Manucher, and Roxane Farmanfarmaian. *Blood and Oil: A Prince's Memoir of Iran, from the Shah to the Ayatollah.* USA: Random House, 1997.
Faruqi, Omar. *Nazari Be Tarikh Wa Farhange Saqqez* [A Glance at Saqqez's Culture and History]. Saqqez: Muhammadi Publication, 1369 [1991].
Forgacs, David (ed.). *The Gramsci Reader: Selected Writings 1916–1935.* New York: New York University Press, 2000.
Foroughi, Mohammad Ali. "Modernisation of Law". *Journal of Persianate Studies* 3 (2010): 31–45.
Foucault, Michel. *The Archaeology of Knowledge.* London: Routledge, 1972.
Fraser, James B. *Narratives of a Journey into Khurasan in the Years 1821 and 1822.* London: n. p., 1825.
Frewshi, Dr Bahram. "Zabanhaye Irani Dar Kharej Az Iran". [Iranian Languages Outside of Iran] *Nashriye Adabiyate Daneshkade Tehran* 12, no. 3-4 (1344 [1965]): 32038.
Frierson, Elizabeth B. "Unimagined Communities: Women and Education in the Late Ottoman Empire 1876–1909". *Critical Matrix: The Prinston Journal of Women, Gender, and Culture* 9, no. 2 (1995): 55–90.
Gellner, Ernest. *Nationalism.* New York: New York University Press, 1997.
Giddens, Anthony. *The Consequences of Modernity.* UK: Polity, 1990.
Good, Byron J. "The Transformation of Health Care in Modern Iranian History". In *Modern Iran: The Dialectics of Continuity and Change*, edited by Michael E. Bonine and Nikki R. Keddie. USA: State University of New York Press, 1981.
Hanioglu, M. Sukru. *The Young Turks in Opposition.* Oxford: Oxford University Press, 1995.
Hassanpour, Amir. "Farhangi Zaraki Le Khuli Teknolozhiy Zamanda". [Oral Culture in the Age of Technology], http://en.calameo.com/read/0011170694fd3b13133a7, accessed 6 November 2017.
Hassanpour, Amir. "Raparini Verzerani Mukriyan, 1331–1332". [The Peasant uprising of Mukriyan, 1952–1953] *Derwaze* 1 (Apr.–May 2017): 94–125.
Hassanpour, Amir. "The (Re)Production of Patriarchy in the Kurdish Language". In *Women of Non-State Nation: The Kurds*, edited by Shahrzad Mojab. Costa Mesa: Mazda Publishers, 2001.

Hawar, Muhammadrasul. *Simko W Bzutnawey Natawayeti Kurd* [Simko and the Kurdish National Movement]. Sweden: APEC, 1995.
Hesami, Karim. *Khaterate Karim Hesami* [Karim Hesami's Memoirs]. Sweden: Arzan, 2011.
Hesami, Karim. *Le Bireweriekanim* [From My Memoirs]. Vol. 1. Uppsala: Jina Nu Forlaget, 1986.
Hilmi, Rafiq. *Yaddasht* [Notes]. Iraq: Roshinbiri Lawan Press, 1988.
Hoare, Quintin, and Geoffrey Nowell Smith (eds.). *Selections from the Prison Notebooks of Antonio Gramsci*. London: Lawrence and Wishart, 1971.
Hobsbawm, Eric. *The Age of Revolution: Europe, 1789–1848*. London: Weidenfeld & Nicolson, 1962.
Hobsbawm, Eric, and Terrence Ranger (eds.). *The Invention of Tradition*. Cambridge: Cambridge University Press, 1983.
Homayun, Dariush. "Eslahate Arzi Dar Iran". [Land Reform in Iran] *Tahqiqate Eqtesadi [Economic Research]* 5 & 6 (Khordad 1342 [June 1963]).
Howe, Stephen. "Historiography". In *Ireland and the British Empire*, edited by Kevin Kenny. Oxford: Oxford Unviersity Press, 2004.
Howe, Stephen. *Ireland and Empire: Colonial Legacies in Irish History and Culture*. Oxford: Oxford University Press, 2002.
Huntington, Samuel. *Political Order in Changing Societies*. New Haven and London: Yale University Press, 1968.
Huzni, Husein. "Ghunchai Baharistan: Tarikhi Kurdan". [Blossoms of Spring: The History of the Kurds] In *Collected Works*, edited by Badran Ahmad Habib, Vol. 1. Aras: Hawler, 2011.
Inkeles, Alex, and David H. Smith. *Becoming Modern: Individual Change in Six Developing Countries*. London: Heinemann, 1974.
Jami. *Gozashte Cheraghe Rahe Ayande Ast* [Past is the Torch of Future's Path]. Tehran: Qaqnus, 1998.
Javadi, Hasan, and Willem Floor. *The Education of Women and the Vices of Men: Two Qajar Tracts*. New York: Syracuse University Press, 2010.
Karimi, Ali. *Zhiyan W Basarhati Abdulraham Zabihi* [The Life and Fortune of Abdulrahman Zabihi]. Sweden: Zagros Media, 1999.
Karimi, Fatema. *Tragediye Tan: Khosunat 'Aleyhe Zanan* [The Tragedy of the Body: Violence Against Women]. Tehran: Roushangaran, 1389 [2010].
Karshenas, Masoud. *Oil, State Ad Industrialisation in Iran*. Cambridge: CUP, 1990.
Katouzian, Homa. *State and Society in Iran: The Eclips of the Qajars and the Emergence of the Pahlavis*. London: I. B. Tauris, 2000.
Kazemi, Farhad. *Poverty and Revolution in Iran: The Migrant Poor, Urban Marginality and Politics*. New York: New York University Press, 1980.
Keddie, Nikki R. (ed.). *The French Revolution and the Middle East* [Iran and the Muslim World: Resistance and Revolution]. London: Macmillan Press, 1995.
Keddie, Nikkie R. *Modern Iran: Roots and Results of Revolution*. New Haven: Yale University Press, 2003.
Keddie, Nikki R. "Secularism and State: Towards Clarity and Global Comparison". *New Left Review* 226 (1997): 21–40.
Kedouri, Eli. *Nationalism in Asia and Africa*. London: Weidenfield and Nicolson, 1971.
Khanlari, P. N. "The Situation and the Future of Education". *Amuzesh wa Parvaresh* New Era, Year 33 [Esfand 1341], no. 1 (1963): 9–22.
Khansalar, Fatemeh Mehr. *Joghd-E Barfi* [The Snowy Owl]. Tehran: Markaz, 2018.

Khaznadar, Maref. *Mezhui Adabi Kurdi La Saratawa Ta Sadai Chwarda* [The History of Kurdish Literature: From the Beginning until the Fourteenth Century]. Vol. 1. Kurdistan, Hawler: Education Ministry, 2001.

Khaznadar, Maref. *Mezhui Adabi Kurdi: Sadai 19 W Saratai Sadai 20* [The History of Kurdish literature: The 19th Century and the Early 20th Century]. Edited by Dr Kurdustan Mukriani. Vol. 4. Kurdistan, Hawler: The Education Ministry Publication, 2004.

Khaznadar, Maref. *Mezhui Adabi Kurdi: Sadei Nozda W Bistam* [The History of Kurdish Literature: the Nineteenth and Twentieth Centuries]. Vol. 4. Kurdistan, Hawler: The Education Ministry, 2004.

Khezri, Muhammad. *Laparayek La Tekoshan W Julanaway Salakani 42–47 Hezbi Dimukrati Kurdistan* [A Page from the Struggle and Movement of the Democratic Party of Kurdistan (1963–68)]. Sweden: n.p., 2003.

Kia, Mehrdad. "Persian Nationalism and the Campaign for Language Purification". *Middle Eastern Studies* 34, no. 2 (1998): 9–36.

Ko, Dorothy. "Gender". In *A Concise Companion to History*, edited by Ulnika Rublack. Oxford: Oxford University Press, 2012.

Koohi-Kamali, Farideh. *The Political Development of Kurds in Iran*. New York: Palgrave, 2003.

Koyi, Haji Qadir. *Diwan*. Stockholm: Nefel, 2004.

Kurdistani, Mastoura. *Tarikhe Ardalan* [The History of the Ardalans]. Kermanshahan: Bahrami, 1946.

Kwestani, Said Kawa. *Awerrek La Basarhati Khom* [Looking Back on My Life] (1996), http://said.kurdland.com in PDF format, Accessed on 23 May 2018.

Lambton, Ann K. S. *Landlord and Peasant in Persia*. London: I. B. Tauris, 1991.

Lapidus, Ira M. *A History of Islamic Societies*. 3rd ed. Cambridge: Cambridge University Press, 2014.

Lerner, Daniel. *The Passing of the Traditional Society: Modernizing the Middle East*. USA: Free Press, 1958.

Linklater, Andrew. "The Problem of Community in International Relations". *Alternatives: Global, Local, Political* 15, no. 2 (Spring 1990): 135–53.

Lloyd, E. M. H. *Food and Inflation in the Middle East, 1940–45*. California: Stanford University Press, 1956.

Lockman, Zachary. *The Contending Visions of the Middle East: The History and Politics of Orientalism*. 2nd ed. USA: Cambridge University Press, 2010.

Louis, William Roger. *The British Empire in the Middle East 1945–1951*. Oxford: Clarendon Press, 1984.

Makki, Husein. *Tarikhe Bist Saleye Iran* [Twenty Years History of Iran]. Vol. 6. Tehran: Entesharat Elmi, 1374 [1995].

Malek, Rahim Rezazade (ed.). *Enqelabe Mashruteye Iran Be Rawayate Asnade Wazarate Kharejeye Englis* [Parliamentary Papers, Correspondence Respecting the Affairs of Persia]. Iran: Mazyar, 1377 [1998–9].

Mamedi, Sanar. *Khaterat Wa Dardha* [Memorandom and Pains]. Vol. 1. Sweden: Alfabet Maxima, 2000.

Marashi, Afshin. *Nationalizing Iran: Culture, Power and the State*. Seattle, London: University of Washington Press, 2008.

Mardin, Şerif. *The Genesis of Young Ottoman Thought: A Study in the Modernisation of Turkish Political Ideas*. Syracuse: Syracuse University Press, 2000.

Mardūk, Abd-Allāh. "The Madrasa in Sunni Kurdistan". In *Encyclopaedia Iranica*, http://www.iranicaonline.org/articles/education-vi-the-madrasa-in-sunni-kurdistan, accessed 15 March 2017.
Mardukh, Muhammad. *Mezhui Kurd Wa Kurdistan* [The History of Kurd and Kurdistan]. Hawler: Rozhhalat Press, 2011.
McDowall, David. *A Modern History of the Kurds*. London: I. B. Tauris, 2004.
Meho, Lokman I., and Kelly L. Maglaughlin. *Kurdish Culture and Society: An Annotated Bibliograph*. Westport: Greenwood Press, 2001.
Mehrpaima, Bahram. *Pishineye Warzesh Dar Saqqez-Kordestan* [The Genesis of Sport in Saqqez-Kurdistan]. Tehran: Tavakoli, 1390 [2011].
Menashri, David. *Education and the Making of Modern Iran*. Ithaca and London: Cornell University Press, 1992.
Messerschmidt, James W. *Hegemonic Masculinity: Formulation, Reformulation, and Amplification*. London: Rowman & Littlefield, 2018.
Mill, John Stuart. *The Subjection of Women*. London: Longman, 1870.
Mirsepassi, Ali. *Political Islam, Iran, and the Enlightenment*. Cambridge: Cambridge University Press, 2011.
Moarefi, Akbar. "Behdāštbarā-Ye Hama". [Health for All] In *Encyclopaedia Iranica*, http://www.iranicaonline.org/articles/behdast-bara-ye-hama, accessed 02 August 2017.
Mofid, Kamran. *Development Planning in Iran: From Monarchy to Islamic Republic*. England: MENS Press, 1987.
Mohammadpur, Ahmad, and Taqi Iman. "Taqhirate Ejtemai Dar Sardasht". [Social Chang in Sardasht] *Nameye Ensanshenasi* 1, no. 5 (1383 [2004]): 11–39.
Mojab, Shahrzad (ed.). *Women of Non-State Nation: The Kurds*. Costa Mesa: Mazda Publishers, 2001.
Momeni, Baqer. *Masalaye Arzi Wa Jange Tabaqati Dar Iran* [The Land Question and Class Struggle in Iran]. Tehran: Payvand, 1979.
Muftizadeh, Ahmad. *Hokumat-E Eslami* [Islamic Government]. Sanandaj: Shuray-e Modiryat-e Maktab-e Qoran, 1979.
Mustafasultani, Fuad. "Dar Bareye Chegunegiye Ijade Etehadyeye Dehqanan". [On the Foramtion of the Peasant Union] In *Kak Fuad Mustafasultani*, edited by Malaka Mustafasultani, Reza Mustafasultani and Heshmat Mustafasultani. Stettin: Print Group, 2017.
Nafisi, Hamid. "Cinema as a Political Instrument". In *Politics of Modern Iran*, edited by Ali M. Ansari, Vol. 1. New York: Routledge, 2011.
Nafisi, Said. *Babak Khorramdin*. Tehran: Asatir, 1384 [2005].
Nafisi, Said. *Tarikhe Ejtema'i Wa Siyasiye Iran Dar Doreye Mo'aser* [The Social and Political History of Modern Iran]. Tehran: Ahoura, 1383 [2004].
Nashat, Guity (ed.). *Women and Revolution in Iran*. Colorado: West View Press, 1983.
Nashat, Guity. "Women in Pre-Revolutionary Iran: A Historical Overview". In *Women and Revolution in Iran*, edited by Guity Nashat. Colorado: West View Press, 1983.
Natali, Denise. *The Kurds and the Stat: Evolving National Identity in Iraq, Turkey, and Iran*. New York: Syracuse University Press, 2005.
Nikitin, Vasili, *Kord Wa Kordestan* [Kurd and Kurdistan]. Trans. M. Qazi. Iran: Nilufar, 1363 [1984–5].
Nohekhan, Hamed. "Me'yarhaye Taqsimate Keshwari Dar Doreye Pahlavi". [Criteria of Administrative Divisions under the Pahlavi] *Kheradnameh* 4, no. 9 (1391 [2012]): 113–36.
Noqrekar, Masud. *Bakhsi Az Tarikhe Jonbeshe Rowshanfekrie Iran* [A Phase of the Enlightenment History of Iran]. Vol. 1. Sweden: Baran, 1382 [2002–3].

Oremar, Kakshar. *Dimana Lagal Mina Qazi* [Interview with Mina Qazi]. Sulaimaniya: Karo, 2013.
Pahlavi, Mohammad Reza Shah. *Mission for My Country*. London: Hutchinson, 1991.
Pappe, Illan. *A History of Modern Palestine*. 2nd ed. Cambridge: Cambridge University Press, 2004.
Pappe, Ilan. *The Modern Middle East*. New York: Routledge, 2005.
Parvin, Gonabadi Mohammad. "Amuzeshe Zabane Farsi Va Hadafe Tarbiyatie An". [Teaching Persian Language and Its Educational Aim] *Amuzesh wa Parvaresh* 35, no. 9 and 10 (1344 [1965]).
Perry, R. John. "Language Reform in Turkey and Iran". *International Journal of Middle East Studies* 17, no. 3 (Aug, 1985): 295–311.
Piramerd. *Diwani Piramerdi Namir* [The Eternal Piramerd's Collection of Poetry]. Edited by Muhamvmad Rasul Hawar. Hawler: Shivan, 2007.
Plan Organization. *Report on the Operation of the Second Seven-Year Plan*. Tehran: 1964.
Presidential Office Document Centre. *Documents on Truman's Point Four in Iran (1946–1947)*. Tehran: Vizārat-i Farhang va Irshād-i Islamī, 1382 [2003].
Qaderzade, Omid, Ahmad Mohammapur, and Omid Qaderi. "Tejarate Marzi Wa Tafsire Mardom Az Taghirate Jahane Ziste Khanevade". [Border Trade and People's Perception of Family] *Rahbord Farhang* 6, no. 22 (Summer 1392 [2013]): 61–84.
Qane, Burhan (ed.). *Divani Qane* [Qane's Poetry Collection]. Iran: Dalaho Publications, 2014.
Qazi, Muhammad. *Khaterate Yek Motarjem* [A Translator's Memoir]. Tehran: Zenderud, 1992.
Qazi, Qader Fattahi. "Chand Baite Kurdi". [Some Kurdish Couplets] *Nashriyeye Adabiyate Daneshkadeye Tabriz [the Journal of the University of Tabriz Faculty of Literature]* 16, no. 3 (1343 [1964]): 307–20.
Qubadi, Gulrukh. *Shaqayeqha Bar Sanglakh: Zendegi Wa Zamaneye Yek Zane Kord Az Kordestane Iran* [Poppies on Rocks: The Life and Times of a Kurdish Woman from Iran] (2015).
Rae, Heather. *State Identities and the Homogenisation of Peoples*. Cambridge: Cambridge University Press, 2002.
Rahmani, Jamil, , Said Hossein Sarrajzadeh and Omid Qaderzadeh. "Motale'eye Kaifie Mazhab Wa Qomgaraiy Dar Mian Kordhaye Shi'e". [A Qualitative Study of Religion and Ethnicity Among Shia Kurds] *Jame'eshenasi [Sociology]* 15, no. 4 (2015): 3–29.
Ranaiy, Shahin. "Barresiye Ejraiye Eslahate Arzi Wa Payamadhaye an Dar Ostane Kordestan". [Land Reform in the Kurdistan Province and Its Consequences], PhD Thesis, University of Shahid Beheshti, 2017.
Rezayi, Mehdi. "A Study of Low-Birth Rate in Iranian Kurdistan". PhD Thesis, University of Tehran, 2011.
Rezayi, Mehdi, Rasul Sadeqi, Latif Partowi, and Ahmad Mohammadpur. "Sonnat, Nosazi Wa Khanewade". [Tradition, Modernisation and Family] *Pazhoheshe Zanan* 7, no. 4 (2010: 71–93.
Rich, C. *A Narrative of Residence in Koordistan*, 2 vols. London: W. Clowes and Sons, 1836.
Ritchie, Donal A. (ed.). *The Oxford Handbook of Oral History*. Oxford: Oxford University Press, 2011.
Rostam-Kolayi, Jasmin. "Expanding Agendas for the 'New' Iranian Woman". In *The Making of Modern Iran: State and Society under Reza Shah, 1921–1941*, edited by Stephanie Cronin. London: Routledge, 2003.

Rostow, W. W. *The Stages of Economic Growth: A Non-Communist Manifesto*. Cambridge: Cambridge University Press, 1990.
Rustayi, Mohsen. *Tarikhe Nokhostin Farhangestane Iran* [The History of Iran's First Academy]. Iran: Nei Publications 1385 [2006-7].
SaVedi, Gholamhossein. *Azadarane Bayal* [The Mourners of Bayal] (1964).
Sahabi, Izzat-Allah. *Nim Qarn Khaterah Va Tajrubeh* [Half a Century Memoirs and Experiences]. Vol. 1. Tehran: Farhange Saba Publication, 2009.
Said, Edward. *Culture and Imperialism*. London: Vintage Books, 1994.
Said, Edward. *Orientalism*. New York: Vintage Books, 1978.
Saidi, Bahman. *Khabat Baraw Sarkawtin: Didarek Lagal Ebrahim Alizada* [Struggle Towards Victory: A Meeting with Ebrahim Alizadeh]. Kurdistan: Komala Central Committee Publication, 2012.
Saidi, Bahman. *Penj Sal Lagal Abdulla Muhtadi* [Five Years with Abdulla Mohtadi]. Sulaymaniya: n.p., 2010.
Sajjadi, Abdulhamid Heyrat. *Pishineye Amuzesh Wa Parvaresh Dar Kurdistan (1320-1357)* [The History of Education in Kurdistan (1941-1957)]. Vols. 2 & 3. Sanandaj: Kurdistan Publications, 2004.
Sajjadi, Aladdin. *Mezhui Adabi Kurdi* [The History of Kurdish Literature]. Sanandaj: Kurdistan, 2013.
Sajjadi, Ziyaedin. "Sa'id Nafisi and Shenasandane Farhange Iran". [Sa'id Nafisi and Introducing the Culture of Iran] *Nashriyeye Adabiyat wa Olume Ensanie Daneshkadeye Tehran* 14, no. 3 (1967): 361-4.
Saleem, Hiner. *My Father's Rifle: A Childhood in Kurdistan*. New York: Picador, 2006.
Salih, Mohammed A. "Internal Cultural Imperialism: The Case of the Kurds in Turkey". *The International Communication Gazette* (June 2020): 1-20. https://doi.org/10.1177/1748048520928666
Scott, Joan Wallach. "Gender: A Useful Category of Historical Analysis". In *The Feminist History Reader*, edited by Sue Morgan. New York: Routledge, 2006.
Sharafkandi-Hazhar, Abdulrahman. *Cheshti Mijawir* [A Mosque Servant's Stew]. Iraq: Kitebi Mehregan, 2007.
Sharzayi, Reza Azari (ed.). *Asnade Baharestan (1): Gozideye Asnadi Az Waqaye' Mashroote Dar Kordestan Wa Kermanshahan* [Bahrestan Documents (1): A Selection of Documents Pertaining to the Constitutional Events in the Kurdistan and Kermanshahan [Provinces]]. Tehran: Library of Islamic Consultative Assembly, 1385 [2007].
Sheikholeslami-Hemin, Mohammad Amin. *Tarik W Roon* [Dark and Light]. n.p: n.p, 1970.
Sheyholislami, Jaffer. "Language Varieties of the Kurds". In *The Kurds: History - Religion - Language - Politics*, edited by Wolfgang Taucher. Austria: Austrian Federal Ministry of the Interio, 2015.
Smith, Anthony. *National Identity*. London: Penguin Books, 1991.
Smith, Anthony. *Nationalism and Modernism*. New York: Routledge, 1998.
Smith, Peter. *The Babi and Baha'i Religions: From Messianic Shiism to a World Religion*. Cambridge: Cambridge University Press, 1987.
Stevenson, John. *British Society 1914-1945*. London: Penguin, 1984.
Sullivan, William H.. *Mission to Iran*. USA: W.W. Norton and Company, 1981.
Swartz, David. *Culture and Power: The Sociology of Pierre Bourdieu* [Culture and Power]. Chicago: University of Chicago, 1997.
Sykes, Sir Mark. *The Chalifs' Last Heritage*. UK: Garnet Publishing, 2002.

Tafsiri, Said Borhan, and Mansour Ahmadi. "Ile Galbakhi". *Pazhoheshname Tarikhe Mahalie Iran* [*Journal of Iran's Local History*] 8, no. 1 (1398 [2019]): 259–70.

Talajooy, Saeed. "Rostam and Esfandiyar: From a Heroic Age to Page, Stage and Screen". unpublished article, 2011.

Tapper, Richard. *Frontier Nomads of Iran: A Political and Social History of the Shahsevan*. Cambridge: Cambridge University Press, 1997.

Taqizadeh, Hassan. "Nokat Wa Molahezat". [Points and Observations] *Kaveh* 5, no. 11 (1920).

Thompson, John B. *Ideology and Modern Culture: Critical Social Theory in the Era of Mass Communication*. UK: Polity Press, 1990.

Tudor, Henry. *Political Myth*. London: Pall Mall Press, 1972.

Vahabzadeh, Peyman. "A Generation Myth: Armed Struggle and the Creation of Social Epic in 1970s Iran". In *Iran in the Middle East: Transnational Encounters and Social History*, edited by H. E. Chehabi, Peyman Jafari and Maral Jefroudi. London: I. B. Tauris, 2015.

Vali, Abbas. *Kurds and the State in Iran*. London: I. B. Tauris, 2011.

Waters, Malcolm. *Modern Sociological Theory*. London: Sage Publications, 1994.

Weber, Max. *Economy and Society: An Outline of Interpretive Sociology*. California: University of California Press, 1978.

Wiesner-Hanks, Merry E. "Gender". In *Writing Early Modern History*, edited by Garthine Walker. London: Hodder Arnold, 2005.

Williams, Raymond. "From Base and Superstructure in Marxist Cultural Theory". In *New Historicism and Cultural Materialism: A Reader*, edited by Kiernan Ryan. London: Arnold, 1996.

Williams, Raymond. *Problems in Materialism and Culture*. London: Verso, 1980.

Williams, Raymond. *Television*. New York: Routledge, 1974.

Wills, C. J. *In the Land of the Lion and Sun or Modern Persia*. London: Ward, Lock and Co., 1891.

Wilson, Sir Arnold. *Sw. Persia: A Political Officer's Diary 1907–1914*. London: Oxford University Press, 1941.

Wimmer, Andreas. *Nationalist Exclusion and Ethnic Conflict: Shadows of Modernity*. Cambridge: Cambridge University Press, 2002.

Yapp, M. E. *The Near East since the First World War: A History to 1995*. London: Longman, 1996.

Zahed, Fiaz. "Gozari Bar Qanune Eslahate Arzi Dar Iran". [A Review of Land Reform in Iran] *Pazhohesnameye Tarikh* [*Historical Research*] 3, no. 11 (Winter 1394 [2016]): 92–122.

Zakaryayi, Shoeib. *Tharikhe Bazandeh: Naqdi Bar Husein Moradbegi's Tarikhe Bazandeh* [The Lost History: A Critical Review of Hossain Moradbegi's 'Living History']. Sulaymaniya: Rawand, 2010.

Zubaida, Sami. *Islam, the People and the State: Political Ideas and Movements in the Middle East*. New York: I. B. Tauris, 2009.

INDEX

administrative divisions   28, 29
Afshar, Iraj   121
Afshar, Mahmud   44, 46
agha class   68, 80
Akquyunlu   13
Ale Ahmad, Jalal   130
Amin, Qasim   147
Ardalan, Mastura   17, 147, 162
armed struggle   47, 103, 105, 106, 108, 143, 170
   rebellion of 1968–9   105
Arsanjani, Hasan   68
Astarabadi, Bibi Khanom   147
Ayyubiyan, 'Ubeidulla   120, 136
Azeris   14, 38, 119

Baluchis   14
Barahani, Reza   53, 118, 129, 130
Behrangi, Samad   119
Bekas, Fayaq   148
Bekas, Sherko   173
Blouryan, Ghani   105
Britain   6, 13, 20, 41, 97

Centre for Iranian Writers   129
city   81

Democratic Party of Iranian Kurdistan   105
development plans   2, 31, 58, 61, 63, 77, 95, 132

Ebtehaj, Gholamhosain   55, 59, 64, 77
education
   hojra   37
   khanaqa   37
   modern   41, 83

Failis   30, 68, 170
Fattahi Qazi, Qadir   120
Fedayyan   109

gender   31, 149–64
   and language   149–50
Gramsci, Antonio   5, 36, 138

Hassanpour, Amir   149–50
healthcare
   bime-ye ejtema'i   95
   daneshkade-ye Pezeshki   97
   edara-ye koll-e behdasht   95–6
   expansion   92
   history   35–7
   hospitals   95
   Iranian Nurses Association   95
   social welfare   97
Hilmi, Rafiq   163
homogenisation
   cultural   115–18
   and *Kurdayeti*   103
   resistance   141–3
Huseini, 'Abdulhamid   120

Ilkhanizada, Swara   112, 126–7, 140
Iran
   Constitutional Revolution   18
   Great War   20
   Islamic Republic   171–2
   nationalisation of oil   163 (*see also* Musaddeq)

journals
   Amuzesh wa Parvaresh   84
   Ayandeh   22
   Barresihay-e Tarikhi   121
   Gowhar   121
   Health for All   95
   Health Today   95
   Kaveh   20, 26, 37
   Kurdistan   30
   Kurdistan (Tehran)   127
   Nashriye-ye Daneshkade-ye Adabiyat-e Mashhad, Tabriz and Tehran   119

Nishtiman 30
Rahnemay-e Ketab 121
Rega 36
Sokhan 121
Sur Esrafil 14, 25
Tahqiqat-e Eqtesadi 66
Ta'lim va Tarbiyat 84
Vaqaye' Negar-e Kordestani 17

Komala
Komala-i Zhiyanawai-i Kurd 19 (*see also* Zhe Kaf)
Revolutionary Organisation of the Toilers of Iranian Kurdistan 110
Kurdayeti 22
Kurdish Emirates 13, 23, 28
Kurdish language 24, 43, 115, 120, 142
Kurdistan
 anjoman-e Eyalati 18
 Iranian 9
 Kurdistan Province 10
 Mrs Bishop in 14
 non-tribal 15, 18–22
Kurdistan Republic 9, 19, 30, 35, 38, 42, 46, 104

landless peasants 77
land reform 65, 75–6
Lurs 14

Mahabad. *See* Sujbulak
Mala Awara 109
Mardukh, Muhammad 26
Ma'refat, 'Aziz Al-Muluk 90–2
Middle East
 Department of Britain's Ministry of Overseas Development 97
militarisation 44, 46–7, 103, 107, 124, 167
Mina Sham 109
Minorsky 20
modernisation
 cultural 131
 infrastructural 31
 rural areas and 80
 state-led 75
 touse'e and 172
 urbanisation and 76
Mu'eini, Suleiman 107–9, 111

Muftizada, Ahmad 110, 139–40
Musaddeq, Muhammad 28, 46, 57, 66–7, 71, 105

Nafisi, Sa'id 119
Naqib, Hapsa Khan 157, 162
new means of communication 28
 and education 115
 institutionalization and management 117
 rural areas 131–3
 visual and audio 113
 White Revolution 122–30
 women 158–9

Ottoman Empire 13, 18, 20, 28, 146–7

Pappe, Illan 4, 16
peasantry
 jutbanda (sharecropper) 57
 rashaiy (landless) 69
Persian language 5, 26, 84–6, 103, 115, 117–21
Persians 14, 38, 44
Piramerd 147–8
Plan and Budget Organisation 64, 67, 96, 97
Plan Organisation 55, 59
political Islam 138. *See also* Muftizada

Qajars 13, 17–8
 literacy 39
Qane' 39–42, 127, 148
Qaraquyunlu 13
Qazi, Mina 154

radio 126
 Kurdish music 142
 Kurdish radio programmes 126–7
Russia 13–14, 20–1, 30

Safavid 13
Sajjadi, Hayrat 83–4
SAVAK (Sazman-e Amnyat va Ettelaat-e Keshvar) 57, 65, 105, 110, 136
 and the Barzani Movement 108
Sepehri, Sohrab 95
Shah, Muhammad 'Ali 25
Shah, Muhammad Reza 25, 27, 53

Shah, Reza   19, 25, 27–36
Sharafkandi Hazhar, Abdulrahman   27, 40, 42
  Hambana Borina   150
Sharifzada, Esmail   107, 109, 112, 164
Sheikhuleslami-Hemin, Muhammad Amin   21, 33, 38, 40, 42
  Memory of Shirin   148
  Tarik w Run   133
Shikaks   18
  Simko   45
Sujbulak   14

Tawfiq, Ahmad   106
television and cinema   128
theatre   126, 131–7
trade   13–17, 30, 34, 64, 81–2
  carpet weaving   17
  cross-border   14
tribes   14–22, 33, 45, 47, 69, 79, 149
Tudeh Party   105–6, 159
Turkomans   14

The Union of Kurdish Students   56, 108

vaqfs   39, 139

Weber, Max   6, 90
White Revolution   54–6

reaction   56–8
Williams, Reymond   5, 122–5, 173
women
  collective agency   159
  elopement   163
  legal and economic changes   155–8
  modern education   154
  nehzat-e zanan   160
  new means of communication   160
  the new science   153
  resistance   161
  and sport   158
  unveiling   148, 156, 161–2
  and White Revolution   153
  of working class   156
  Yakiati Afratani Kurdistan   154
working class
  child labour   77
  fa'las   77
  hammals   77
  mahallas   64
  seasonal workers   68–9, 72, 78
  unskilled   68, 78, 82, 169
  urban   82

Yousefi, 'Aziz   105

Zhe Kaf   19, 23, 42, 44. *See also* Komala-i Zhiyanawai-i Kurd

www.ingramcontent.com/pod-product-compliance
Lightning Source LLC
Chambersburg PA
CBHW062220300426
44115CB00012BA/2154